What People Are Saying About
The Soul of Success . . .

"*The Soul of Success* gives us a glimpse of what can happen when we dare to be ruthlessly honest with ourselves and live in alignment with our deepest values."

—**Cherie Carter-Scott, Ph.D.**, author of *If Life Is a Game, These Are the Rules* and *If Life Is a Game, These Are the Stories*

"Jennifer Hawthorne weaves people and themes together impeccably, creating a rich and transformative experience. I wept many times, laughed out loud, and felt deeply at home in myself as a woman in connection with her tribe. The women in this book are worthy models."

—**Melissa Michaels**, founder and director,
Surfing the Creative^SM youth programs
and developer of international rites of passage programs

"Inspiring and touching. These stories wonderfully illustrate what success really is."

—**Barbara Sher**, author of *I Could Do Anything If I Only Knew What It Was*

"A commendable collection of inspiring stories with the energy and heart to ignite spirits and resuscitate dreams."

—**H. Jackson Brown, Jr.**, author of
the *Life's Little Instruction Book* series

"This book teaches us to seek wholeness, to feed the inner self. Otherwise, we may reach the pinnacle of success only to discover a lost and unfulfilled self."

—**Marva Collins**, award-winning educator,
including Legendary Women of the World
and the President's National Humanitarian Award

D0360607

"*The Soul of Success* is an inspiring book that encourages women to tap their inner gifts. It will be a source of comfort and courage to all who read it."

—Joan Lescinski, CSJ, Ph.D.,
president of Saint Mary-of-the-Woods College

"To find your heart is to find true success. Jennifer Read Hawthorne takes you deep into your heart with a book filled with inspiration, enlightenment, and a new definition of success. I love this book!"

—Terri Amos, Miss USA 1982 and
author of *Message Sent: Retrieving the Gift of Love*

"*The Soul of Success* reveals the deepest strengths of the feminine. It reminds us that divine wisdom is always available to us, if we just take a moment to listen."

—Judy Martin, contributing correspondent
to National Public Radio and World Vision Radio

Also by Jennifer Read Hawthorne

THE
Soul
OF
Success

JENNIFER   READ   HAWTHORNE

Health Communications, Inc.
Deerfield Beach, Florida

www.hcibooks.com

Library of Congress Cataloging-in-Publication Data

Hawthorne, Jennifer Read.
    The soul of success / [written and edited by] Jennifer Read Hawthorne.
      p. cm.
    ISBN 0-7573-0236-X
    1. Women—Psychology.   2. Self-perception in women.
    3. Self-acceptance in women.   4. Self-esteem in women   I. Title.

    HQ1206.H38 2004
    170'.82—dc22
    2004059928

Publisher: Health Communications, Inc.
            3201 S.W. 15th Street
            Deerfield Beach, FL 33442-8190

Inside and cover design by Larissa Hise Henoch
Inside book formatting by Dawn Von Strolley Grove

They can be like a sun, words.

They can do for the heart
what light can
for a field.

—St. John of the Cross

For Orion and Elisabet,
who ignite my soul
with their love and teachings

Contents

Introduction

If your success is not on your own terms,
if it looks good to the world
but does not feel good in your heart,
it is not success at all.

—Anna Quindlen

This is a book about being in the world in a new way.

It all started when I realized that we women may be from Venus, but in our quest to have it all, we have been spending way too much time on Mars! We have bought into the idea that success is about the bottom line, financial achievement, status and winning. We have looked to our relationships, our salaries, our achievements and our possessions to define ourselves and measure our success.

And we have mastered "doing." We have become skilled at working full-time jobs, all the while managing our homes, our families and our primary life relationships.

But at what price? Personally, I reached the point where I had to admit that my level of "doingness" had evolved into full-blown workaholism and was threatening my health, my family and my sanity.

I first set out to master the material world years ago when I attended a seminar called "Yes! To Success," an intense three-day program where I learned how to set goals (daily, weekly, monthly, one-year, five-year, even lifetime), how to manage time and how to "dress for success." I still find many of the techniques I learned then to be valuable tools for managing life today.

But somewhere along the way something shifted inside me. Going over my goals once or twice a day in the hope that I could somehow *make* it all happen, I began to see that activity like this was mostly about doing, often characterized as a "masculine" quality.

And about three years ago, the effect of this approach to living started to become clear when I found myself frustrated and dissatisfied with the person I was becoming. Despite having done a great deal of work on myself, I was still critical, judgmental and controlling, I didn't like my husband, and I spent a lot of time pretending that he was responsible for my unhappy state. My body hurt all the time.

Our circumstances were trying. I spent half my life (so it seemed) making the six-hour drive between two homes in the Midwest—one in Minnesota, one in Iowa. We had uprooted our comfortable, small-town living situation when the company my husband worked for moved everyone to their Minneapolis headquarters (we kept the Iowa home because it was my base of business). Just months later, my husband was laid off. But by this time, my stepson was thriving at his new high school.

Together, we decided that my husband would not look for another job, but take time to do some writing and pursue interests he had never had the time for. My income was sufficient for us to live on at the time, and I loved my speaking work, so it was not a pressure for me to support the family—in fact, I was happy to do it.

Then, like so many industries and professions, the speaking field was hit hard when the events of 9/11 occurred. Slowly, what had been my primary livelihood began drying up.

"What more can I do?" would have been my normal response to this situation at one time. But I didn't want to do more. I was exhausted, as I had been for years—mentally, physically and emotionally—from all the driving, managing two homes, and the stagnation that seemed to be settling into my marriage as my husband and I sat in front of our laptops all day. And although I had very little work, I always seemed to be working.

Instinctively, I felt that if I were to find balance in life—that elusive thing most women in our society are struggling to find—it would have to be by culturing whatever was the opposite of masculine drive, energy and focus: the so-called "feminine" aspects of nature. As I sought to learn more about the feminine, I became more and more intrigued by the possibility that the deeper, feminine principles at play within every human being are as much a part of successful, happy living as the so-called masculine ones.

I began talking to women and collecting their stories. And my discoveries were both surprising and life changing.

I discovered simple themes like *compassion, self-love, forgiveness, integrity* and *surrender,* which you will see in the contents of this book. You may look at some of these words and immediately think, *Oh, I already have that one, and I've got that one down—and that one, too.* Some of these words may make you react strongly. I understand because I, too, am a woman who does not do well with a word like "surrender"! Even the word "feminine" is one that can push a woman's buttons these days, conjuring up images ranging from frills to submission.

But far more than qualities, these words are principles that, when operating in a person's life, can deeply influence and enliven the soul's destiny.

I am learning that these feminine principles are, simply, more about "being" than doing. As many writers and speakers have pointed out, we are human beings, not human doings. When we combine the receptivity, the intuition, the healing and the humanity of the feminine with our ability to act in the world, life changes for the better. We get to relax. We get to feel at peace with whatever is going on around us. We get to tap into the magical river of life where our days seem to flow.

And we are able to know, with the deepest understanding possible, that these are the things that make life truly successful. This is the innate and authentic power of the feminine—and the true soul of success.

Of course, the masculine and feminine aspects of life are available and present within all human beings, male and female. The principles discussed in this book and illustrated in the accompanying stories are truly genderless. Whether male or female, when we allow ourselves to be guided by the inner feminine part of ourselves—the deepest impulses of our being—then the inner masculine part of ourselves can manifest these impulses in an easy, effortless way. It's a beautiful marriage of the inner feminine and masculine, the *yin* and *yang*. As a male friend told me, he likes "doing," but he wants the principles described in this book to be the basis of his activity. Somehow, it just feels like a better way to live.

I speak to women because I believe our very nature makes us more open to a different way of looking at success. As part of my own process in understanding the feminine, I have interviewed and gathered stories from women I find to be beautiful, vibrant, awakened and powerful beyond measure. Represented here are "successful" business executives, mothers, yoga teachers, speakers, actresses, financial planners, social activists, peacekeepers, professors, artists, writers and dancers. I asked each of them for a story of personal transformation, and, in their heartfelt revealing of themselves, I have learned and grown so much.

I have learned that self-love is harder than we think—and the key to everything. That the relationship between the physical, mental, emotional and spiritual is more than a New Age platitude—it's the key to healing on every level, which is fundamental to true success. I've learned that how I live my life *at this moment,* no matter what I'm doing, is more important than any plan for the future. And I've learned that divine grace is at work in the universe 24/7—all we have to do is be open to it.

Don't get me wrong; I care about money and being admired by others, too. But these days, I find that I care much more about other things—like spirituality, passion for living and trusting the never-failing guidance of my heart. I don't want to lead a mundane existence. I want to feel that most of what I do is meaningful, and I want to explore new territory all the time. For some time now, my mantra has been: *I want to be in the world in a new way.*

I believe that most of us long to return to a more balanced way of living. We want a new barometer of success that includes *inner* experience. In fact, we hunger for inner riches along with outer ones, and we feel ourselves poised to break through to a different and *deeper* experience of success in our personal and professional lives—success that includes a sense of peace, freedom and deep fulfillment.

Ever and always, I want to be in the world in a new way. Please, come with me.

1·Intention

was fried. I had once loved my job leading business-writing seminars. But after too many days standing in front of corporate managers from 8:00 to 5:00, entertaining them, educating them and practically *willing* them to write better—well, it had gotten old. And the luxury of room service had long been overshadowed by an aching desire to sleep in my own bed. It was definitely time for a change.

I had learned through study and personal experience that if you want to do something great, you have to start with a clear intention. So I sat down one day with paper and pen at hand, closed my eyes, and asked myself what I really wanted to do with my life. The answer came easily and quickly: I wanted to speak—not about how to write a better business letter, but how to live a better life. When I opened my eyes, I wrote down my intention: to start speaking to audiences about how to create the life we want. I then launched into designing the flyer that would describe in detail the first presentation I wanted to give on "Women, Power and Happiness."

A couple of weeks later, my friend and colleague Marci Shimoff was in my office. Like me, Marci taught business writing in the corporate world, and, like me, she was up to her eyeballs in dangling modifiers. We were discussing some fine point of punctuation when she suddenly saw my flyer and grabbed it off my desk.

"I've been wanting to start a speaking business for the past four years," she practically shouted. And just like that, our speaking partnership, which we called The Esteem Group, was born.

The first thing we did was to write down our intention. Our mission was "to help women understand and experience their inner power and self-worth, so they can create and live their own vision." Little did we know what power those words contained.

We began building our speaking business, specializing in self-esteem presentations for women. One of our best resources was Jack Canfield, a renowned expert in the field of self-esteem, with whom Marci had studied. So when his book *Chicken Soup for the Soul* became a national bestseller that year, we immediately got his permission to share stories from it with our audiences.

It turned out to be a powerful combination: women and *Chicken Soup*. We saw what an impact the stories had, how deeply they moved women and how much they helped them with the changes they were trying to make. So the following January, when Marci approached me with the idea of coediting a volume for women, I didn't hesitate. We faxed Jack a proposal. He said it sounded like a good idea—and then we all got busy and let it drop.

But Marci and I kept getting clearer about our intention: We wanted to touch the hearts of women all over the globe. We wanted to inspire them, uplift them, give them a vision of life lived from the heart—and show them the magnificent support we can be to one another.

We finally flew to Los Angeles and sat down for a meeting with

Jack. With our vision clearly in mind and heart, we told him that we wanted to touch the hearts of women around the world through a *Chicken Soup for the Soul* book just for them. Jack asked us why he should let us do the project, when his office already had a successful track record (they were working on number two in the series). Marci and I looked at each other across the table and simultaneously realized we hadn't prepared a thing to say!

For a moment, we sat speechless. Then, all of a sudden, the words started pouring out: We both taught business writing and understood the principles of good writing, I had majored in journalism, we understood the "Chicken Soup" genre because we'd been using stories in our public presentations, we were connected with women through our business and felt that we understood what women were hungry for, the women's market was huge, and finally, Jack and his coauthor Mark Victor Hansen couldn't coauthor a book for women without women coauthors!

Jack didn't even hesitate. He said yes, and sixteen months later, *Chicken Soup for the Woman's Soul* became a reality. Within two months, it hit No. 1 on the *New York Times* bestseller list. A million copies had been sold.

But we didn't understand the real implication of the numbers until the mail started coming in. We soon found we had fulfilled our intention beyond our wildest imagination. We were deluged with letters from women literally all around the globe telling us how our book had affected their lives. Estranged mothers and daughters were reconciled; abused women found the courage to get help; women changed careers, adopted babies; confronted their bosses, their illnesses, their fears, their mothers-in-law. We toured all over the country, speaking and signing books, and everywhere women shared their stories with us. Marci and I wept with them, cheered with them, and most days felt we were the luckiest women alive.

I still feel that way! I have learned that when intention comes from the heart and is coupled with the willingness to work, miracles can happen. We may not know how they're going to happen, but we don't need to. We just need to be awake to opportunities and willing to show up and do what's needed. To say that Marci and I worked extremely hard on that first book would be an understatement. The learning curve was steep, and we had to put the book together while still building our speaking business and teaching in the corporate world to earn an income. Even finding days when we were both in town at the same time was challenging! But we knew it was the opportunity of a lifetime. What a perfect vehicle we had found to fulfill our desire.

In the following story, by Dr. Christine Horner, we see another example of the extraordinary power of intention. Christine was moved to political action by her outrage over an injustice she encountered as a plastic surgeon helping women recover from breast cancer. She wanted to empower women, and she knew that helping them gain the ability to have their health-care needs met would be a significant way to do that.

She also knew that her greatest chance for success with her idea was to get very clear about her intention, so she wrote it down: "All women will have reconstructive surgery available to them." And then she watched as the universe began to organize around her intention. As she points out—and as Marci and I found out—this is usually far beyond anything we could ever imagine or plan!

For those of us with a history of breast cancer in the family, Christine Horner's story is particularly relevant. But I believe everyone who reads this story will be inspired by her wholehearted desire to serve others—and her willingness to go all the way to the top.

CHRISTINE HORNER'S STORY
Make It So

When I heard the news on October 21, 1998, that President Clinton had signed the Women's Health and Cancer Rights Act into law, I wiped the tears from my eyes and gave my mom in heaven a high five. "We did it, Mom!" I exulted.

It had been a tough five-year battle to get this legislation passed, but it was worth every frustration, every late night and every dime. The new law meant that if a woman had to have a mastectomy, her insurance company would have to cover reconstructive breast surgery. In the early 1990s, many insurance companies, in a misguided effort to save money, had decided to stop paying for this essential restorative operation. Now coverage would be required, and every patient could be made whole again.

This story begins seven years earlier, in the fall of 1991, when I opened my own solo practice in the greater Cincinnati area. At age thirty-three, I had finally completed twenty-seven years of education to realize my childhood dream of becoming a plastic and reconstructive surgeon. It was so fulfilling to finally be able to help people with my surgical skills!

As I developed my practice over the next two years, I felt a special passion for serving a particular group of patients. They struck a deep personal chord in me because my mother was one of them. These were women with breast cancer.

One day in 1993, a young woman in her thirties sat in my office and told me how the treatment of her breast cancer had required mastectomies of both breasts. She wanted me to reconstruct them.

Following her consultation, as required, I sent a letter to her insurer, Indiana Medicaid, requesting authorization to perform the reconstructive surgery. I thought the letter was a mere formality since insurance companies had always routinely paid for breast reconstruction after a mastectomy. But several weeks later I received a reply saying that the surgery was "not medically indicated." That's insurance jargon that usually means, "There's no medical reason to deny this surgery, but to cut costs, we're not paying for it."

I thought it was a mistake and wrote them another letter. It was not a mistake. The Medicaid insurance executive was unrelenting. This businessman declared that the surgery was "not medically necessary."

I was outraged and decided that, no matter what it took, I would fight this decision. Not because it was a threat to my practice or my personal finances; I had plenty of patients with other needs. In fact, after several months, I realized that the appeals process would require enormous time and almost certain financial loss. But I didn't let that stop me. I refused to abandon my patient. I could relate too well to what she was going through.

Just imagine being told you have breast cancer. You're told you must have one or both of your breasts surgically removed. You're also told you'll be treated with chemicals that will make you very sick, cause you to lose all your hair and possibly damage your organs. Death is a real possibility. You fear the treatments and the pain, and on top of all of that, you have to wonder if your significant other will still love you and still find you sexually attractive. Thank God, you learn, you can be restored to wholeness with reconstructive breast surgery. Then you find out that your insurance company refuses to pay for this surgery. Imagine.

A few months later, armed with stacks of published research, I argued my case to the judge presiding over my final appeal. I presented the studies documenting the enormously beneficial effects of breast reconstruction. They all showed that when women undergo breast reconstruction in the same operation as the mastectomy, they suffer far less emotional trauma. The judge was a woman, and I won my case.

This wasn't the end of my battle, though—far from it. A short time later I was shocked to discover that this case did not set a precedent and had no bearing on any other future cases. Every Medicaid case is evaluated separately. That meant I would have to go through the same draining, time-consuming, financially costly administrative slugfest for every single Medicaid patient who needed breast reconstruction! Worse still, private insurers started jumping on the denial bandwagon. The final straw came one day in the form of a letter from Blue Cross and Blue Shield of Kentucky. It declared that breast reconstruction for my thirty-three-year-old patient was unnecessary because there was no medical need to reconstruct "an organ with no function."

My eyes fixed on those five words: "an organ with no function." I started yelling, "An organ with no function? What kind of callous, coldhearted idiot could say such a thing?" I vowed then that every woman who must have a mastectomy would also have insurance coverage for reconstructive breast surgery.

In order to achieve that, I knew laws would have to be passed. For me, this was no simple task. I knew nothing about the political process, and even with a doctorate, I was hesitant to speak up, out of fear of sounding stupid. But I knew if I kept following my heart and remained clear about my intention, somehow I could make this happen.

And so, the adventure began. And what an adventure it was—awe-inspiring, magical and profoundly spiritual. At times, everything and everyone I needed for the project seemed to fall effortlessly into my lap. Seemingly random offers of essential help, perfectly timed meetings and serendipitous events happened so routinely that I came to expect them.

For example, deep into the project, I realized that Senator Ted Kennedy should sponsor the federal bill because of his success in getting health-care bills through Congress. I didn't take any action or speak to anyone about this thought, but a week later, at a state medical meeting, a surgeon from Boston walked up to me and said, "I'm operating on Ted Kennedy next week. Do you want me to ask him to sponsor your bill?"

It seemed as if I had a direct line to God. Ask and ye shall receive—no kidding!

But it was also difficult, frustrating and sometimes even shocking. It required enormous perseverance and strength, which I had to develop over time—and at times the challenges seemed insurmountable. When I launched the project, it made sense to me to focus on passing one federal law. Unfortunately, the Clintons' national health-care plan had just failed, and the word in Washington was that no federal health-care bills would even be considered. I soon realized that, somehow, I would have to pass fifty individual state laws. I took a deep breath and began planning, organizing, calling and writing. Within a year I had enrolled the help of plastic surgeons, breast cancer survivors and numerous organizations in every state. And, one by one, state laws began to pass.

Then, one morning in 1994, I got the darkest news yet. I learned that our successes in the states meant nothing, thanks to a legal loophole. It seemed that a law called ERISA, the Employee Retirement Income Securities Act, exempts most people from the protection of state health-care laws. In order to fulfill my commitment, I realized that a federal law would have to be passed after all.

The challenge and chances of success seemed as intimidating as climbing Mt. Everest, shoeless. But then something personal and tragic happened that renewed my resolve. My mother, the vibrant, extraordinary woman who had taught me to reach for the stars, lost her fifteen-year struggle against breast cancer. The disease had stripped her of her dignity and cut short her life. I held my mother's hand and felt her spirit go free as she took her last breath. At that moment, I vowed to let nothing stop me. I dedicated the project, now called the Breast Reconstruction Advocacy Project (BRA Project), to her memory. I pledged to myself that her untimely death would be a pivotal event in the worldwide fight against this disease.

By this time, I had grown more politically savvy, and I realized that it was now time for me to go straight to the top. I had to meet President Clinton. I'd heard it said that we are all only three people away from meeting anyone, so everywhere I went I started asking, "Do you know how I can meet President Clinton?" Within two weeks, a friend introduced me to a member of the Federal Trade Commission. I met David for lunch and told him all about my plans. He told me he went to Washington to meet with the president four times a year, and the next time he went, I could go.

Two days later, he called me and announced, "We're going on Tuesday."

"What?" I said, looking at my calendar with about forty patients scheduled for the office that day.

"Your patients will understand," he explained. "You're meeting the president. Oh, and by the way," he added, "there's one other thing. It will cost you $10,000. It's a fund-raiser for the 1996 election, and that's the minimum contribution."

"There's no way!" I yelped. "I can't do that."

"Look," he reasoned, "this is a once-in-a-lifetime opportunity. You can fund-raise from your friends. It's for a good cause."

Suddenly, I felt a strong feeling in my gut that said, "Do it." Because my gut rarely fails me, I listened. And so, a few days later, I was in Washington to meet the president.

Wanting to make an impression, I opted to wear a perfect black strapless dress and elbow-length black velvet gloves. I felt like a million bucks as I walked into the Mayflower Hotel. After walking through the metal detector, I gave one final check and adjustment to my gown and gloves and entered the room—where I immediately saw that everyone was wearing business suits!

Mortified, I stopped to get my seat assignment and was told, "We needed another woman at the president's table, so we moved you there. Is that okay?" Absolutely! But as I headed for my table, my embarrassment returned as heads swiveled in my direction.

"Thanks for dressing for us," one of David's friends said as we walked by.

"Oh, you're welcome," I said with a smile. "It was really no trouble at all." I realized I might as well just enjoy myself.

An hour later, the president arrived. He was taller than I had imagined, with a ruddy complexion and gray hair, and yes, he was as charming and charismatic as legend said.

"I'm Dr. Christine Horner," I said, as I finally made it to the front of the receiving line and was shaking the president's hand.

"Yes, I know who you are," he replied. "You live across the river from Cincinnati and you're working on legislation about breast cancer. And, I believe you're sitting at my table tonight, aren't you?"

"Why, yes, I am," I answered, trying not to show my astonishment. He really was good! I had been asked to send information about myself before the event because the president liked to be briefed about everyone he would be meeting. I had heard that he never forgot a name or a face, but still, I was impressed.

"I'll see you later at the table," he said as the next person in line took my place.

I ended up sitting directly across the round, twelve-foot table from the president—too far away for a conversation. Endless streams of people came up to speak to him throughout the meal. As the evening passed and the time for him to give his speech rapidly approached, I was struck with the thought that I had just spent $10,000 to talk to the president, and I might not get to do it. In a mild panic, I leaned across the table, caught his eye and yelled, "I want to talk to you!" He jumped a little, and then yelled back, "Okay. I'll come and get you after my speech and we can talk."

He stood up and went to the front of the room. After giving his twenty-minute speech, he left the stage and, as promised, came by my table and signaled to me to follow him. I rose from my chair and walked behind him. He shook hands, smiled and bid good-bye to everyone with sweet, laid-back Southern charm. We walked into the hallway and the doors closed behind us.

Swarms of secret service agents descended. He began snapping his fingers at his assistants. "Give it to me now," he demanded. Papers were thrust at him from all directions, and he began signing them furiously, while at the same time, streams of young men updated him on the latest happenings in quick sound bites. Tension was high, and he was working at frenetic, lightning speed.

Suddenly, he turned to me and said in a relaxed tone, "Now, what is it you want to say?"

I was still reeling from what I had just witnessed. My knees were knocking. I felt like Dorothy trembling before the Wizard of Oz. *Hi, I'm Dorothy, the meek and mild,* I thought. One minute of presidential time seemed equivalent to an hour, so I started talking as fast as I could. I told him about the problem with insurance companies not covering breast reconstruction, and our efforts to get a bill to Congress. He took notes and appeared to be very interested. He said he would look into it and see what he could do. And then he turned around and walked out of the building, surrounded by his entourage.

Three days later, I received a call from a member of the Democratic National Committee. "We like your spunk," he said. "Normally, a $10,000 contribution is the cost for two people to attend an event. Since you came by yourself, we'd like to invite you to meet with the president again when he comes to Cincinnati in two days."

Wearing just the right business suit, I listened to the president as he gave his speech at the private luncheon. He turned to leave, and I sprang from my chair. As he approached the stairs leading to the men's room, I leaped in front of him and blocked him like a linebacker. Dorothy was gone, and Xena the warrior had appeared! Staring him in the eyes, no more than six inches away, I said, "My mother died of breast cancer, and so did yours. We can make a tribute to our mothers' lives by passing breast reconstruction legislation!"

He snapped his fingers at his assistant, asked for his card, and then handed me his business card with the zip code to the Oval Office. "Send me a packet of information at this address," he replied.

I did. A few weeks later I received a note on White House stationary, personally signed by the president, thanking me for the information and promising he would look into the matter.

That meeting led to more meetings, including several with Hillary Clinton and her staff in the West Wing of the White House, and suddenly doors began to open. Media coverage for the project exploded. Several major women's magazines called for interviews, including *Glamour, Allure, Ms.* and *Elle.* There were dozens of television, radio and newspaper interviews. It seemed that everyone wanted to get on board across the whole country.

I was buoyed with optimism when the bill was introduced to Congress in 1997.

Then, it stalled. It was promptly put into legislative committee— or, "a black hole," as it's also known—where it sat for two years, seemingly dead. I knew that bills rarely, if ever, pass on their own merit; they only make it through by being tagged onto a larger, "moving" bill. But even that wasn't working. The reconstruction legislation was tagged onto every moving bill, but none passed. With only one day of the 1998 congressional session left, it looked as if the situation was hopeless. Sure enough, I received a phone call that day from the staff legislative liaison for the national plastic surgery society. His words cut through me like a knife, "Bad news, Christine; it's all over. There aren't any other bills to tag it onto."

My heart sank. I couldn't believe that all those years of hard work with such clear, divine support could end like this. We had come so close!

The next day, my secretary knocked on the door while I was examining a patient. She rarely interrupted me, and I thought something must be terribly wrong.

"You have an urgent phone call you must take now," she said. My heart raced as I picked up the phone. Then, I heard the voice of the same staffer, but his tone was entirely different. He sounded elated.

"It passed!" he said.

"What?" I said. "What did you say?"

"It got tagged onto the budget bill at the last minute, and it passed!" he exclaimed.

In a daze I thanked him and hung up the phone. Then I burst into tears and gave my mom that symbolic high five. My heart spoke the words, "We did it, Mom!" and her spirit filled the room. My mother's great sacrifice *had* made a difference. Her life and death would help millions of women. At least now they could be spared the trauma of not being able to have reconstructive surgery.

But as the days passed, I felt unsettled. One problem was solved, but another, much greater problem remained and clouded the cele-bration—the epidemic of breast cancer. Why was it still growing? What was the cause? How could it be stopped? Thus began a new and far more important mission in my life: to trace this killer back to its root causes and help protect women from ever developing this disease in the first place.

I studied hard and unearthed many answers, and soon my intu-ition told me to jump off another professional cliff. I sold my plastic surgery practice in 2002 to dedicate my life full time to teaching people what I had discovered. I wrote a book describing the best natural approaches that research has proven substantially lower the risk of breast cancer. When used in conjunction with standard medical treatments for women with breast cancer, these same techniques can help to improve their chances of survival.

This amazing journey has taught me that when we make a commitment to a greater possibility for the world, the universe rises up in support. All we have to do is surrender to its infinite organizing power and listen to its guiding messages.

"One problem was solved, but a much greater problem remained. Thus began a new and far more important mission in my life: to trace this killer back to its root causes and help protect women from ever developing this disease in the first place."

—Christine Horner

2 · Intuition

oon after graduating from college in Baton Rouge, I moved to Washington, D.C. I wanted to experience life in a big city, and our nation's capital seemed liked a perfect match for my journalism skills and political interests.

On my own for the first time, I loved living in a place where the national news was also the local news! Every day I walked from my Dupont Circle apartment downtown to various temporary secretarial and office jobs. I was a "Kelly Girl," as they were called in those days, and the great thing about being a Kelly Girl in Washington was that I had jobs like a three-month stint with a Presidential Commission. I also fell in love, and my boyfriend and I were so compatible that we never had an argument. Life was grand!

One day while walking to work, the thought passed through my mind: *There's got to be something more to life.* I didn't think much of it, but the thought began to recur every morning, as I walked past beautifully landscaped homes and impressive government buildings.

Then one morning, passing the Peace Corps building on my usual route, something made me stop. I stood outside the building for a moment, asking myself what I was doing, then walked in. I asked for an application, filled it out that evening and dropped it off the next morning on my way to work.

A couple of months later, I was accepted. My mind couldn't make sense of it. Was I really going to leave this wonderful, rich life to go to Africa for a couple of years? I felt as if I were standing on the edge of a precipice, wondering whether to jump.

I jumped. I couldn't help myself. Although I didn't know a thing about intuition at the time, the impulse to expand my life beyond "the box" could not be denied. I left my boyfriend, my family and my friends—not to mention electricity and hot running water—for an adventure into the unknown. On the surface, I was terrified, but nothing could stop the voice inside that compelled me forward to a new life.

This "voice inside"—our intuition—is a basic faculty within every human being. Unfortunately, in our society the mind is cultivated far more than intuition. In fact, intuition is so undervalued in the West that our parents don't cultivate it in us as small children, and our educational system ignores it completely. But whether we "hear" it or "feel" it or just sense it, like the proverbial sixth sense, our intuition guides us at life's turning points, as well as in the small daily choices we have to make. And, even if it has not been fostered, it is always there.

The trick is, can we pay attention? I am learning that intuition is something I feel in my body. I am also starting to realize that when a thought comes into my mind, it's for a reason. Let's say, for example, it occurs to me to send a copy of my latest book to a client I haven't spoken with for a couple of years. My usual response would be immediately to have a dialogue with myself, maybe second-guessing myself or trying to figure out why I would want to do this. But I'm learning that even mundane thoughts like these are not random; they are inner guidance, based on my soul's knowingness of a much bigger picture of my life than my mind can possibly grasp. The more I practice listening to my intuition, the surer I become that my life is being guided by something much bigger than I am.

It is thrilling to watch intuition manifest itself in the material world. In the following story by Lynne Twist, the intuition of a group of African women astonishes and delights. Although we often hear the word in conjunction with women, as in "women's intuition," I do not believe intuition is the proprietary faculty of women alone. But because it is a quality of the feminine, something that can only become useful when one is in "receiving" mode, women may naturally be more open to it.

If you feel out of touch with your intuition, you might be overlooking it just because it's so close at hand. There are a number of great books available on how to awaken your intuition. But it might be easier just to remember the words of Naomi Judd, who said about intuition: "Honey, that's when your gut gets it before your head gets around to figuring it out."

The story you are about to read confirms my belief that to honor intuition, and to encourage it in our children, others and ourselves, is literally to invite the divine into our lives.

One final note: A couple of years ago, my mother handed me a shoe box containing every letter and postcard I had written home during my three years in the Peace Corps and traveling around the world. There were about 125 all together. "I thought you might want to write a book some day," she said.

LYNNE TWIST'S STORY
Well of Strength

A large portion of Senegal is covered by the massive and encroaching Sahel Desert, which expands each year, toward the sea. The Sahel is a harsh environment, not friendly to life, or even to the plants and animals that typically live in desert environments. The sand is fine, like dust, and a shade of pale orange. It is so fine and so pervasive that everything near the edge of the desert is covered with the yellowy orange sand: the streets, the houses, the plants and the roads—even the people.

We were there, eighteen Hunger Project contributors and leaders, to meet with the people of a village several hours into the desert about their need to find a new source of water or a new place to live. As our drivers took the vehicles down the road from town and deep into the desert itself, we became covered with this very fine silty sand. It burrowed into our lungs with every breath. As we drove on the rough road into the orange wind, we saw fewer and fewer people, plants and animal life, and pretty soon there was nothing but barren land. It was hot and dry, over 95 degrees Fahrenheit, and I wore a hat and had a bandanna across my face to keep from breathing in the sand. It was so bleak that it seemed unimaginable that any human being could live in this climate.

For a while we were on a rough, unpaved road. Then it disappeared into the sand, and our drivers began driving on the open desert by compass only. Our Senegalese drivers knew the desert well, and there was a point at which the lead driver in the front vehicle stopped and turned off the engine. Then the other two did the same. After listening awhile, we could hear the faint sound of drums. Our lead driver smiled, turned on his engine and began driving toward the sound of the drums. As we drove, the drums grew louder and louder, and soon on the horizon we could see tiny moving specks. As we drove closer and closer, we thought the specks were animals of some kind. Then as we grew near, we saw that they were children, dozens of children running toward our vehicles, bursting with excitement.

Here we were, in a place that showed no signs of life, being greeted by exuberant, cheering children brimming with vitality and aliveness. Tears welled in my eyes, and I could see my traveling companions were moved in the same way by this jubilant greeting. More little ones kept streaming toward us, and beyond them in the distance were two large baobab trees standing alone in the desolate vastness. The baobab is a lifesaving tree that can grow with almost no water and provides shade and a windbreak for people who dwell in the desert.

Ahead of us, under the two baobab trees, about one hundred twenty people were gathered in the precious shade. Drummers were in the center of an opening in the crowd, and we could see that inside the circle some women were dancing. As the distance between us closed, the drumming filled the air with a vibrant energy, and the celebration appeared to grow more intense. We picked up some of the children and gave them a ride in our cars. Others ran alongside. It seemed that this incredible scene had risen out of nothing. Here they were—men, women and children—dancing, drumming, cheering, clapping and shouting greetings of welcome to our small visiting delegation.

We climbed out of our vehicles, and dozens of women ran to us dressed in beautiful traditional Senegalese clothing with headdresses and long cotton boubous—long, loose, colorful dresses. The drums were beating, the children were shouting, the women were squealing with delight, the men were singing. It was a welcome like no other.

They seemed to know that I was the leader, and they pulled me into the center of the circle, where the women danced around me and with me. I was swept up in the moment, moving my body in concert with theirs in a freeing, natural rhythm. They cheered and clapped. My fellow travelers joined me, and we danced and clapped and laughed together. Time and space seemed suspended. It wasn't hot or dry anymore. It wasn't sandy or windy. All that disappeared, and we were enveloped in celebration. We were one.

Then the drums suddenly stopped. It was time for the meeting to begin. People sat down on the sand. The chief identified himself and he addressed his comments to me. With the help of our translator, the chief explained that their village was several kilometers away, and that they had come to welcome us and were grateful for our offer of partnership. He said that they were strong and able people and that the desert was their spiritual home. But they and sixteen other villages to the east were at a point where the scarce water resources were pushing them to the edge of their options. Their people knew nothing but life in this desert, were proud people of this land, but knew they could not continue without some change in the water situation.

Government services were not extended to these people, even in times of crisis. They were illiterate people who weren't counted in the census. They couldn't even vote. They had little or no cachet with their government. They had tremendous resilience, but their shallow wells were nearly dry, and they knew they would need something outside of their current thinking to see themselves through this next dry season.

The people were Muslim, and as we sat together in a circle to discuss the situation, the men did all the talking. The women were not in the primary circle, but sat in a second circle where they could hear and see, but they did not speak. I could feel the power of the women behind me and sensed that they would be key in the solution. In this barren orange land, it didn't seem possible that there could be a solution, but the attitude, sense of resilience and dignity of these people argued differently. There was a way through, and together we would find it.

Then I asked to meet only with the women. It was a strange request in this Muslim culture where the mullahs and the chief were empowered to speak for all, but they allowed it. The women from my group and the tribal women gathered together on the hot ground and drew in close. Our translator was a man, and the mullahs allowed him to join us.

In this circle of tribal women, several women assumed leadership and spoke right away, saying that it was clear to them that there was an underground lake beneath the area. They could feel it; they knew it was there. They had seen it in visions and needed our help to get permission from the men to dig a well deep enough to reach the water. The men had not permitted it, as they did not believe the water was there and also did not want the women to do that kind of work. In their tradition, only certain kinds of labor were allowed for women. Weaving and farming were allowed. Planning and digging a well were not.

The women spoke with convincing vitality and strength. It was clear to me that they knew what they knew, and they could be trusted to find the water. All they needed was permission from the men to pursue their clear instinct. That was the help they needed from an outside source. That was what they needed from us.

There was a rush of collective energy and commitment. I looked around me. It was baking hot. There were thousands of flies. I had silt in my mouth and lungs. It was about as uncomfortable a place as you can imagine being in, and yet I remember that I did not feel any thirst or discomfort—only the presence of possibility amidst these bold and beautiful women.

When we set out into the Sahel Desert, I had feared we were going to encounter people who were hopeless, starving, sick and poor. These people definitely needed more food and water, but they were not "poor." They were not resigned. They were eager to create a way through this challenge, and they burned with the fire of possibility. They were a well of strength, a wealth of perseverance and ingenuity. They wanted our partnership—not handouts or money or food—and respect and equal partnership is what we brought.

After many conversations with both the women and the men, we made an agreement with the mullahs and the chief that we would start our work with the women because the women had the vision. With our partnership, the men agreed to allow the women to begin the work of digging the well. Over the next year, as the community rationed its existing supplies of water carefully, the women dug both with hand tools and the simple equipment we brought them. They dug deeper and deeper into the ground, singing, drumming and caring for each other's children as they worked, never doubting that the water was there.

The men watched skeptically but allowed the work to continue. The women, however, were anything but doubtful. They were certain that if they dug deep enough, the water would be there. And it was! They reached the underground lake of their visions.

In the years since, the men and women have built a pumping system and a water tower for storage. Not just one, but seventeen villages now have water. The whole region is transformed. Women's leadership groups in all seventeen villages are the centers of action. There is irrigation and chicken farming. There are literacy classes and batiking businesses. People are flourishing, and they are contributing members of their country. They face new challenges now and meet them with the same dignity and commitment. The women are now a respected part of the community in a new way, with greater access to leadership, and the tribe is proud that it was their own people, their own work, and the land they lived on that proved to be the key to their own prosperity.

"It was baking hot. There were thousands of flies. I had silt in my mouth and lungs. It was about as uncomfortable a place as you can imagine being in, and yet I remember that I did not feel any thirst or discomfort—only the presence of possibility amidst these bold and beautiful women."

—Lynne Twist

3 · Medicine

had just given a "Chicken Soup for the Woman's Soul" presentation for a client company on the Mississippi Gulf Coast. It was a deeply connecting experience for everyone present, and the audience was still applauding as I walked off the stage and over to my table to get a pen out of my purse, before being whisked to the back of the room to autograph books.

Just before I turned to walk to the back of the hall, a woman came up to me and opened and closed her mouth several times, as if she wanted to say something but couldn't. When she finally spoke, she told me that I had really messed up her plans. Confused, I asked what she meant. She told me that she had been planning to commit suicide the next night, but that now, after hearing me speak, she was going to have to rethink everything.

I took her hand and looked deeply into her eyes. I knew that far more than what I had said, this woman had felt and received the transmission of love that had been so palpable in the room, generated not only by me, but also by everyone present. This love had healed, as love always does.

Jeremy Geffen, M.D., knows well the connection between love and healing. Before retiring from clinical practice in 2003, Dr. Geffen ran a remarkable cancer center in Vero Beach, Florida, for ten years. The Geffen Cancer Center and Research Institute was well known for the unusually high survival rate of its patients. It was a place people often went to as a last resort. In many cases they had been refused treatment at other places and told that their cancer could not be cured or even meaningfully treated. Many had been referred to hospice. But at Dr. Geffen's clinic, in case after case, patients lived longer than their former doctors had predicted, often happily and gratefully.

What made this clinic so effective? For one thing, the waiting room was sunny and graced with orchids, and the chemotherapy suite had soft lounge chairs where patients could sit comfortably to receive their treatments while listening to music through headsets. But what made the experience most different from other medical offices was the clinic's real specialty: blending high-tech medicine with the healing power of love and kindness.

The waiting room was like a living room, with staff and patients, friends and relatives all connecting with one another. Almost no one read magazines—they were too busy interacting and looking after one another. The feeling of family was strong. Numerous scrapbooks in the waiting room were filled with cards, letters, photos and other expressions of love and gratitude received from hundreds of individuals who had been cared for at the center over the years.

If someone didn't show up for a scheduled appointment, everyone knew it and asked about him or her. The staff was so kind and caring that patients and family alike found the clinic to be a refuge in a difficult time. In one case, a patient's wife wanted to go shopping, so he asked her if she'd drop him off at the clinic so he could hang out there while waiting for her! Can you imagine? In another case, a UPS deliveryman was seen sitting alone in the waiting room after he had finished dropping off a package. After some time, the man was approached by a receptionist who gently asked him if he was okay. "Yes," he said quietly. "I've had a rough day. But it feels so good in here that I just don't want to leave."

Why would someone want to hang out at a cancer clinic? Because "medicine" was in the air! For Dr. Geffen, love was an essential part of the medical protocol, and his staff at the cancer center had been carefully chosen and trained to give love, the sweetness of life, along with the other forms of treatment. His high success rate shows the difference it made.

But *how* does love heal exactly? It almost sounds like a cliché, but I recently heard a simple explanation from Dr. Wayne Dyer in a special PBS presentation called *The Power of Intention*. In it, he described the relationship between our behavior and our bodies specifically in terms of serotonin, a chemical produced naturally in the body that is associated with a sense of well-being. He noted that research has found that when a person is a recipient of an act of kindness, his or her serotonin levels increase, strengthening the immune system. But interestingly, the serotonin level also increases in the person *performing* the act of kindness, strengthening his or her immune system as well. And amazingly, if someone simply *witnesses* an act of kindness performed by another, he or she also experiences the same physiological results and benefits!

Finding one's own medicine means finding that ingredient in ourselves—that spark in our essence and our own souls—that allows us to administer to others. "Ministering" is taking care of another's soul. When we allow our essence to administer to another, that person is healed and uplifted to some extent on one or all levels of mind-body-spirit.

Everyone has the ability to heal others—and finding one's own medicine comes naturally. For some people, their medicine might be humor, the ability to laugh at life and to find lightness of spirit in the midst of suffering. Some people are good cooks, and that's their medicine; they cook out of kindness and joy. The movie *Babette's Feast* offers an exquisite look at a woman whose cooking is a sacred act of love and generosity, deeply affecting all those who eat the food she has prepared.

I asked an herbalist, a modern-day "medicine woman," to describe medicine. She said it's the spirit with which you do something. She told me that she can talk to people, counsel them and recommend herbs to them, but only if she does these things with love and devotion can they be true medicine.

Rarely do we think of our behavior or ourselves as medicine. Typically, the word "medicine" refers to a substance we take to get well, in either mind or body. But medicine was always intended to heal mind, body and soul, and, like Dr. Geffen, in the next story Vicky Edmonds gives us insight into the power each of us has to heal others through our own natural impulses and gifts. Vicky shows us that anything we do, if done with the sweetness of love, becomes medicine.

VICKY EDMONDS'S STORY
Food for Each Other

My story is in two parts, both of which came out of a third part, my childhood—but don't all stories? My family was poor and my father so abusive I didn't expect to live to eighteen. He once told us he would kill us and hide our bodies, and no one would even notice we were gone, we were so insignificant. I tried to convince my mother to leave him, but she said, "If I leave, he'll kill us all." I said, "He's going to anyway. Wouldn't you rather die trying?"

She did leave him, and we did survive. But I grew up feeling very small.

Part One: Somebody Should Do Something

I was a young mom without a clue how to be one. My husband Ken was working for a subsidiary of Holland America, the cruise company, while I was mostly staying at home for the first time in my life with our four-and-a-half-year-old son, Lucas, and another son, Ean, just born. Occasionally I helped out at a friend's Montessori school in exchange for Lucas's tuition. But like that of many young moms, my world was small—consistent with the life I had grown up with. That suited me just fine because, deep inside, I felt I had absolutely nothing to give anybody.

However, I always delighted at the opportunity to break out of my world to go on our annual cruise. One of the employee benefits at Ken's company was that we could apply for a cruise once a year. We had applied to go in September 1989—and they had said yes! We were thrilled to be taking our children on a Caribbean cruise to Cozumel, Mexico, and the islands of Grand Cayman and Jamaica.

Four weeks before we were to leave for our vacation, I was watching the news and saw that Jamaica had been struck by Hurricane Gilbert, one of the most devastating hurricanes ever to hit the area. I saw footage of a five-year-old girl with big tears in her eyes, sitting on the steps of a building as water rushed by in the streets. She couldn't find her family, and she couldn't get anywhere. The news report said that all the water was contaminated, and the people were cut off from food supplies. A state of emergency had been declared.

The image of that little girl moved me to tears. As a child, I had felt abandoned too, so my heart and attention were completely with her. I thought, *Somebody should do something to help these people!*

Suddenly, everything shifted. I was the one speaking and also the one witnessing my speaking. I heard myself say this, and then the larger me heard the echoes. *Somebody should do something* was immediately followed by, *I wonder if I'm somebody?*

Thoughts started butting up against each other. *Who do I think I am? How dare I?* These were immediately followed by, *How dare I not?* And then, *I can think big thoughts, but I'll never really do anything or amount to anything.* Part of me was still the small, helpless child.

But it was one of those lucid moments where something explodes and suddenly there's an opening. I saw a possibility of what I might do if I were big enough. I thought maybe I could do something, even if it was small. *Even a small something might be something.* It was terrifying even to think that I might try. What would happen if people laughed at me? How much smaller would I get? But I thought, *I'm going to try.*

The next day as I drove Lucas to school, I tried to teach him that we are citizens of the whole world, and that "taking care of our own" means everything on the planet. I told him about what had happened in Jamaica and said, "Why don't we ask all your friends to bring something for us to send to the people who don't have any food. Let's ask the kids to bring a canned good to school."

Lucas's teacher okayed the plan, so I sent a note home with each of the fourteen children in the class. Over the next week, the children brought in canned goods and put them in a box I had placed in their classroom. They were so sweet and excited. Everybody wants to feel they can give something valuable, and this was the first contribution many of them had ever made. I could actually see the light in their eyes.

One of the moms couldn't get to the store, so she sent a $50 check. I thought, *Oh, my gosh,* and realized that I could go to Costco and buy several large cans of food and dried foods in bulk. But how would I send it all? Our income had been cut in half because I was staying home for the most part with my newborn child. We couldn't even afford heating oil for our house that week and were living mostly in the kitchen where there was a wood stove.

Then over the next week, several other parents sent in checks— one for $75, one for $25. They were all talking about it. I finally decided just to keep some money out for postage, since I couldn't afford to send everything on my own. I was calling UPS and the airlines to find out the cost of shipping canned goods to Jamaica when a writer from *The Seattle Times* called.

He said he'd heard I was collecting food for the children of the hurricane. He wrote a small but very kind article that appeared deep on an inside page of the paper—you know the kind, one of those "human interest" stories.

Suddenly people started showing up at our house to donate food. One older woman and her son drove up in a beat-up, old pickup filled with bags and bags of food. I was standing on the porch when they pulled up, and tears started streaming down my face. The woman just shook my hand and said, "God bless you."

We kept moving the boxes of food into our living room until there was no more room. I had thought I was going to be sending $20 worth of food to Jamaica, and now all of a sudden, we could barely walk through the house because there were giant piles of bags and boxes everywhere.

I started calling airlines. Some of them could get it to Florida, but it was going to cost a fortune—and I didn't have a clue how we'd get it to Jamaica even if we got it that far. I felt so guilty because I didn't know how I would be able to get the food back to the people who had donated it if I wasn't able to get it to the hurricane victims.

But the week before we were to leave, everything started to fall into place. Eastern Airlines told us they'd ship the food as far as Florida—for free! I was told how to package it and how to fill out the complicated paperwork. I took the $75 I'd put aside for postage and went out and bought more food. We borrowed a truck and made a couple of trips to the airport, where the food was put on a pallet and weighed—and we learned we had collected 1,454 pounds of food!

Then, miracle of miracles, Holland America said we could take it with us on our cruise from Florida to Jamaica. Yes, we were still going there. One of the wonderful things about cruise lines is that they visit the places on planned tours even when they've been affected by a natural disaster like Gilbert. With 1,500 people on board, the tourism can contribute significantly to the rebuilding of an area that's been hit.

The big day came, and we set off on our cruise. After a lovely voyage, we were excited to arrive in Jamaica. The customs agents met us as we got off the ship and asked us where the food should be delivered. I had no idea! I had never done anything like this before, and all I had thought about was getting it to Jamaica. The customs agents told us that if we couldn't give them an address by 5:00 P.M., they'd have to seize our shipment.

A man standing nearby overheard what was going on and told us about a church that was housing 40 children who had lost their homes. We couldn't get through by phone, so we got in the man's car, and he drove wildly for about twenty minutes to the church. When we arrived, the minister was too busy to help, but a missionary who had come from Minnesota to help with the disaster volunteered to get some of the teenage boys from the church to come and pick up the goods.

We went back to the ship and waited nervously until, just before customs closed at 5:00, the missionary arrived with a bunch of boys and a big truck. After loading up the truck, they all thanked us profusely, and assured us that the food would all go to help children. Watching that truck drive away, we felt an awful emptiness. I had felt that way after I gave birth to my son: all of a sudden it's over, and there's a profound silence. I was dazed, trying to believe it had all worked.

Ken turned to me and said, "Well, would you like to see any sites before we leave? After all, we are on vacation!" So we got back into tourist mode and toured the island. There was devastation everywhere. Roofs were blown off, broken glass and pieces of rooftops were all over the place, and major reconstruction was going on all around us. But we ended up having a wonderful vacation. Even as we continued our cruise to the other spots on the tour, the feeling of having been a part of something bigger than ourselves stayed with us.

About three weeks after we got home, I called the missionary and learned that a third of our donation had gone to the church housing the children, a third had gone to an orphanage, and the rest had gone to a hospital where mothers had given birth prematurely due to the stress of the hurricane. It had all gone to children! I thought about how no one had come to help me when I was a child. But I had exposed the myth that one person alone can do nothing, and it healed something in my heart.

I had felt that somebody should do something, and I had turned out to be that somebody. But I was hardly prepared for the impact of the shift that had occurred in me.

Part Two: Seeds of Our Souls

Having had the experience of the impossible becoming possible in Jamaica, I got the courage to publish my first book of poetry shortly after returning home. I had been writing poems since I was eleven, trying to survive my own hurricanes. In my family children weren't allowed to have thoughts or feelings, and we were not allowed to tell the secrets of what went on in our house—under threat of death. So mine spilled out onto paper, and writing became my lifeline. I am proof that if we have one place where we can be tethered to the truth, we won't capsize in the storm.

I had written at least eight thousand poems in my life up to this point, and until now I had almost never dared to share any of them with anyone, not even Ken. So, perhaps it's not surprising that my book, *Inside Voices*, was about being barely able to open my mouth at all. I got the courage to break the silence by again asking myself, *What can one person do?* I still wondered. But I thought, *Maybe if I break the silence it will change the way future generations in my family are treated.*

And I remembered Jamaica and thought, *Maybe it always has to start with one person—maybe one person is the only person who can do something.* As Margaret Mead said, "Never doubt that the work of a small group of thoughtful, committed citizens can change the world. Indeed, it's the only thing that ever has."

Part of my fear was that no one would want to read my poems. But then I realized that these poems had been successful when I had had the courage to write them at all. They were successful when people were kind enough to stand in a room while I read them out loud, giving me the opportunity to be witnessed and no longer in isolation with my truth. And then they were successful when I had the courage to put them in a book.

And so I thought, if the book sells, it'll just be icing on the cake! They had already done their job—they had helped me break out of prison. I went again from *How dare I?* to *How dare I not?*

My deeper fear was of my family's anger. And, in fact, some of them were furious at the publication of these secrets. My mother and sister were proud that I was an author, but they wouldn't talk about the book. Then a local television station did a segment called *If Words Could Kill* that featured a poem I had written called

"Cutting Room Floor" about trying to edit the abusive words from my psyche. Some of my aunts saw it and called my mom, saying I was telling lies on television about the family. I learned from my mother that none of them had ever known the extent to which my father had abused us. Ironically, the event brought my mother closer to her sisters than ever before. She got to tell them the truth and be comforted for the first time.

Realizing that trying to keep the secrets inside me was killing me, I published my second book of poetry a year later, titled *used to the dark*. This one was about opening my mouth wide and screaming, an even deeper surgery on my pain and isolation. I donated some copies to a project called Books for Prisoners and a few weeks later got a call from a woman working at the local juvenile prison. She said she had a group of girls she had been trying to reach in many ways, but "nothing had been happening except attitude." Then she had started reading the girls my poems, and she said, "They get really quiet and then just fall open. Suddenly they're saying, 'That happened to me!'" My writings had given them permission to break their silence.

When the woman asked me to give a reading at the prison, I asked if I could give a poetry class at no charge instead. I wrote with that group of girls for twelve weeks and then made a book of their writings. We called it *Confinement: The Things We Keep Locked Up Inside.* Many of the poems explored an idea I had given them: If you lock up your secrets and your thoughts of worthlessness, you can't see through them to your good qualities, your beauty and your potential. If you hide the parts that you think are ugly, you don't let yourself see your beauty, either.

I gave some extra copies of the book to a friend who worked at a treatment center for kids with drug and behavioral problems. One thing led to another, and I've been giving poetry classes there for the last nine years. In fact, I've worked with hundreds of thousands of adults and children now: battered women, prisoners, gang kids, sex offenders, at detention centers and halfway houses—you name it.

One of my most amazing experiences was at a community center where gang and street kids aged twelve to twenty would come on Fridays and Saturdays between 10:00 P.M. and 2:00 A.M. to get food, play board games and shoot hoops. The kids literally had to check their guns and knives at the door with an off-duty police officer to come in. They knew they wouldn't get their weapons back, but they came in anyway. Grandmothers volunteered to cook for the kids—who, for a change, got to be kids. The youth crime rate went down 53 percent in the neighborhood during the time this program was operating. I was brought in as part of the high-school general equivalency diploma (GED) program, expecting six or seven kids. But at times we had as many as twenty-eight kids sitting on each other's laps, writing poetry. At the end of the course, I published their poetry in a book they named *Lost Between the Cracks*—because they felt they were "throw-away kids."

One of my neighbors asked me one day, "How can you work with sex offenders? They should be locked up and the key thrown away." I told her that some would be out when they were eighteen—about five minutes from now! If I could get them to rage on paper about their own abuse (96 percent of child sex offenders are victims themselves), they could have compassion for their own victimization and possibly make a shift. And if just one of them got enough out of his system that he didn't rape someone in an alley one night, would that be enough for my whole life's work? It absolutely would!

Over time I found it wasn't just the gang kids who had painful secrets. A group of eighth-graders at my son's middle school wrote poems I published in the book *Between the Lines: Things We Still Can't Say Out Loud*. Even in these more advantaged kids at this nice middle-class school, I found the same sense of worthlessness—which I regard as the biggest mistake in human thinking and the biggest lie ever told. I always feel that if I can get them to consider that it's a lie, then they can look for the ideas and the seeds they hold inside.

My own boys are growing up healthy, whole and self-confident. Lucas is now a hip-hop artist, who composes amazing music and lyrics and produced an album with his best friend for their senior project in high school. Ean doesn't like to sit down long enough to write anything, but when he does, it's wonderful. A poem he wrote in middle school begins: "Knowing we two would be the same, I looked for you in the places I would be."

For me, everything started when I had the thought, *I wish somebody would do something,* and answered it with the question, *Could I be somebody?* I went from believing I had nothing to give, to seeing that I could feed hundreds of Jamaican children, to now knowing that there aren't enough days in the year to give all the gifts I have to give. When I work with adults and kids, I try to prove to them that they, too, are somebody and they, too, have boundless gifts to give. In fact, their very presence is a gift waiting to be opened. They may think they're worthless, but they're not. They are themselves gifts of nourishment and healing that the world desperately needs.

I tell everyone I work with, "You cannot prove your worthlessness to me." We all have inside us delicious food and healing medicine that the world is dying from the lack of. Every single person I see now, I wonder, *What medicine is hiding inside them? What food is waiting there to be given to us all?*

Becoming Food

I am a pear.
I want to be
soft on your lips,
easily swallowed,
taken and digested

each bite completely
until I am a part of you.
Until I can add
myself holy
into your growing,
into your strength,
into the lack of hunger
of knowing.
I am a bowl of pears
offered
to each one in the room,
plenty for everyone,
never empty,
if you're still hungry,
there is more.
I am an orchard
of pear trees,
strong and rooted,
wood in the sun,
flesh of fruit
ready for picking
many different times
through the summer,
many sittings,
many meals.
I am the pear on the ground
giving in, giving myself in
to the soil
so that I can grow
from the seed and the pulp
into new ways
of being.
And I am the full mason jar

on a grandmother's shelf
ready to offer myself
still to you
in the dead of winter
so that you will be nourished
and I
will still be
food.

—Vicky Edmonds

"I went from believing I had nothing to give, to seeing that I could feed hundreds of Jamaican children, to now knowing there aren't enough days in the year to give all the gifts I have to give."

—Vicky Edmonds

4 · Self-Love

sat in my therapist's office, crying. "It doesn't matter how much I do—it's never enough!" I shouted angrily. "I take my supplements, I do yoga every day, I come regularly for my appointments. I still can't balance my pH, and my cancer still won't go away."

Ali, my therapist, sat in compassionate silence while I sobbed. Then quietly he said, "I think the problem, Jennifer, is that you make healing an item on your to-do list. You think it's something you can 'do'—like going to the grocery store or picking up the dry cleaning—then check off your list when you've completed it. But you're not willing to change anything about your routine, your habits, your workaholism, your thriving on adrenaline. You don't make taking care of yourself a priority, and you're not willing to live your life any differently." I left his office in despair, knowing he was right.

Three years earlier, a doctor had discovered I had a basal cell carcinoma on the side of my nose. Although not life threatening, it was still enough to demand attention. Chemotherapy had cured it—for one year. Then it came back. I knew that another round of chemotherapy or surgery would likely take care of it again, but the underlying cause of the cancer was clearly not being addressed.

So I had determined to change my diet and work with Ali, a psychologist and health practitioner, to see if I could eliminate the cause of the disease. At this point I had been trying for a year and a half, but the cancer was visibly growing. In complete frustration, I finally scheduled an appointment to see a doctor for a biopsy. I hated admitting that I had failed.

I was relieved to be going on vacation to Hawaii before the appointment. I desperately needed a break, having recently completed a manuscript for a book and working twelve to fourteen hours a day in the final days before deadline. I was exhausted— physically, mentally and emotionally. I knew that what Ali was saying was true, but I didn't have a clue how to change my life. To make matters worse, my frenetic pace had been completely at odds with what I was writing and speaking about—topics like balance! But I couldn't see how I could have done things differently and still met my deadlines. *Not* meeting deadlines and speaking demands would have been unthinkable for me.

Once in Hawaii, I did almost nothing but rest. I walked on the beach at beautiful Lanikai on Oahu, then slept, then walked some more. I had little energy for anything else, and I cried every day. I prayed for answers and met frequently with friends in a support circle.

And one day I met Ginny. My friends had told me about her, and I wanted to interview her for this book, which was in the beginning stages. We sat in the hot Hawaiian sun as she told me her story and changed my life forever.

Before I met Ginny, I thought I knew what self-love was—despite what Ali had said to me. I had been speaking professionally about self-esteem for more than ten years, always defining it as how much you like yourself. But as many times as I had stood in front of audiences and talked about how self-esteem is deeper than achievements, deeper than possessions, deeper than relationships, I was defining my own self-worth by exactly that: my material and outward success. I knew that I was successful *in terms of the way our society defines success*, so it was easy for me to think of myself as having high self-esteem and to like—if not actually *love*—myself very much.

But when you really love yourself, you do not put your healing on your to-do list. You get very real, willing to go deep within yourself, to expose yourself, to become vulnerable *to yourself* and to show yourself that you care.

This will mean different things to different people. But I'd like to share Ginny's story with you. Perhaps, like me, you will read it and come away with a deeper understanding of what self-love means—for you.

As for me, Ginny helped me understand that self-love is really compassion directed towards one's self. Her story went so deep into my mind and heart that one month after meeting Ginny, I canceled my doctor's appointment. My cancer was gone.

GINNY WALDEN
Olympic Heart

t was ten o'clock at night and all was silent on the hospital ward. I went to the bathroom to wash, and as I filled the sink, I looked into the mirror. I saw my bald head, my skinny body and the dark circles under my eyes. I saw a body wounded from six months of cancer treatment. The irony of my situation was not lost on me.

As a child I was an avid swimmer and athlete. To get away from my difficult family life, I poured all my energies into my dream of being on the Olympic team someday. By the time I was fifteen, I had started training myself by swimming between the buoys and the small islands in Long Island Sound at Rye, New York, where I grew up. At seventeen, I was training seriously for the 1964 Olympics. I had already qualified for the 100-meter freestyle when, at an unofficial meet two weeks before the Olympic trials, my coach asked if anyone wanted to swim the 1500-meter. I timidly raised my hand—and then proceeded to break the national record for this event. I would later learn that my unofficial time was only thirty-five seconds behind the men's world record!

At my coach's urging, I called my family and asked if they would send me to Los Angeles to compete in the last meet in the nation where I could qualify to go to the Olympics in this event. But, no surprise, they refused. So I didn't get a shot at qualifying for the 1500. And ultimately, my time at the trials was not fast enough to make it in the 100-meter event either. I was truly a long-distance swimmer, but I had learned that too late.

Angry and frustrated, I gave up training for the next Olympics. But I continued to swim and then coach swimming, just to stay in shape—and for the joy of swimming. For the next thirty years I led a very active life. I spent a lot of time outdoors in nature, ate healthy meals and rarely ate junk food. I stayed in peak condition and eventually went on to break five national Masters swimming records for my age group!

Meanwhile, my professional life was also flourishing. When I was twenty-one, I had moved west to Santa Fe, New Mexico, to pursue my other calling as an artist. Now, at the age of fifty, I was a regionally known sculptor and loved my work—carving stone and creating bronzes. I also wrote poetry and performed and taught classical and flamenco guitar. In my personal life, I was in and out of relationships and therapy, learning about myself through the school of hard knocks.

Then, in August 1997, I was diagnosed with Stage 3 advanced breast cancer. A mammogram three years earlier had shown a pea-sized spot, but I had been told it was no big deal, nothing to be alarmed about, and to come back in three years, which was the norm at that time. I increased my commitment to wellness by adding emotional healing to my fitness program. I started "working on myself," letting go of many of the destructive patterns in my life related to my work and relationships. I had always had trouble seeing the value of my work or myself. I had typically lost myself in relationships in an effort to please others and tended never to ask enough for my artwork. After a life of much inner and outer conflict, however, I was finally beginning to feel truly happy.

But in three years the spot had grown into a lump; the doctors told me it had probably been growing for eight to ten years. The thought of cancer was so far removed from my healthy, fitness-oriented reality that I couldn't even relate to the diagnosis. And I felt so good that I couldn't quite buy into the fear of the illness. I told my doctors that I was not going to stop being happy just because I now knew that I had had cancer for ten years. My oncologist approved. He said with great seriousness that the American Medical Association (AMA) now approved a positive attitude. I laughed and asked, "And how much does that cost?"

For the next nine months, I embraced conventional treatment with the attitude that I would pull out all the stops and take a stand for my life. I had surgery, during which my doctor removed a tumor from my breast the size of an orange. Then I sailed through three months of chemotherapy with no ill effects. I believe I did so well because I had researched alternative options, and I had embraced acupuncture, meditation and a macrobiotic diet as an important part of my healing regimen. At one point, a Native American shaman told me that my illness was leaving because I was not giving it a home. I also asked Dorje, a Tibetan monk in Santa Fe connected with the Dalai Lama, about cancer. He said, "Ginny, do not be fearful. Fear increases illness. Do whatever medicine you choose; it does not matter. Just be joyful, be happy! Do what makes you happy!" This appealed to me, and I continued to maintain a truly joyful attitude throughout the nine months of treatment.

I also continued to search for alternative therapies, hoping that I would not have to go through more of the conventional treatments. My doctor assured me I'd die if I chose the alternative approaches at the expense of the traditional. He recommended a risky new treatment called "stem cell rescue," in which stem cells are extracted from bone marrow, frozen, and later put back into the body after high doses of chemotherapy have theoretically destroyed all cancer cells. I elected to do the treatment as an outpatient, believing I'd be more exposed to infection in the hospital.

The treatment was brutal. I threw up, fainted, had epileptic fits and suffered internal bleeding as well as a nosebleed that lasted seven hours—my platelets were so low that my blood couldn't clot. I couldn't hold down food, so I lost fifteen pounds and was skin and bones. After the stem cells were reintroduced, I was just waiting for the tenth day, at which point the stem cells should have kicked in and started rebuilding my immune system. But on day nine my white blood cell count was so low that I had to be admitted to the hospital. My doctor said my immune system was so depleted that if I scratched myself, I could infect myself and die.

In the hospital room there was a large red notice on my door stating "Neutropoenic"—which, loosely translated, meant that I could die if someone breathed on me. The nurses and doctors looked at me gravely and said I would need to be there a month and a half or two before my immune system could return to normal—*if* it returned to normal, I read between the lines. I could not have visitors and would be alone a lot. But I told myself I could do it and proceeded to fix up my room.

Now here I was, late at night, regarding myself in the mirror, as bald as Tweetie Bird. I looked like Death.

And then something odd happened. Friends had always told me, "Ginny, you need to love yourself." Never having experienced unconditional love, I had no idea what it felt like. But in that moment, looking in the mirror at my wounded body, a deep feeling came up from my belly, through my chest and up to my eyes, and I started to cry.

For the first time, I felt compassion for *me*. Tears came down my cheeks as I slowly and gently bathed my body the way a mother would bathe an infant. I pressed the hot washcloth against my skin with love and compassion, saying "I love you" and "thank you" to my body with every touch. I bathed my whole body in this manner. And for the first time, I felt unconditional love for myself.

Afterwards I felt light and happy. I tucked myself into bed, somehow knowing I would make it. I had seen cancer treatments kill so many people, and deep inside, I knew that there *had* to be other ways to heal—the body is always healing itself naturally. But how could I facilitate that process? I made a promise that I would help teach others how to heal if I were shown how to do it. I went to sleep feeling safe and happy.

That night I dreamed of the Dalai Lama. He came to me inside a tall, clear crystal, his head bowed, his hands in praying position as he said, "Now, Ginny, remember—be joyful!" When I woke up it was sunrise, all gold and blue over the Sandia Mountains. I felt so good that I danced around the room singing my favorite song, Bobby McFerrin's "Don't Worry, Be Happy," which I played daily to inspire me.

The nurse came and took my blood sample. Minutes later, the doctor returned with my report. Suddenly, he threw up his hands and shouted, "What?" All the nurses came running; they probably thought I had died! He said, "Yesterday her blood counts were 600. Today they are 7,700. They are normal!"

He said the only reason they would be so high was if I had a fever or an infection, but I had neither. And I had been there only three days! The doctor and nurses looked at me as if I were a ghost. The nurses said they had not seen anyone recover so quickly in the entire five years they had been there. The next day my count was again normal, and they sent me home.

Less than two weeks later, I heard about a Chinese exercise called Chi-Lel, the form of medical *qigong* (pronounced "chee-gung"), considered the number-one self-healing method for chronic illness in China. Watching a videotape, I gazed in awe as an ultrasound showed a patient's malignant bladder tumor, the size of a tennis ball, disappear in forty-five seconds while four teachers practiced the techniques, saying affirmations and moving their hands over the area of the tumor, never even touching his body!

Thrilled by this discovery, I went to a workshop to learn Chi-Lel for myself—and found that the personal technique involved patting the body with the center of the palms methodically and rhythmically, all the while "talking" to the body. It was almost identical to what I had done spontaneously that night in the hospital.

At the workshop, my teacher suggested I begin teaching others, as healing takes place faster in a group. She said I was a natural, so, before even starting the radiation treatments that followed my release from the hospital, I began practicing the techniques myself *and* teaching them to others. Over the next four months I taught eight hundred people for free or by donation, all while I was receiving radiation and recovering from the stem cell procedure. A fitness center donated space for my group's Chi-Lel practice: we had as many as fifty people at a time. Healings occurred regularly. I had been shown a way to help others, as well as myself.

I had been advised that I would be in bed with severe burns on my chest for two weeks, but after six weeks of radiation, I was not burned at all. I also healed the devitalized tissue inside my right breast from the scars of the lumpectomy, which my doctor said was impossible.

In the following years, practicing Chi-Lel would help me complete my physical, emotional and mental healing, as well as detoxify my body from the conventional treatments I had received. My oncologist said that the cancer would probably be back within a year, but I have now been cancer free for six years. I call my new hair my $100,000 haircut! In 2002, I was honored to be promoted to Senior Instructor of Chi-Lel, one of only five worldwide, and I have now had the joy of teaching the Chi-Lel self-healing method to more than 3,000 people.

Most important is the emotional healing I've experienced. My heart has opened and I feel like everyone is my family. When I learned how to feel compassion for myself, I learned how to feel compassion for everyone and everything. Compassion is the essential flow of the heart that connects us to the world. It has allowed me to feel a oneness with all of life—and this has empowered me as a woman, an artist and a human being.

"When I learned how to feel compassion for myself, I learned how to feel compassion for everyone and everything. Compassion is the essential flow of the heart that connects us to the world."

—Ginny Walden

5 · Faith

f you're old enough to have watched *The Ozzie and Harriet Show,* the popular television program of the late fifties, you probably saw actresses Sara Buckner (now O'Meara) and Yvonne Lime (now Fedderson), who had feature roles on the show playing Ricky and David Nelson's girlfriends. Real-life best friends and roommates, Sara and Yvonne had plans for big careers in Hollywood.

When they auditioned for an entertainment tour of Korea and Japan, they were selected out of 500 girls because they "looked like the girls next door." The story you are about to read tells of an experience they had in Japan that changed their lives—and, ultimately, the lives of thousands of children.

Sara and Yvonne say that they owe their success to faith. In their case, faith is connected to their understanding that they are never in charge of what they are doing, "God is."

But faith is not necessarily religious, nor does it necessarily have to do with belief. Dr. James Fowler, a Harvard-trained expert in the psychology of religion and the author of *Stages of Faith*, says that faith is a person's way of making sense of life. He says that everyone operates by some basic faith, whether it is associated with religion or not.

For example, I experience faith as a feeling of being at home in the universe, an undeniable knowing that all is well and that all will be taken care of. For me, faith means living in a reality that sees everything that happens as having a purpose, and everything that happens to me personally, good or bad, as contributing to my understanding about life. As my friend Father Tom Miller puts it, "Darkness is my candle."

For my sister Heather, faith is not merely having hope—it is absolute belief. She describes her faith in God as something that can release burdens and worries, and that has helped her keep her sanity time and time again. She says that faith is "a condition of the heart in which you have no doubts, but rather certainty and trust. Faith erases anxiety and doubt, and creates or builds inner peace and happiness."

It's my experience that, if we can face the hard times in life with a willingness to learn from them, more and more light is revealed. In this way, we become freer and more open, with an ever expanding view of life. When we have faith in something, whether religious or not, we can act with the certainty that no matter what happens, the outcome will be right, even perfect.

In the case of Sara and Yvonne, they say faith allows them to put one foot in front of the other toward every next goal, always knowing that, on the other side of obstacles, there are miracles.

SARA O'MEARA & YVONNE FEDDERSON'S STORY
Silence Broken

Yvonne and I were warm and safe in our hotel room in Tokyo, Japan, after four days of a severe typhoon—one of the worst the city had ever seen. We had never experienced such fierce storms in our lives. For a couple of those nights, we had sat in our hotel room in total darkness with the high winds pounding at our windows—all power had gone out. We had all been under strict orders not to leave the hotel, and we were more than glad to comply. It was considered a "red flag" alert. No one in the city was to go outside because of the high level of destruction that had also produced dangerous and unsanitary conditions.

But at the first sign of clearing, coupled with feeling tired of being stuck in our room for days, we decided to bundle up against the cold and venture out to explore the storm's aftermath. Our youthful curiosity had gotten the best of us and fueled our sense of adventure. As we walked through the lobby of the hotel, the desk clerk asked if he could help us.

"Oh, no! We are just going out for a walk," Yvonne replied.

"But, ladies, there is a red flag alert! You're not supposed to leave," he protested, coming out from behind the desk.

"Oh, we'll be fine. We're just going out for a short walk and getting some fresh air," I shot back as we quickly exited.

Up and down the streets we wandered, amazed at the devastation before our eyes. Trash and debris were scattered everywhere; people were cleaning up whatever they could salvage. Some were loading baskets with what we guessed might be food. In some places where we stepped, the mud mixed with who-knows-what oozing up over the tops of our shoes. At times, the stench almost took our breath away. After about a mile's walk, we turned down a small side street deciding it might be wise to start back. This initial little adventure for the two of us had already been quite an eye-opener.

Suddenly, we came upon a group of small children huddled in a circle under a fallen awning in an attempt to fend off the freezing winds. The look on their faces at the sight of these two white women coming toward them expressed a silent plea for help. They were shivering; some barefooted, most with tears streaming down their faces. As we moved closer, we noticed their knuckles were cracked and bleeding from the cold, their light cotton clothing torn, tattered and soaked through. We counted eleven of them, ranging in age from what seemed to be about two to twelve years old.

Horrified by the sight, our motherly instincts instantly flooded us as we unbuttoned our coats and beckoned them to come inside to get warm. Without hesitation, the children dove under one by one, our coats ballooning as they squeezed in. Feeling the shivering cluster against us, Yvonne and I stood there in silence for a moment looking into each other's eyes. We didn't know what to do to comfort them and pulled out our English to Japanese dictionary in a desperate effort to translate, "Where are your parents?"

Having no luck, all we could think of saying to them was, "No papa sans? No mama sans?" The children just shook their heads and cried harder.

We knew, right at that moment, what we had to do. Without speaking, we turned and slowly began shuffling our bundles the mile back toward our hotel. As we maneuvered our cargo back through the streets, we kept trying to figure out what we were going to do. What a sight we were as we maneuvered along through the mud- and debris-filled streets. We had no idea whether these children had been lost or abandoned during the typhoon. All we knew was that they needed a hot meal, a warm bath, a chance for their clothes to dry and a good night's sleep—and that's exactly what we were going to give them. We were sure that when we got back to the hotel, we could find out where they belonged. At the moment, there was no time for any thoughts other than to keep moving. We were all soaked through by now and cold to the bone. But we had started this trek, and there was no turning back.

When we arrived at the hotel, we stopped outside for a moment to uncover the children. Yvonne and I agreed that we would just walk them in with us right through the lobby—hopefully dodging any resistance—and take them up to our room. We put our fingers to our lips in an attempt to signal them to be quiet. With a couple of the children in our arms and the others clinging to our coats, we entered.

To this day, I distinctly remember the rush I felt going through my body as we just walked straight through the lobby with frozen smiles on our faces in hopes no one would say anything—or notice. It amazes me how naïve we were as we led this disheveled parade, smiling and nodding at the hotel staff and other guests. After all, we were actresses, weren't we? We hoped we could carry this off. (Years later, we would laugh as we shared what each other was thinking at that moment.)

In my mind's voice, I kept repeating, *Children? What children? Just keep moving, Sara.* Yvonne said she just kept thinking, *I hope no one stops us,* and *I hope we don't see the colonel.*

Lucky for us, we didn't see him, or our mission would have stopped right there, immediately. After all, we weren't even to have been out of the hotel with the red flag alert still in effect.

When we made it up to the floor of our room, Yvonne and I stopped for a moment to take a breath before heading down the long hallway.

"We made it," I said to her with a nervous giggle.

As we proceeded down the corridor to our room, the maids on the floor just looked at us curiously, wondering what it was we were doing. We closed the door behind us. With the children still clutching on to us, we looked at each other and simultaneously said, "Now what?" What we had done really hit us in that moment. We had become so caught up in our impulse to help these children that we obviously had thought through nothing more than getting to this point; we just did the next thing that seemed natural.

We began to undress and bathe the children—two and three at a time in the tub until all were clean and wrapped in whatever we could find for makeshift clothing. By the time we were through, our room looked like a laundry with clothing hanging everywhere to dry. Then we called room service and ordered up food for all. We were surprised when the order came with exactly enough plates, glasses, and utensils for thirteen people. We hadn't asked for those, in an effort to keep our visitors a secret. Needless to say, by that time, the whole hotel was abuzz about the two women and eleven children. So much for going unnoticed.

We decided it was time to approach the colonel about what to do with the precious cargo in our room. We realized we needed some direction on how to find out where the children belonged. Surely, we thought, they were only misplaced by the frenzy of the typhoon, and all had homes somewhere. There certainly must be parents looking for these darling children. We persuaded the maids to look after the children as we set off to find the colonel.

When we found him and began unfolding the story, his reaction wasn't what we'd expected. He hit the ceiling and informed us that this was one of the worst things we could have done. He was horrified that we had brought the children into the hotel, much less to *our* room. He explained our actions could bring about major problems for all of us because we knew nothing about these children—who they belonged to or where they were from.

We halfheartedly apologized for not thinking more before we had brought the children with us, but we refused to abandon them back into the streets. We asked whether it was true that he also had children. We remembered he had spoken about them. Would he want them abandoned if something happened to him?

We just kept at him until he finally caved in and said, "Okay, okay."

He informed us that the best thing we could do was to get them dressed and take them to one of the orphanages in the city. He would quickly compile a list for us. We were to go get the children and be back downstairs in a half hour. There was a certain tension in his order that we didn't comprehend at the time.

With a speed that would have made anyone dizzy, we gathered the children and were back downstairs where the colonel ushered us out to a waiting taxi van he had obtained driven by an English-speaking Japanese man. The colonel and driver agreed that the driver would act as our interpreter in our attempt to find a safe haven for these children. After a brief conversation with the colonel, he handed us the list of orphanages, and we were off on our search.

By this time it was midafternoon, and we had little daylight left for our pursuit. As we moved down our list, orphanage by orphanage, we were told time and again that because of the typhoon, many Japanese children had been orphaned; thus, the orphanages were at capacity. When the sun began to fade, we wondered what were we to do. We still had several orphanages on our list. We were steadfast to this commitment and agreed that we could not leave the children out in the night.

"Back to the hotel," we instructed our driver.

That time, we stopped along the way and purchased some food to take with us so we wouldn't have to call room service. We also made an agreement with our driver to meet us at a designated place near the hotel early the next morning.

Yvonne and I decided that to avoid being caught by the colonel, we would take the children up the back fire escape to our room for the night. On our return, we had the driver drop us off in the back of the hotel. We *knew* we were asking for big trouble if we were caught. As we climbed the fire escape, I felt the adrenaline rush through my head. The two young maids on duty began giggling as they watched us pass the children through the window into the hallway of our floor. This was the funniest scenario they had ever seen. To ensure that our "stowaways" were not revealed to anyone and to get some extra blankets for the night, we tipped them with cashmere sweaters we had brought along from home.

As the morning light streamed across the city, we exited via the fire escape and set out on our search once again. Hour after hour, our troop rambled through the streets in our taxi with no success. The story was always identical—no room. It was early afternoon as we approached one of the last orphanages on the list. We drove up and stopped at the entrance. While we ushered the children out of the taxi toward the door, they started pulling back and crying in unison. Although confused by their reaction, we proceeded to knock on the door. The children began speaking in gasping clips through their tears, pointing at the door.

When the door opened, we were greeted by a gentle-looking man with a surprised look on his face at the very sight right before him. After a brief exchange with our taxi driver, our driver-translator informed us that the children had been living in this very orphanage before they were sent into the streets as a result of the typhoon's destruction.

"How could this be?" we asked. "Then why were they turned away?" we also asked.

It was at this point that the truth of these children's plight was made clear to us. Our driver explained that the orphanage could no longer keep these children because they are half-American and half-Japanese. The disaster had created a situation wherein so many full-blooded Japanese had been left homeless and parentless, that the Japanese government would only subsidize them—not any children who were of mixed blood.

As we stood there listening, we couldn't believe what we were being told. The head of the orphanage went on to explain that he had actually taken these children in before even though he wasn't authorized. After the typhoon, he had been instructed to take in the full-blooded children only and send these eleven children out. He apologized with a face that looked somewhat embarrassed, yet he said there was nothing he could do. He wished us luck in finding a place, turned and closed the door.

Stunned and speechless, Yvonne and I stood in the street frozen for a moment. We had difficulty comprehending what we had just been told. So this was the reason they were abandoned—because they were half-American. Prior to this, we had just been two young girls living in what was the America of the late 1950s who knew something about the rising voice surrounding discrimination but had never witnessed it personally. The issue stared us directly in the face. We had never understood the possible complications for children born of parents of different races. These children—who were fast becoming our children—had become "throw-aways." They had no value—not even to the parents from whom they were born. We were enraged! This gave us the courage to go back and face the colonel.

We had no thoughts of the possible implications that these half-American, half-Japanese children would have on our lives. We had no way of knowing at that time what breaking the silence of these children's plight was going to mean to our lives. Our innocence was beginning to have cracks running all through it.

When we returned to the hotel, we explained to the colonel all we had been through and adamantly told him we were not going to walk away from the children. He took a deep breath, shook his head and then gave us the name of a doctor—a half-American, half-Japanese man—who had been running the Tokyo Gospel

Missions and who, in the past, had taken such children into his establishments. The colonel then confessed to us that he had known that the half-American children were a problem. We hit on an issue that both governments refused to deal with at the time. It was growing to be a "hot topic."

Fueled with a newfound energy, we immediately contacted the doctor. Sadly, we found that he was leaving for the United States. But he directed us to a Japanese woman known as "Mama Kin," who he felt might be able to help because she had already taken other mixed-blood children into her home. Once again, we loaded the children back into the van and struck out to find Mama Kin.

We were very encouraged until we arrived at her threadbare, one-room hut with no front door in the doorway. Even the windows were without windowpanes. She wanted to help but pointed to the ten other orphans for whom she was already caring—whose looks, oddly enough, resembled the children we had in tow. Her roof was leaking, and two small hibachis were fired up—one for cooking and the other for warmth. She was just serving the last of her food. She explained that she had no money to take care of her ten, much less to take in eleven more. She showed us that she only had two jackets that the children took turns wearing outside and to school.

Through our driver-translator, we learned that Mama Kin's children had also been turned away by their families in shame, and had been living, unwanted, on the streets. She had turned this little dirt-floor shack into a refuge for them. Although her place was meager, we could readily see that she was filled with love and light. We told her if she would help us with our children, she could trust that we would also find help for the other children. We could look into her eyes and see she was someone *we* could trust. Finally, she agreed to keep our children, and we promised to return the next day. (Later we discovered that her name meant *golden one* in the Japanese language. She proved to be every bit that—and then some.)

Yvonne and I decided that the only place we could ask for help was from the servicemen attending our show that evening. We weren't sure what might happen when we broke the silence about these half-American children we had found wandering the streets. Yet we were sure that some of their fathers, if not the majority, were quite possibly the result of some of the servicemen on R and R (rest and relaxation) from Korea where they were stationed. We were there to entertain and didn't know whether they would take offense if we brought this up, causing us to be in trouble. But that chance we had to take. We had made a promise to Mama Kin—and the children.

As we went through the show that night, Yvonne and I could hardly concentrate on our performance. When it was over, instead of leaving after our applause, we just stayed center stage. Our hearts pounded; I don't remember who started talking first. But by the time we were done, we had spoken out about these children.

"Some of these might be your children, for all you know," we said. "Please, won't you help these innocent little Amerasian orphans?"

We then passed the hat as we pleaded with them to meet us at our hotel the next morning and come help us make the children's home warm and more comfortable.

The response was fantastic. Somehow—and somewhere—we had clearly hit a nerve. The next morning, more than a dozen soldiers arrived at our hotel in an army truck filled with blankets, C-rations and lumber to help upgrade the makeshift orphanage—most of them young men. We spent the entire day at Mama Kin's. Some of the servicemen put in a front door and windowpanes and did general repairs to the hut, while others accompanied us to an open-air market to buy more bedding, tatami mats, warm clothes, food and other things those desperate children needed.

We discovered that these kind men were more than willing to help. In fact, they even came back on different occasions while we were in Japan. Some came back to help again, while some just came to play with the children when they could. Sometimes, as I watched them interact with the children, I wondered if one of them might be part of their own story. But it didn't matter; the ones who came clearly cared. For the rest of the scheduled tour, whenever we weren't entertaining the troops, we continued to help the homeless Amerasian children and the kind-faced woman who had dedicated her life to housing them.

As word got out, more Amerasian children were left on the doorstep of Mama Kin's hut with notes pinned on them that read, "For the Orphanage of Mixed Blood." Mama Kin's home came to be our first orphanage, eventually housing more than one hundred children after the various expansions and renovations that we were able to pull out of thin air with God's help.

As our particular goodwill tour was coming to an end, we went to the persons-in-charge and asked, "Is there a way that we could extend our trip and do other shows?"

They were thrilled because they wouldn't have to send for other actresses to come and do the shows. They paid us a per diem. Although it wasn't much, it allowed us to remain in Japan an additional two months and continue to stabilize the orphanage. Doing our shows at night gave us the opportunity to go to Mama Kin's during the day to work with her and the children. We continued to have the servicemen pass the hat and obtain whatever help we could beg or borrow.

Our adventures in Japan were filled with red tape and stumbling blocks. Who knows what would have happened without the kind financial support we received from our families in the States and those servicemen? Most Americans weren't as supportive at the time: The reality of just how many children had been fathered by some of our soldiers over there did not come to full light until some years later when we dealt with the same issue in Vietnam. Yet we were determined to stay with this project even after we returned to the United States.

One of our biggest obstacles was the red tape we continuously faced, which set into motion major trials in our laborious efforts to manage what we were giving birth to. It was difficult for anyone to imagine that our efforts would amount to anything. After all, we were only a couple of young actresses. To this day, we still run up against walls. Little did we know back in those first days in Japan that this journey would be such a challenge. Yet the driving force behind our mission is that we have always known we are not alone. Although there have been obstacles and people who have stood in our way throughout, we knew that we had dedicated this mission to God. As such, we will always have him by our side, along with some very special "earthly angels." For that, we are truly grateful and owe our success.

The truth is we don't think much about whether we can do something. When we got this first "call" from God, we answered— no questions asked. We've never really stopped to look at the big picture. We've never bought into the fear and resistance we met along the way. We've just kept putting one foot in front of the other toward our next goal with a lot of faith, prayer and trust. We have seemed to go from obstacle to miracle, over and over. We then came to realize that somehow, the miracle will always show up on the other side of the obstacle—if we just hang in there long enough and keep the faith. We've tackled roadblocks as if they were to be expected. We have simply remembered at all times that we are not in charge, God is. We started to break the silence of child abuse in Japan, and we're not about to let it go silent again.

We consider our work with the children in Japan to be a per- fectly natural beginning, as the events have continued to unfold over the years. Although the work there was enormous, we, along with our wonderful volunteers, managed to build and maintain four orphanages exclusively through private funding. Together with others who cared, Yvonne and I were also able to launch a nonprofit organization and create chapters around the United States to help expand the visibility of our mission. We called it International Orphans, Inc. (IOI). This organization eventually became Childhelp USA as we brought our efforts homeward. We know that this is what God wants us to do. Someone has to give these children a voice. And it's our privilege to continue to do so.

POSTSCRIPT: By 1964, it appeared that virtually all of the Amerasian orphans in Japan had found homes, and Sara and Yvonne thought their work was done. But then General Lewis Walt asked if they could help the orphaned children in Vietnam, where war was beginning to heat up. Once again, the two friends didn't hesitate. From 1966 to 1972, under the banner of International Orphans, Inc., they raised funds to build and maintain five orphanages, schools and children's hospitals in Vietnam.

At the close of the war in 1972, another urgent need arose when U.S. troops were about to pull out of Vietnam. Along with other humanitarian associations, Sara and Yvonne helped organize "Operation Babylift" to rescue the Amerasian orphans who would likely be killed by the Vietcong if left behind. By the end of the war thousands of children had been airlifted to safety and placed in homes.

Sara and Yvonne shifted their humanitarian efforts to their own country in 1978, when asked by Nancy Reagan if they could help with the problem of child abuse in America. They researched the issue and discovered, to their horror, that there truly was an epidemic of child abuse throughout the country. They responded by founding Childhelp USA, the mission that has been the focus of their boundless energy and determination to this day. It is one of the largest national nonprofits dedicated to the treatment and prevention of child abuse and neglect. Additional contact information is available in the Contributors section at the end of this book.

"The truth is we don't think much about whether we can do something. When we got this first 'call' from God, we answered—no questions asked."

—Sara O'Meara
and Yvonne Fedderson

6 · Courage

ear the end of my two years in the Peace Corps in West Africa, I began to have the desire to learn more about myself and what I was made of. Aware that it was a perfect metaphor for "going deeper" within myself, I requested to spend a third year deep in the bush of the small, impoverished country where I lived. My application to transfer had been accepted when I suddenly got an even stronger calling to head to India, where I hoped to find someone who could teach me the "meaning of life." I know—it sounds like something you'd see on a greeting card!

With money from my Peace Corps "readjustment allowance," which ultimately allowed me to travel the world for a whole year, I headed first to East Africa, where I joined friends from college. Two of them had been Peace Corps volunteers living in Western Samoa, and the three of us converged on our other Peace Corps friend Karen's apartment in the city of Nairobi, where we spent three months in search of adventure.

Sometimes we'd take off in the afternoon and drive to the Nairobi Game Park, just four miles outside the city limits. In fact, some of our most exciting, indeed, adrenaline-producing experiences occurred there, such as the clutch going out in Karen's tiny Morris Minor just as we came across some lions (she had to get out of the car to fix it with a paper clip). At one turn we came around a bend and startled two male rhinos fighting. The rhinoceros is one of the few animals that will attack without provocation—and these two were already mad! Then, just as we were leaving the park at the end of the day (you are required to vacate before dusk or you'll be locked in), we startled a mother elephant crossing the dirt "road" to the stream where others were drinking and cooling off—with their babies. You may have heard the stories about female elephants fearing for their kids. This one turned to us and began walking toward our little car. Karen put the car in reverse, and slowly we began backing up. The elephant would stop, then come toward us again. We'd back up farther. The standoff seemed interminable, but eventually the pull to join her children was stronger than the desire to crush us.

But one of our most memorable experiences was renting a Land Rover to go on "safari" through the other game parks of East Africa. We had been to Tsavo East and Tsavo West, the parks that comprise ten million acres of wilderness in Kenya, and to the Serengeti in Tanzania. We had seen Mt. Kilimanjaro, more beautiful than any photo could ever capture. We were heading home when we decided to visit the Ngorongoro Crater, a volcanic crater in the valley where the earliest human remains have been found.

What happened next is best described in a poem I wrote about the event, which I share with you here. For a moment, fear almost paralyzed me. But I was so determined to make the most of the moment that, thank God, courage took over.

Ngorongoro Crater

All day the Land Rover made dizzying loops
through the crater basin, like patterns on the zebras
we scattered by the thousands.
Reedbuck, waterbuck, klipspringers, kudu—
we followed them, circled them, chased them.
We ran with wildebeest, hartebeest, oryx, impala,
imagined stalking elephants and elands
while monkeys watched and
we sensed lions and leopards stalking us.
We saw the fallen gazelle eaten by jackals
and hyenas, creatures of carrion.
We watched the vultures dine,
felt as if we were devoured.

Two thousand feet up on the crater's ledge,
we pitched our tent under the sign
No Camping on the Rim of the Crater.
Perched at the edge of night, I imagined
my arms encircling this ancient place, earth's cradle.
Sleep was chased by hoofbeats,
heartbeats racing through my blood,
the roar of lions, too close.
I left the tent in search of warmth,
climbed into the Rover's backseat,
scanning the African sky for a hint of light.

In the equator's half-moment between dark-light,
   sleep-wake,
a tapping on the fragile glass,
a pair of eyes watching me.
Heart stopped, then thundered in my ears.
He was not alone, and the two men carried spears.
Bolting upright, I watched as they moved closer.
Leather thongs circled red-throated necks,
ocher hair fell wild and long in corn-rowed plaits.
They smelled of dung and sweat, sour milk,
carried gourds dripping with cattle's blood to drink.
I brought my face closer to the glass.

Tall and thin, the half-naked men wore
the dark shining skin of a long-ago people
copper cloth thrown easily around their shoulders
painted legs, red-smeared arms
beaded earrings, bracelets, headbands dripping
from their bodies blue-red-white.
They shone red and copper,
reflected in the light of their tall spears
still tapping against the window.

Slowly I climbed into the cold morning.
I did not call to the tent. I stood and met
the Masai. Then soundlessly, as they had come,
they turned and walked away,
two spots of blood pulsing against the sky.

One of my friends in the tent that night was Pam George, author of the next story. Pam is an artist and a scholar. Through the years since Africa, I have watched her lovingly paint canvases, carve woodblock prints, tie-dye fabrics—even build houses.

Observing her in her studio, you'd never suspect the fierce side of this gentle university professor.

But when the events you will read about occurred, I watched Pam "morph" into the embodiment of a spear-wielding warrior. Like Erin Brockovich, Pam took on a corporate giant to fight for justice. In doing so, she put her career on the line, facing one of the darkest, most fearful times of her life.

When we hear about corruption and the blatant, widespread misuse of power in the world, it can be devastating. It hurts our hearts to see people unwilling to behave honestly and for the good of all. So, to women like Pam, and many others in this book who are devoting their lives to the betterment of the human condition, I say thank you for standing up for what is right, and for bringing your time, your energy and your vision to things we all care about!

I believe that justice does exist in the universe, a sort of cosmic law of balance that we can't always see or know. But it is through the courage of women like Pam that this law of justice is made manifest.

One final word about Pam. As I write this, she is about to retire from a thirty-five-year career in university education and administration. True to her spirit, she applied for—and has been granted—one more Fulbright assignment, this time to teach in Sri Lanka. Her paintbrushes will have to wait just a bit longer as she continues to carve a legacy of excellence in the field of education.

And if she encounters any wild adventures along the way, I have no doubt that she'll be equal to them.

PAMELA GEORGE'S STORY
Testing the Sleeping Giant

W hen I chose my life's work, I knew it would demand that I work hard and be creative. I could do that! But little did I know that it would also ask me to be brave. I mean really brave. That turned out to be the hard part.

As a professor of educational psychology, my job is to train teachers, counselors and principals to evaluate students and school programs. But my *work* goes well beyond that job. For nearly three decades, my dream has been of schools where students are judged by their actual performances, and test scores are only a small part of their educational records. I teach about assessments that are less harmful to kids than most standardized IQ, aptitude or achievement tests. I also document schools' misuses of standardized tests.

My mission began the day my eight-year-old daughter, Kemen, came home from school with tears streaming down her face, a test results form in her hand.

"Momma, I failed the math test!" she cried. "I got the worst score in the class!"

I calmed her down, confident that she was mistaken. Kemen had always liked math. She breezed through her homework and tutored other kids in her third-grade class. But as I studied the scores for the standardized end-of-grade test, I saw that she was right. She had scored 6 out of 100—the lowest score of her class! Stunned, I searched futilely through the complicated report for some clue to this terrible result.

Kemen was devastated. She had been hoping to qualify for classes for academically gifted students; now she might have to repeat third grade! I vacillated between being the supportive mom and the angered professional. Because I knew both Kemen's strength in math and the pitfalls of standardized testing, I began to search out the cause of such a questionable test result.

I asked to view the exam. My request was curtly denied. I asked for a retest—also denied. I then asked to have her original test scored by hand. Thank heavens they complied! It was discovered that the answer sheet she was given had been a photocopy, probably made when the test proctor ran out of originals. The scoring machine could not accurately read the photocopied score sheet, yet it did not flag the test. Rather, it reported a false, low score in math.

That was the end of that problem for Kemen. Today she is a proud young woman happily studying applied math and statistics in college. But for me, this experience was only a beginning.

I became committed to helping other parents and teachers prevent such misuses of standardized tests. My dedication grew as I counseled parents whose children were mistakenly labeled mentally retarded based on IQ scores. I worked with teachers whose good judgment concerning students was often trumped by standardized tests. I observed classes where the curriculum had become "drill and kill" test preparation that bored the kids to death. And I worked with students at all levels whose educational futures were diminished by exams that clearly underrepresented their abilities.

I saw much misuse of testing because I live and work in the South, which has long led the nation in aggressive testing of children. Though other regions would follow, the South was first to require kindergarten ready-or-not testing, first- and second-grade testing, grade-retention based on test scores, high school competency testing, and more! The testing business was gigantic. Testing and publishing companies were selling millions of standardized tests to state departments of public instruction, school boards and legislatures.

I knew I had to alert other parents and teachers to the problems I had found with testing. I felt neither brave nor assertive, but it was clearly the next step to take. And so I wrote a book called *Testing Our Children*. It was one of the first of what would later become a popular trend in consumer-oriented books calling for test reform. I wanted it to be readable, with testing statistics simplified and test questions demystified. It steered parents and teachers to published records of court cases in which test items had been contested. It illustrated common errors in test items and testing practices. It taught parents about their rights in testing and test use situations.

The book was reviewed favorably in the education media and regional press. As I had expected, primarily because there were few test resources for students or parents at the time, the book was popular and the first edition was soon sold out.

But just when I thought the path of my work was clear and that justice had been served, a sleeping giant awoke! One of the country's wealthiest test companies brought legal action against me for *Testing Our Children*. As publisher of a commonly used IQ test, it claimed my book, by telling readers about specific test items hitherto kept confidential from parents and teachers, encouraged parents to violate the company's copyright laws. In addition to claims of enormous financial damages, they demanded that my book be taken off the market and that I never write, teach or lecture about standardized testing again.

The combative language of the company's New York lawyers stunned me, for I am Southern and by nature polite. I read the lawyers' certified documents over and over again, searching for some mistake. Dazed, I finally put them down and frantically thought of ways to run away. The vehemence with which they pursued me frightened me, for I did not have tenure at my university and this action would surely jeopardize my prospects. The company's demand for financial reparations astounded me, for it represented more money than I, or my whole family, could earn in a lifetime.

What was I to do? If I caved in to the industry's legal pit bulls, I would certainly lose my *work*—which provided meaning and a sense of "calling" beyond a job. But if I fought back, I would most likely lose my *job*—a professorship for which I had worked hard and earned a Ph.D. For a few days I was so worried that I didn't eat anything at all. My friends called me "trauma trim," but they worried about me. Night after night, anxious thoughts crowded my mind and I didn't sleep beyond nodding.

In the small hours of one morning, I lay curled in bed feeling as if I was lost in a dark and frightening cave, when a ray of light finally broke in. I sat up in bed, suddenly energized by a realization—I was *not* in this situation alone. For years, I had met or corresponded with colleagues around the country who had shared my concerns about the misuse of standardized tests. A coalition had developed of like-minded educators and civil-rights advocates across the country. I needed to call on their support!

After my first breakfast in days, I picked up the phone and got started. I called John (the energetic test reform advocate), Diana (the social justice attorney), Bob (the great networker), Page (the smart rural educator) and Chuck (the journalism professor). Each colleague called a few more. By the end of the second day, messages of support were flooding in from coast to coast.

Soon, the news reverberated out from our coalition to a broader audience, to civil rights groups and universities across the country. My colleagues told a simplified version of my story in their circles —that "the large testing industry was trying to set a dangerous legal precedent for copyright superiority by beating up on a well-meaning teacher from a public university in the South who was unlikely to fight back."

By the end of the week, an education advocacy center based at Harvard began coordinating my defense. Soon a famous law firm in Washington, D.C., took the case *pro bono*. This team of lawyers chose to fight the case using the First Amendment's safeguarding of the right of a teacher or parent to criticize test materials and practices.

As my battle continued, something strange happened—I started to feel brave! The battle to continue my work and the encouragement of others who thought that this work was important was changing who I was deep down. I could stand my ground. I didn't always have to be polite—especially when I was threatened. I did not have to give in to the powerful testing industry. And I did not have to do this all by myself.

We settled the case favorably out of court in a few months. The book again was available for sale, and today I continue to write about, lecture on and publish criticisms of inappropriate uses of standardized testing.

One day near the end of the deliberations, I was looking around the Washington conference room at the group of powerful advocates from Boston, New York and D.C. They were colleagues, and now friends, who championed *Testing Our Children* and who shared my dream of better measures for kids. I felt so grateful for their support, their knowledge, their skills and their energy. I felt braver than I ever had in my life. And I smiled as it occurred to me that the testing industry had picked on the *wrong* woman!

"I sat up in bed, suddenly energized by a realization—I was not in this situation alone. I needed to call on others' support."

—Pamela George

7 · Honesty

henever I speak to a group of women, we talk about honesty. Even though I know I'm among honest people for the most part, I also know that being honest with *ourselves* is one of the hardest challenges for women. We say yes when we mean no, we take on projects that keep us up late and deprive us of badly needed rest, and we are often so busy taking care of others that we don't have a clue how we ourselves are truly feeling.

Perhaps one of the most difficult things we face regarding honesty is committing to a particular life path, then realizing somewhere along the way that it's the wrong path, or that we've outgrown it, or simply that it's no longer serving us. When we've invested a lot of time, money, education, intimacy or belief in something or someone, it can be extremely hard to change direction.

There is often an added element of pressure from family or others as well, perhaps to follow in someone's footsteps. But when a person gets so real about her feelings that she's willing to give up her investment—whether it's a project or a life direction—the rewards can be far greater than she ever imagined. This kind of honesty is raw and likely to leave a person feeling very vulnerable. But the resulting freedom and joy will far outweigh the perceived rewards of remaining attached to the current situation.

Something along these lines happened to me when I first started working on the original version of this book. I had met a wonderful woman, an author and world-renowned psychologist, at Book Expo of America in New York. We hit it off so well in that brief meeting that we talked about writing a book together. A few weeks later, we began working on a book proposal, and two months later we completed it and sent it to my publisher.

The very day our proposal was considered, the senior editor called me to say it had been accepted. I was ecstatic. We talked about next steps, deadlines, publication date, etc. But over the next couple of days, I began feeling uneasy. I found myself struggling with the realization that, after giving 100 percent of my time, effort and devotion to the book proposal for two months, I no longer wanted to do the book. My vision had changed since starting the project, and what I valued and wanted to convey was different from the original impulse and plan for the book.

At a crossroads, I knew I had to be willing to throw away the hard work, to hand it over graciously to my coauthor and tell both her and my publisher the truth: that I did not want to go forward with this project. And I did.

I felt humbled and vulnerable. It was hard to admit that I had made a mistake. And I was troubled about breaking a commitment and appearing unprofessional.

But I find that when honesty comes from the heart, with clarity and the desire to create a winning situation for all involved, it usually serves everyone, even though it might not be apparent at first. It will never work if we use honesty to manipulate or as an excuse to get out of an obligation without being accountable. It will never work if we blame or judge others in the name of telling "our truth." But once we are fully honest with ourselves, then we can be honest with others. And I find that the more honest I am—with myself and others—the freer I become.

This was certainly the case with my decision regarding the book I withdrew from. My publisher agreed to go forward with the book with my coauthor if she wanted to; thus, I was a fortunate link in a potential collaboration that could serve them both. This also opened the opportunity for me to proceed with my own book, which ultimately came to represent something much deeper than even I had originally conceived, evolving into the book you are reading now.

I have known people who have changed life directions after much greater investments than two months of their time, like author Arnold Patent, who gave up his twenty-five-year law practice and "the perfect life" to pursue something else, because he was honest enough to admit he was no longer happy. That takes guts. But there is no question in my mind that people like Arnold would agree with the author of this anonymous quote about honesty: "Honesty is not something to flirt with. We must be married to it."

In the following story, Jacqui Vines had been committed to the life of a single, high-powered businesswoman. She thought she had become all that she wanted to be in terms of success. But the events of September 11, 2001, changed everything, and Jacqui finally had to tell the truth.

Jacqui Vines' Story
9/11 Legacy

When Cox Communications acquired AT&T in Baton Rouge, Louisiana, I was sent in as Vice President and General Manager—the first and only Cox employee on the scene. My job was to get acquainted with the managers and employees who had stayed on from AT&T, hire new employees, build a senior team, and oversee the transition from a bottom-line culture to a customer-service culture—all while running a $150 million business with 550 employees.

I had a lot to prove. I had come in with a Human Resources background, and from a corporate perspective, anybody in HR is assumed to be "touchy-feely." I had to prove that I had the necessary financial acumen and functional knowledge of the depth and breadth of the financial world if I was going to be accepted as a bona fide general manager.

I had always believed in my heart of hearts that God was preparing me for something great and that it had to do with working with large groups of people, especially bringing people together. I had vast experience with this as a child. My mother had me out of wedlock; for four or five years, I lived with her on and off in the "'hood," then with various uncles and cousins. At 14 I was finally taken into the Connecticut Family Services system as a ward of the state. I grew up in foster homes and group homes; although I was African-American, I was sometimes placed with black foster parents, sometimes with white. I went to an all-white high school after going to an all-black high school. I learned through therapy from the age of 14 to 18 how to look inside myself and understand myself, so I developed a real self-awareness at an early age. I learned to survive through intuition and detachment. And when you have to survive in an environment, you pick up subtleties and celebrate the differences, more so than if you are just a passive observer.

At Cox, I felt I was doing what I was meant to, because I was working with a highly diverse group of more than five hundred employees. It's still very polarized here—black and white—so I was in my element. I thought I was living my purpose and walking the path that had been laid out for me, and in doing so I was successful. That's what I thought success was.

It was an intense period in my life, not unlike my life in general, but even more so than usual. And I loved it! I became very involved with the employees, the customers and the community, then shifted my focus to productivity, and ultimately, to innovation. I was always trying to prove to corporate that I could get the job done, and prove to our people that, not only could we do everything I said we could—but that we were actually doing it and delivering the results. It was a kinetic, high-powered environment. And I was so busy that I didn't even have time to consider that there might be anything more to life than my work. I was grateful that, as a single woman, I could focus entirely on my job. I didn't have any interest in dating, or the time or energy to see much of old friends and family members. My life seemed completely full.

I had taken over the system in March 2000, and in September 2001, I flew to Atlanta, where I was to give my first budget presentation at Cox headquarters. I had spent the whole budget period really trying to understand the numbers, making sure I was asking the right questions of the organization, trying to anticipate the questions corporate would ask—and all while being a new GM. So much was on the line, trying to impress my boss and my boss's boss, that prior to leaving, I didn't really talk to anybody, I was so immersed in the budget and getting my game face on.

Even in the limo on the way to the Cox corporate office, I was still trying to nail down the presentation with one of my directors, making sure it would be perfect.

But this was the morning of September 11, and when we walked into the office, we arrived just in time to join a group riveted to a TV set and watched with horror as the second plane hit the second of the Twin Towers in New York City.

Almost at the same moment, everybody left the room to call someone or answer a call on their cell phone. I remained, sitting there alone. I had no particular person to call and no one was calling me. I had been so focused on preparing for this presentation that I hadn't returned calls or even told anybody I was going to be traveling. I hadn't been connected with anybody in my family for a long time, and there was no one even to ask where I was or to worry about me. Nobody had a clue whether I was on one of those planes—and no one was frantic to find out.

For the first time in my forty-two years, I realized that all the "successes" I believed I had had up to that point meant nothing—because there was no one to call. After all the achievements and opportunities I'd had and this wonderful journey I'd been on, here I sat alone. I could be looked up to by many, put on a pedestal by others, but the long and the short of it was that I stood alone as a woman who had "successes."

I sat there and waited for everyone to come back. As they did, I once again put on my game face, readying myself as the group decided to go forward with the presentation.

By the time we finished and prepared to go home, all the airports had been closed, so we rented a car to drive back to Baton Rouge. It was an eight-hour drive, and the whole way home, I carried on a conversation with my financial director, one of many who reported to me. But beneath the conversation with him, I was having a conversation with myself. I could no longer see any reason for the legacy I was creating. I may have impacted people and things, but all I could ask was the big question: What was this all for? I had never had a notion to get married and had never really wanted to have children. But now I was having an epiphany: It's really about passing on who you are and what you've created, both from a spiritual and financial perspective—and I didn't have that.

Soon after 9/11, I got a call from my 19-year-old niece. Samantha was the single mom of an 18-month-old daughter, and she needed help. Living with her parents wasn't working out, and she had no place to go. She asked me if she could come from Colorado and take me up on my "one-month" offer.

My one-month offer is the one where, if someone in my family is down and out and has nowhere to live, I say, "As long as you want to help yourself, you can come stay with me for a month until you can get on your feet."

As one of the few successful people in my family, I had long ago had to learn how to set boundaries. I still have people I consider sisters and brothers, not in the traditional sense, but foster and half-brothers and -sisters—and they usually call me only when they need something!

So I said yes and told Sam that she and her daughter could come—for one month.

Almost immediately I had to take over to get the baby on a schedule, as much for my survival as anything! I'd get home from work at 7:00 or 8:00 in the evening, and little Jennifer wasn't going to sleep until anytime between 10:00 and 12:00. So I started parenting quickly and discovered that it came naturally to me.

We soon realized that Sam was five months pregnant. There was no way I was going to put her out on the street after one month, so four months later, Gracie was born, and I accepted the rearing of an infant along with her toddler sister. I also told Sam I would send her to school in the fall. By that time, I had been child-rearing for six or seven months.

Sam often said how much she loved her children, but intimated that she didn't feel capable of raising them. More than once she commented, "You just seem to do this naturally." She raised the issue again one night after the girls were asleep, when she and I were sitting on the couch having one of those conversations you have with a young adult about the meaning of life and goals and what matters. I knew there was something she wanted to say but didn't know how to. Finally, looking down at her hands in her lap, Sam said, "I love my kids, but I don't know if I can raise them."

I knew she was asking me if I could take them. I looked at her, a young woman in such turmoil, and something stirred in me. I knew I would take her children.

I didn't say anything, and we began talking about something else. But as I lay in bed that night, I thought about that moment and said to myself, "This is something I need to do, for myself and for the children." I knew this was the lesson of 9/11 for me—I had received God's message that day and it was affirmed in our discussion that night.

Certainly, if this had happened prior to 9/11, I would have said no. I would have said, "I'll help you find some other family member who can do it, and we'll put you in school." But by now I had realized a lot of things. I didn't want work to be my entire life. When the doors closed at the office, there was much more to who I was and what was out there. And success was not just about being a VP, GM, CEO or anything else—it was about how much you give back to someone or something else, whether community, people or children.

I realized that, in the end, when the doors closed and the lights went out, I wanted to be able to touch someone. The truth came when I was willing to say, wait a minute, this isn't necessarily the path. I had to become painfully honest to accept the fact that I had a major gap in my life and had not even had a clue it was there. I had been looking at my life through a lens in order to be okay with what I was doing. And it just so happened that it took one of the most tragic things ever to happen to America to lift that lens.

So the next morning at breakfast I said, "Sam, if you would like me to, I will take the girls." And from that moment, I permanently took on the rearing of my girls.

I am continuing to raise them, and I plan on raising them for the rest of their lives. In a way, it's like having another job, because I have them on a schedule just like mine. My day starts at 5:30 in the morning with a cup of coffee and my spiritual readings until they wake up. Then we have from 7:00 to 9:00 to be together and get ready for work and day care. Everyone at work knows I will not have a breakfast meeting! I always spend half an hour alone with each of them, snuggling and talking about the day and what they want to wear.

But our most special time of day is the drive home from school, when we talk about what happened today. From then until their 8:30 bedtime it's all about bikes, games, homework, supper, phonics, princess movies, music, bedtime stories, prayers and goodnight kisses. After that, I return e-mails and phone calls to the West Coast, and I'm in bed by 11:00. If I absolutely have to work late, I get someone to watch the girls and go in after they're in bed. One night a week and one weekend evening a month I'll schedule community-oriented work, usually speaking to groups in town. Otherwise, work has me 150 percent from 9:00 to 6:00, but then it's my time with my girls.

I don't care if a child is born to you or given to you; when you accept the role of parent, formally or informally, a special bond is formed. Frankly, there was never any doubt that these were my children; they were in my heart. Jennifer is introspective and dainty. She has her moods, but she's a beautiful child and spirit. Little Gracie is as wild as she can be, has no fear, wakes up with a giggle and goes to bed saying, "Sweet dreams." What a discovery to learn that I could give a 2-1/2- or 3-month-old child a bath and a warm bottle at night—and she'd sleep all night! I watch in awe as I learn that I can actually help someone be more comfortable at the beginning of this life and sense that I can be a positive guiding influence for them throughout their lives. That's the legacy I care about.

My direct reports tell me they're very happy I have the girls in my life, because they used to feel that they were my extended family—and they went on one too many team-building trips! What these children have done is create balance for me.

They've also helped me understand the needs of working parents and their children in a deep and significant way. When Cox needed to move into a larger office space, a developer sold me on the idea of establishing a commercial business community that could share certain amenities in the facility, such as a fitness center. At this writing, we are about to move into what was at one time the first shopping mall in Baton Rouge, along with several commercial businesses and some university offices.

But we are also going to have a Boys' and Girls' Club, which will provide after-school care programs for employees' children until 8:30 at night. And the YMCA will have a day care center there for children who haven't started school yet. My children helped me understand how *really* important it is to be able to walk down the hall and look in a window and see how they're doing during the day.

Raising these children is far more challenging than anything I have ever faced at the office, or anywhere else. It is a humbling experience to parent—to know that I can run a $150 million business, but I cannot get a two-year-old to eat her broccoli!

And yet, it is the core, the one part of my life that I think God made sure I got, even though I was too ignorant to know that it was important. It has added a whole new understanding to what I call success: Achievement is only complete when the heart is full.

"I had to become painfully honest to accept the fact that I had a major gap in my life and had not even had a clue it was there. I had been looking at my life through a lens in order to be okay with what I was doing."

—Jacqui Vines

8 · Integrity

 know almost as much about integrity from the times I *haven't* been in integrity as the times I have. I once began dating a man who was getting divorced—only his wife didn't know about it yet. I later felt that I had betrayed her. I have had significant relationships that I took for granted, using workaholism as an excuse to avoid intimacy with a friend or even my husband. And I have sometimes asked things of my children that were not fair or reasonable, just because they were demanded of me when I was a child.

Integrity is what happens when your inner voice and values line up with your words and actions. I found a wonderful example of this when I came across a *Life* magazine from 1995 and opened to an article about the NBA basketball player, Hakeem Olajuwon. When he developed his namesake shoe with Spaulding, he insisted it be sold for no more than $35. He felt that $120 was too much for a working mother with three boys to pay for a pair of athletic shoes. That's integrity: being so clear about your values that you make sure everything in your life lines up with them— even if it means giving up financial gain or prestige.

The *Flower Essence Repertory*, a book that describes the healing properties of flowers, says, "Consciousness must also include conscience; as the soul gains greater awareness of itself it also acquires an inner voice or moral life. This morality must be generated from within; as long as laws or dictates are stamped on the personality from the outside, the Self will not develop real strength of character."

This idea of the soul awakening to its inner voice and adopting a morality based on what's inside rather than outside feels like the essence of integrity to me. Being out of integrity occurs when the heart and mind are not aligned, resulting in confusion, which takes the passion out of life. When the mind, heart and soul are totally aligned, then passion flows naturally, powerfully and directly.

Linda Chaé's mark on the world of business feels as if it has integrity at its core. I met Linda through a mutual friend, who had introduced me to several skincare products that had been developed by Linda. Although I was used to buying products at the health food store, these products were definitely different! After using a body cleanser and lotion based on her formulas for a couple of months, my skin became so soft that anybody touching it, even inadvertently, would comment about it.

So I feel very lucky to have discovered Linda, for obvious personal reasons! Her products feel as if they actually feed my body and skin. But her story feeds my spirit, and models a way of being that inspires and encourages me to listen more deeply to the voice of my conscience.

LINDA CHAÉ'S STORY
The Beautiful Truth

W hen my family moved from our farm into the city in the mid-sixties, the look at my new junior high school was ironed hair and miniskirts. There I was with home-permed hair and dresses my grandma had made me, generously decorated with rickrack. I longed to fit in, but I couldn't seem to "get it right." And my father constantly reinforced that idea, often thumping me on the head when he thought I was out of step. It took me five years to realize how I could make my dream come true.

I was in my senior year of high school when one day, I overhead the girls talking about classes they were taking at modeling school. They were learning how to turn and pirouette properly, and one of them was talking about how your blush was supposed to go on at *this* angle. They were all so cool, and I was just standing there with my lunch tray trying to find somebody to sit with.

Then something clicked in me. If I could go to modeling school, I could be cool, too! My family couldn't afford to send me to something so frivolous, so I got a job to earn money for the tuition. I could hardly keep my feet on the ground that first day of class—until I met with Kathy, the make-up artist, who told me I needed at least another $300 to purchase the required makeup.

I had already quit my other job, so I jumped at the chance to work for Kathy when she said she needed an assistant. I started by keeping her workstation clean at the modeling school. Before long I was working at the beauty care products company she owned, ordering her products; sticking on labels; delivering products to modeling schools, beauty schools and salons; and doing everything but the books.

By the time I was twenty, I was in college working on a history degree and, at the same time, basically running Kathy's company. Then one day she told me she wanted to sell the business. I knew immediately that I wanted to buy it, but where would I get the money? I found out that I could get a Small Business Administration loan for the $18,000 I needed, if someone would co-sign. My dad had died and left my mom some money for her retirement, but it wasn't a whole lot more than the amount I needed. That night I sat at the kitchen table and told my mom about the opportunity. She was happy to be able to help me get started in a business. I knew my father wouldn't have liked the idea, but she agreed to co-sign for the loan.

A few days later I was the proud owner of my own make-up and skin care line. Now I needed a place to showcase my products, so I quit college and went to work at a beauty salon doing makeup and facials with my own line. I was thrilled to be selling such a fabulous line of products. Kathy had always told me how natural and yummy it all was. "Yummy" was her favorite word. She didn't make the products herself; she bought them from a manufacturer, from whom I continued to buy. Everything was named after fruits and vegetables—like Cucumber Eye Cream and Peach Day Cream—and smelled, well, yummy! The Peach Day Cream was my favorite, and the best seller among my customers. My dream of doing something right was finally coming true.

The same year, still only twenty, I got married. My mother-in-law, Julia, was battling breast cancer, and she came to live with my husband and me so we could help take care of her. Julia was just miserable from the swelling in her arm caused by the removal of her breast and lymph nodes. Every night I would say, "Let me massage you and see if we can relieve that pressure." I had a natural gift in my hands and could find the lymphatic congestion points and relieve the swelling. I lavished her with my Peach Day Cream every time I got the chance.

But I began to notice something odd. Whenever I massaged Julia, she'd get a hard lump, sometimes two, near where the breast had been and halfway down her arm.

One day when I was getting ready to give her a massage, I realized I had run out of Peach Day Cream at home. So I took some almond oil and avocado oil, added some nutrients and essential oils, and used them instead. The lumps disappeared.

We began to experiment. I kept doing the same massage but tried different creams. For three or four months I didn't use the Peach Day Cream. Sure enough, no lumps, and I could always get the swelling down. Then one night I ran out of the pure oils, so I said, "Let's try the Peach Day Cream again." Within an hour she had two painful lumps that lasted three days.

During one of Julia's checkups, I told the doctor what we were finding with the massages and the creams. "There's no way a cream could be doing that," he said, clearly irritated by the very idea. "You're massaging differently. And you shouldn't be massaging a cancer patient anyway. You must stop that immediately."

Julia begged me to continue massaging, as it eased her suffering. And at the next checkup I mentioned it again because I was still finding the same results. The doctor was furious that I had ignored his instruction, and once again, he totally dismissed the idea that a cream could have that effect. But I knew there must be something wrong with the Peach Day Cream. What could it be? All I had ever been told was that it was peaches in a cream.

I contacted the chemist at the manufacturing company that made my products and asked, "What ingredient in here could cause lymphatic fluid to harden?" He said he couldn't tell me the ingredients. I called back again and again, asking politely, sweetly, sternly, even angrily for a list of ingredients. Finally, with great reluctance, he gave me a list of ingredients, but would not give me any information about them. And much to my surprise, there weren't any peaches in my Peach Day Cream.

Keep in mind that this was 1970, and there was no Internet where I could easily research ingredients. But I had to know more. So I decided to go back to college to see what I could learn. Continuing my full-time job, I started taking night courses in chemistry.

A year and half later I finally found myself in a course studying the material safety data sheets used by manufacturers. Although at the time there were no regulations protecting consumers, these data sheets were created to protect workers in manufacturing plants. For a class assignment, I ordered data sheets for the ingredients in the Peach Day Cream.

A few weeks later my teacher passed out envelopes to all the students. I opened mine with a sense of foreboding, then read with growing horror that the Peach Day Cream contained six ingredients that were either potentially carcinogenic or could contribute to tumors and lumps. I sat at my desk and cried.

The minute class was over, I called the chemist at the manufacturing plant and practically screamed at him, "I can't believe this! You told me that these products were safe and not toxic, and here I am reading about all the carcinogens in them!"

"You don't understand," he said, in a condescending tone. "Those ingredients are just in the products in trace amounts. The material safety data sheet assumes you're handling the ingredient at full strength. If the powder is at full strength and it gets airborne, it's going to create lung cancer. But no one's going to be breathing in your Peach Day Cream."

I argued with him, insisting that he help me understand how this could be okay. He had an answer for everything. But I knew my mother-in-law had those lumps. I had done a human test experiment without really intending to.

Finally he said, "Well, that's fine, you don't need to buy these products. But you're not going to be able to find any other cosmetics without them. This is all there is. You can't hold your cream together or preserve it without them." Then he said, "And, you know, your product isn't any different from any of the others," and he named a number of major brand names. "They're all doing the same thing, and none of them are worried about cancer."

Later, when I called him again with further documentation showing that some of the ingredients caused cancer in animals, he said, "It's not my concern or the cosmetic industry's concern to stop cancer. That's not our job. Somebody else has to do that."

For the next three weeks my Peach Day Cream sat on the shelves collecting dust. I couldn't bring myself to sell it. In fact, I realized that the same ingredients were probably in the whole product line, so I stopped selling everything. My products were displayed in beautiful glass cabinets in the reception area of the salon where I worked, and I didn't have a clue what to do with them. I just did facials with fruits, vegetables and essential oils and worried about my business.

What should I do? I had invested in a lot of inventory. Was I wrong? Could the whole cosmetics industry be selling carcinogenic products? I had my own experience, but all the doctors and chemists I had ever spoken to said I was wrong. What did I know? I was just a chemistry student. I felt that old, sad feeling that I was always wrong. I knew my dad would have thought I was crazy. And I shuddered at the thought of how angry he would have been if I put my mother's financial investment at risk.

A few weeks later, one of my favorite clients came through the door in a wheelchair. She had had cancer for a while, but the wheelchair was new. She looked old and tired from the chemo, and my heart broke to see her. I went over to her, bent down on one knee and held her hand. "How are you, Edna? What can I do for you?"

"Honey," she said. "I just want to get some products. The doctor

says that the cancer's gone everywhere and I only have six weeks,
maybe two months. And I just want to know if you'd come to my
funeral, do my makeup and fix this funny wig of mine the nice
way you do. Could you come and just not let my friends see me
ugly at my funeral? You can't scare your friends."

I tried not to cry. I said, "Of course, Edna. Of course I will."

Then she said, "Honey, I want five Peach Day Creams. My last
six, seven weeks, I'm gonna put that on my feet, I'm gonna put
that everywhere. I love that stuff!"

I sucked in my breath and backed away a little bit. I didn't know
what to say. Finally, I said, "Edna, I don't think you should use
that Peach Day Cream."

"Why, honey, you always had me use your Peach Day Cream,
and I love it!"

"Well, I just learned something. I was at the university and I
learned that there are some ingredients in that cream that look like
they contribute to cancer."

Well, you wouldn't have known Edna had rolled in there in a
wheelchair. She popped out of that thing and stood up. She got
really close to me and said, "What?"

I told her again and she said, "You know, I wasn't so bad a year
ago. I've been using this stuff for a year. Is this why I have two
months to live?"

I was horrified. And scared. I was only twenty-three, but I knew
about liability and lawsuits. Suddenly, it was as if my shadow side
appeared. I found myself saying, "Now, Edna, that's when it's at
full strength, and you're not using these ingredients at full
strength. They're diluted way down in here; they're just trace ingredients. . . ." Blah, blah, blah, blah, blah. I just repeated the
chemist's exact words.

Edna leaned in to me and said, "I don't believe one word of that
and neither do you. I am so ashamed of you." She turned and
pointed, saying, "That's your name on those products. How could

you put your name on those products with those ingredients in them?"

"But I didn't know! I didn't know! I've been looking and looking and trying to find out about this."

She said, "Something made you suspicious—why didn't you protect me?"

I babbled, "I'm sorry, Edna. I really didn't know for sure until I got the scientific information three weeks ago, and I'm not selling those products any more. That's why I told you not to take it."

Suddenly she shifted from being angry. She grabbed my hand and said, "Linda, you do something about this. I'm dying, but you're young and you have the rest of your life. You make me a cream. You make every woman a cream, whether they have cancer or not. We deserve to look beautiful. We deserve to have something that smells nice. And we deserve not to die for it. You do that."

Edna paused for a moment. "You know, Linda," she said, "you changed my life. About a year ago, when I started coming to you, I was so discouraged all I could talk about was dying. You told me what Napoleon Hill said, that 'what the mind of man can conceive and believe, it can achieve.' Honey, I believed you. You listen to those words. You take that as your motto and read that every day. You keep that in front of you and know that, for women like me, you've got to do this, Linda."

"Okay, Edna," I said. "I will."

About ten weeks later I got the call. I went to the funeral home and made Edna beautiful. As I sat with her in that little back room, I started to cry. I patted her cold cheek and said, "Edna, I'm so sorry if I contributed to your cancer. I am so sorry if I had anything to do with your not being here today." I felt her spirit, and I knew Edna was in that room. I said, "Edna, I don't know enough chemistry, but I'll learn it. I don't know if it's possible to make a safe cream, but if it is, I promise you I will do it."

After the funeral, I went back to the beauty salon and got a big trash can. I swept everything off every shelf. I went to my warehouse and bagged all the rest of my inventory. Then I sat down and figured out I had just lost $32,000. I put my head in my hands. How would I make my monthly payments so my mom wouldn't lose her house? I looked up and said, "Edna, they're all gone, they're all thrown away. I'm never ordering them again and I need your help. If you could give me a hand from heaven every once in a while, that would be great. And if there's anybody up there that knows this stuff, please ask them to help me open the doors because I'm on a mission. I'll never, ever, ever again sell something that could hurt any human being, let alone somebody vulnerable with cancer."

From that day on, I dedicated my life to researching and finding ways to make toxin-free beauty products for women. At first I stayed on at the salon doing facials so I could continue to pay off my loan and make sure that my mother was financially secure. But I also started developing my own products. I continued studying chemistry and skin histology so I could have a better understanding of how to make products naturally and help the largest organ of the body contribute to the health and vitality of the whole.

I contacted all the raw material suppliers repeatedly, asking for healthy alternatives, begging them to find a way, for example, to make a product hold together without using toxic polyethylene glycol (PEG) as an emulsifier. And eventually they started calling me back. "Linda," they'd say, "your name and number are imprinted in our company's archives forever! We've got something for you. . . ."

Year after year, as I worked on creating toxin-free products, the demand for more natural products grew. Finally, I started my own company and created products I knew and trusted. Women loved them! One day a New York media firm contacted one of the chemists I had pestered, asking if he knew someone whose products could be featured in an infomercial on natural cosmetics. They were looking for someone engaging, passionate and different. It seemed that none of the New York facialists had enough attitude! The chemist said, "I've got just the person."

Within a week of airing the infomercial on national television, the phone lines were jammed at the major Midwest phone company handling the calls. Within two weeks, we had sold all 25,000 pieces of product, unheard of at that time in the infomercial field. In the first year, we did $70 million in business and broke all the records. *Vogue* magazine took notice and wrote a complimentary article about me. The *Los Angeles Times* interviewed me, as did most of the newspapers around the country. I was given credit for the "go-natural" look. That was the headline: "Linda Chaé takes cosmetics all natural! She's our go-natural girl!"

But even those products weren't as good as what I'm doing today. Eventually I had enough money to invest in my own research laboratories, always searching for ways to develop toxin-free products. And now, thirty years after I entered the world of skin care products, there are huge breakthroughs in the industry. Today there are many raw material suppliers willing to make all-natural ingredients for sophisticated products like anti-aging creams. We're able to make toxin-free products that heal acne and psoriasis. We're able to make deodorants without aluminum and propylene glycol. We can now make a natural toothpaste without toxic ingredients, thus eliminating the need for a warning label to "keep out of the reach of children under the age of six." We even have a shampoo that makes suds without endangering health, which we couldn't do just five years ago. And these are far better than the vast majority of products labeled "nontoxic," which, sadly, means only that less than 49 percent of the lab rats died when exposed to them.

Ultimately, it's the consumer who is really changing the industry. When women see what happens to their skin after using toxin-free products for thirty days, they aren't satisfied with anything less. My goal has never been just to have my own line and be successful; I want every cosmetics company to be able to offer safe products. For example, there's finally been a breakthrough on an all-natural preservative. How wonderful if every company were to use it, rather than the commonly used formaldehyde! I'm for the next generation being healthier thanks to every pregnant mother using pure products because that's all that's sold anymore. That's why, although I have my own product line, I also provide formulas for many other natural-care companies.

And because of Edna's inspiration and the motivation to challenge the integrity of the cosmetics industry, I founded the non-profit ToxicFree® Foundation. This provides families with third-party, unbiased documentation about the toxic, carcinogenic and even poisonous ingredients found in nearly all personal, oral and skin care products. We regularly meet with various senators and representatives in Washington, along with the Federal Drug Administration (FDA), to try to secure "Right to Know" legislation regarding the ingredients in products used by the entire family.

Today, there are other business opportunities and interests that pull at me, but I can't let this one go. At the age of twenty-three, thanks to Edna, I got up the courage to believe I could be right about something. And, thanks to Edna, I made a commitment to do the right thing, whatever the cost. I give her a wink now and then, and hear her saying, "Honey, you done good."

"I'll never, ever, ever again sell something that could hurt any human being. I dedicated my life to researching and finding ways to make toxin-free beauty products for women."

—Linda Chaé

9 · Wholeness

ong before it became popular, my family was reading labels on food products and using herbal remedies to solve problems like hyperactivity and depression. Today, the movement toward alternative medicine, health and exercise is catching on like wildfire in this country. Yoga has gone mainstream, and universities are establishing colleges of alternative healing. "Integrative medicine" is an emerging field of Western medicine that seeks to meld the best of complementary and alternative therapies with the best of mainstream medicine. And "wholeness," a word that describes mind-body-spirit fitness and integration, is no longer the sole property of New Age thinking.

But regardless of the type of healing therapies you are drawn to—traditional, alternative or a combination of the two—it is interesting to see the intense interest on the part of many in becoming more responsible for their own health. Many of the women I interviewed for this book expressed a distrust of Western medicine because it focuses on the symptoms rather than the cause of disease. They expressed the desire not only to take a more active role in their own healing, but also to go beyond the level of symptoms and get to the root of their disease or health challenge. Treating symptoms seems to be the Western way; Western medicine seems to be slow to accept that an ache in one part of the body could be related to a pain in another, seemingly unconnected part of the body.

But the reality is that we are holistic beings, and it is a law of physics that *everything is connected.* So is it really too far a stretch to think that physical symptoms might be connected, or that they might correspond to something else, like emotional or mental stress?

My youngest sister, Wendy, for example, met with every doctor at two clinics over a ten-year period, describing symptoms of fatigue, muscle aches, joint pain and numerous digestive problems, including nausea. The results were discouraging. Tests were done and nothing was found. At other times she was not taken seriously, or told that what she was experiencing was not possible. Even the possibility of there being any connection among symptoms was usually denied.

Constantly researching, Wendy found a doctor, the first woman she had seen, who was distinctly different in her approach. This doctor gave her more time than any other had, listening to her, asking questions, then listening to her answers. For two hours they spoke, instead of the usual five or ten minutes previously given. The doctor then mentioned some possibilities of what my sister might have, including celiac sprue, which immediately caught my sister's attention—our grandfather had died of it.

Nobody in our family knew that sprue was genetic. At her doctor's suggestion, Wendy began a rigorous wheat- and gluten-free diet, the only known cure. And although it takes a long time to heal from this debilitating disease, after several months, Wendy's digestive problems were gone, her fatigue was 80 percent better, and her muscle aches and pains had vastly improved.

Because of Wendy's experience, our other sister, Heather, also suffering from a myriad of serious symptoms, was tested and diagnosed with sprue. After going on the prescribed diet, she too has started to show signs of improvement.

Of course, my sisters' stories address physical symptoms and healings only. The whole field of mind-body medicine goes even deeper than this. Deepak Chopra, a pioneer in this field, says in his book *Unconditional Life*, "Medical science was not being true to reality until it conceded that illness is connected to a person's emotions, beliefs, and expectations."

I know exactly what he means. A few years ago, I was seeing a health practitioner for several symptoms, including a tooth that had hurt for two years if I ate on the left side of my mouth, and a tightness in my hamstring that I had endured for five years, which no amount of stretching or physical manipulation could relieve for more than a few minutes.

My health practitioner at the time, a chiropractor also trained in a mind-body technique that promotes the release of past emo tional trauma, reminded me that whenever a physical symptom does not respond to any kind of physical treatment, it's likely to be emotion based. He proved it when, during one session, after I revealed some of the money issues my husband and I were struggling with, he asked: "Which is more important to you: financial security or your marriage?" I burst into tears and admitted that I didn't know. We used the release I experienced at that moment, however, as a springboard for applying the technique. The next morning, my tooth problem had disappeared and my hamstring was 80 percent improved.

I am well aware of the miracles of Western medicine, including the surgeries I have had that have made my life better. My mother's life has been saved on more than one occasion by the quick thinking and acting of medical professionals. My gratitude is deep and eternal.

But intuitively I feel that we must take a deeper look at what is happening on a collective level when it comes to healing. I am appalled at the take-a-pill mentality we see in every other commercial during prime time television—all ending with the disclaimer about the possible side effects of the drug (a natural outcome of the symptom-based approach). The AARP magazine is so oriented toward articles on prescription drugs that I've stopped reading it.

I'd like to see us start taking care of ourselves in a way that removes the need to take most prescription drugs.

I'd also like to see us start taking more responsibility for the possibility of underlying causes of our physical ailments. I'm not saying that every symptom has an underlying emotional cause, but I do believe that each of has the potential to look at ourselves more honestly, especially if we ask for help. Old patterns bind us, and the willingness to look at those patterns and release them or change them is a step toward freedom.

Mackey McNeil's story, which you are about to read, is an almost unbelievable tale of how a deep emotional wound manifested itself as a frightening physical symptom—and how it was healed. It is a story about healing from the perspective of wholeness, based on the remembrance that everything is connected.

MACKEY MCNEILL'S STORY
Blurry Vision

For most of my life my approach to healing was to take a pill and watch my symptoms disappear. Like magic, I felt better, at least for a while. But a few years ago I experienced a completely different kind of healing. Instead of suppressing symptoms, I went deeper—to find out what in my life was causing the symptoms.

It all started one morning when I was driving back to my office following an appointment. Suddenly the road looked blurry. This lasted a few seconds and then my normal perfect vision returned. A minute or two later, it happened again. I was frantic! Fearing that I might wreck my car and hurt myself or someone else, I got back to my office as quickly as I could. My vision continued to alternate: clear to blurry and back to clear again. My imagination ran rampant—cancer, a brain tumor, some kind of degenerative disease that was taking away my eyesight—and the horrible possibilities seemed endless.

In a panic, I called my eye doctor and went to see him that afternoon. He ran every possible test, but found nothing. He recommended I see a neurologist. Following the appointment with the neurologist, I had an MRI scan and consulted an ear, nose and throat specialist. I was tested, poked and prodded until I was weary, but no one could find anything wrong. The months passed and I continued to have random moments of fuzzy vision followed by panic.

I was sitting in church one day when the blurred vision occurred again. Deciding to experiment, I closed one eye. To my surprise, when I closed my left eye, I could see perfectly. Whatever was happening was only in my left eye! Amazingly, none of the testing had shown this. So with this new information I returned to the neurologist. This time he diagnosed a twitch in the muscles surrounding my left eye. I was relieved to know that my problem was as simple as a muscle twitch—until he offered me a prescription that he said I would have to take "daily and forever."

I went home in despair. I was tired of being viewed in terms of "pieces." I had seen an MD; an ophthalmologist; an ear, nose and throat (ENT) specialist and a neurologist—all of whom tried to view my problem as an isolated occurrence in my body. It didn't feel right to me. It troubled me, for example, that during this time I had also had a tooth problem on the left side of my mouth. I could not understand how the eye and the tooth problems, just inches from each other, could *not* be related! My intuition told me there was something much deeper underlying my eye problem.

But I had no idea what to do next. So I flopped down in my favorite chair and picked up the latest copy of *Body and Soul* magazine, which I had started reading about six months earlier. Normally I didn't have time for magazine reading, but I read this one because I had resonated with it the first time my husband brought home a copy. For years I had been interested in how to generate and sustain real health, and this magazine was the only source I had ever been able to find that addressed this issue.

I came to an article on energy healers. I was intrigued by the article's suggestion that physical symptoms can often be caused by energy blocks resulting from emotional causes. I had always been willing to try anything once, trusting my own experience to know whether it was safe and right for me. Something about the concept of *energy healing* felt true to me. And since I had tried everything I could think of to heal my eye from the physical perspective, without results, this certainly seemed worth a try. But where would I find an energy healer?

Two days later I walked into a party and, catching up with a friend, asked, "Do you know an energy healer?" To my surprise she answered, "Yes I do, and she is great!" I called the next morning for an appointment.

I arrived at the healer's house and nervously knocked on the door. The article said that energy healers were very intuitive. I felt uneasy, wondering if this healer would be able to read my mind. A voice called, "It's open," and I let myself in.

The healer was about my age. Dark-haired and attractive, she looked like a normal person. She smiled, gave me a hug and escorted me to her simple workroom, which contained a massage table, a chair and a table covered with crystals. She asked me to lie down on the massage table and asked if I wanted a blanket. "Yes," I replied. The warm cover acted as a security blanket, helping to calm my jitters in this new and uncertain environment.

She told me that I could sleep or stay awake since her work would proceed regardless of my state. She began by holding one of her crystals in her right hand and swirling it over my body. "I'm feeling your energy," she explained. Her quiet confidence was very reassuring, and I could feel any doubts that I might have had about her methods melting away.

She immediately asked about my left eye, even though I had not told her why I was there. She said she could feel an energy block over my eye and asked me if I'd had an injury of some sort in that area. Startled, I remembered that around four years before, I had lost my balance playing racquetball and hit my head, producing an egg-sized knot and a black left eye, along with a broken left arm and a concussion.

She asked me to tell her more about the events surrounding this injury. I explained that I had been adopted as an infant. A few weeks before the accident, I had met my birth family for the first time. I'd had plans to visit them again the day after my accident, but I had canceled my trip because of my injuries.

She didn't ask any more about it and went on with her work. I relaxed and fell asleep. The session over, I agreed to see her for another appointment. In the week that followed, I had only one incident of blurred vision, which was a huge improvement. Before my healing session, I had been having many blurry episodes a day. I promised myself I would never take the precious gift of sight for granted again.

I arrived for my next appointment feeling both eager and relaxed. While I lay on her table, she asked me about my relationship with my birth parents. I explained that I had met them around four years ago, just after my thirty-eighth birthday. I told her that I had found my birth parents to be wonderful, gracious people who had lovingly welcomed me back into their family. Finding them had been a joyous experience but had also been emotionally unsettling, bringing up feelings of ambivalence and confusion about how to deal with two sets of parents. Still, I continued to stay in touch with my birth parents, visiting them several times a year.

"What is happening now?" she asked.

I told her that in a month my birth parents were taking the entire family—my birth brother and sister, along with in-laws and grandchildren—on a cruise.

"And how do you feel about that?" she asked.

"Grateful," I replied.

"And what else?" she inquired.

I did not want to admit to any other feelings. Raised to be polite, I knew I was supposed to be grateful, and I *was* truly grateful. To feel anything else was not the proper thing to do.

"Do you really want to heal your eye?" she asked me.

"Well, there *are* these little nagging thoughts," I said. "You'll probably think I'm being irrational . . ." and then they tumbled out. "Today my birth parents have enough money to treat us all to a cruise. Yet when I was born, they thought there wasn't enough money for them to keep me. My birth mother admits that, as they look back, they realize they probably could have managed— because they always managed somehow. I have missed my birth parents with a deep physical sense of loss my whole life. I would rather have stayed with them and not have had enough money than be able to go on this cruise now. It seems too high a price to pay, to lose so much time and love—for money. I missed thirty-eight years with them and I feel cheated!"

As I expressed the myriad thoughts and feelings buried inside, I felt guilty. I had great adoptive parents. They had taught me the important things in life and had given me unconditional love. To feel these things seemed to betray them. It also could feel like a slap in the face to my birth parents, who had taken me back into their lives, no questions asked. Yet as my gut wrenched, I could no longer deny the truth: I was angry.

My energy healer stopped me in my tracks with her response. "Don't repress your feelings again and rob yourself of your healing," she said. "Your feelings are not right or wrong, good or bad. They just are. Accept and appreciate them. Here are your options: Call your birth parents and tell them how you feel, or say nothing, go on the cruise and get deathly ill. You choose!"

I was struck with fear. I thought, *How can I possibly call these kind people and tell them I'm angry? They are giving me a wonderful gift.* And then my real fear surfaced: *If I express my resentment, they might reject me again!* That would be unbearable.

"Your choice," she repeated.

Fear or no fear, I knew I had to call. I had to risk their anger and rejection to heal myself.

"When are you going to call?" she asked me.

"Sunday evening at 7:00," I replied.

"Do you want to call me at 6:00 for support, and we can walk through the call?" she asked.

"Yes," I agreed eagerly.

My course set, I headed back to the office, relieved that Sunday was four days away.

Those four days seemed to pass at the speed of light. Filled with anxiety, I called my energy healer at 6:00 on Sunday. She expressed her love for me and encouraged me, and we walked through every step of the call. She reassured me it would all turn out well.

At 7:00 I phoned my birth parents. By the time they answered the phone, I was in tears, my voice jagged between sobs. I began, "I need to talk to you. My request is that you listen. My intention is that love be present at the end of this call." I paused, continuing to sob. I took a few deep breaths. Then the most beautiful thing occurred. My birth parents said, "You can say anything to us, anything at all, and we will love you. We have always loved you and always will."

"You may change your mind," I said, ever skeptical of being loved. Tears flowing, I continued, "I am angry that there is enough money for us all to go on a cruise! I missed so many years and it hurts in my heart." I touched my chest; I could feel the pain. "I would rather have been with you all those years than go on this cruise. I am grateful for the gift, but I am angry and hurt all at the same time." Now we were all crying.

My birth parents told me again, "You can say anything to us, anything at all, and we will love you. We have always loved you and always will."

The pain in my chest began to lessen. Rejection, my worst fear, had not come to pass. More conversation, more tears and our call was complete. My intention had been fulfilled; at the end of the call, love was certainly present. I was elated.

My physical healing from this conversation was dramatic. My left eye never again got the jitters or blurry vision. My heart healing was even better: I went on the cruise and had a wonderful time. I connected with my birth family, really getting to know and love them. My heart could hardly contain my joy—snorkeling and playing with my brother and sister and, best of all, celebrating my birthday surrounded by my birth family for the first time.

Healing with my birth family brought me to new levels of understanding about my body and my inner voice. I see now that the physical and emotional are not separate—in fact, my body provides a way to tap my intuitive voice because it tells me things in concrete terms—and it never lies. I pay attention to my aches and tight spots, recognizing them as messengers, alerting me to look and see what else might be there.

My experience is that developing intuition is like learning any new skill: It feels awkward at first, but if you keep practicing, it becomes as natural as breathing. Mastering my intuition has brought new meaning to the word "trust," for now I see trust as an inward journey of knowing what is perfect for me in any moment.

Everything in my life shifted as a result of healing my fear of rejection. It gave me the strength to invest in personal growth work, therapy and coaching—all types of self-investment that I had previously been incapable of.

It particularly altered the way I interact with money. As a CPA and financial planner, I had worked with people and their money for my entire professional career, always with a sense that something was missing. I had found myself willing to invest huge amounts of money in other people's dreams, but not in my own. For example, the year before, I had invested in a women's venture fund, all the while ignoring several ideas I had about expanding my own business. While I owned the largest woman-founded CPA firm in Cincinnati, I had passed on many ideas for national expansion over the years because they required an investment of *my* money in me.

I see now that this was because of my own "baggage" around money: *I wasn't worth anything* was the belief that had run my life. Talk about blurry vision! As I allowed myself to feel and release my deepest emotions without judgment, my whole attitude about money shifted. I had always been good at saving money. I always had a cushion. Being an entrepreneur, I was willing to take a certain amount of risk. But the minute it meant depleting my cushion in any way, I would shrink back.

After this event, I realized the folly of always thinking someone else's business plan was better than mine. I had been working evenings and weekends on a book about the relationship of joy and money. I now realized that if I were seriously going to write this book, it had to become a priority. Committing to a deadline, I began taking two days a week to write, thereby reducing my days in the office to three. As a CPA, I bill by the hour, and while I had others in the firm billing, this was a serious reduction of income. But without it, the book would have stayed in its infancy, trapped by the fear I held onto of not having money. Once I made it a priority in terms of time and money, I got it done!

By the way, I never even looked for a publisher. I knew I had to self-publish, which required an investment of my own money, including a professional editor, artists and marketing people. To use someone else's money to fund my dream would have sidestepped my own healing and everything I was learning about letting go of fear.

My ability to spend money also shifted. Right after my healing, I received a gift of money, which in the past I would have put directly into savings to build the ever-increasing cushion I needed to feel safe. But this time, I took a portion of the gift to my favorite jewelry store and picked out a present for myself without regard to price.

Today I own four companies, with a fifth partnership currently being formed, all of which required my own capital to grow and build. But underlying all this success is the shift in my self-confidence and my willingness to invest in my inner knowing.

For me this is what it truly means to heal.

"I see now that the physical and emotional are not separate—in fact, my body provides a way to tap my intuitive voice because it tells me things in concrete terms—and it never lies."

—Mackey McNeill

10 · Commitment

ay the word "commitment" and the first thing that usually comes to mind is marriage and men who are afraid of it. A look at books on the topic of commitment shows that most related titles deal with commitment-phobic men, and they focus on advice to men on how to get past their fears to enjoy a happy and lasting relationship.

But while we could talk for days about commitment in terms of relationship, I'd like to talk about commitment here in terms of addiction, and the commitment to self that it takes to recover from some of the deadliest habits in our society. For if we think we're doing everything possible to experience fullness of heart, mind and spirit, we may be deluding ourselves if we have not addressed the issue of addiction.

I never thought of myself as an addict, because I don't use chemical substances, and the only alcohol I drink is a rare glass of wine. But Anne Wilson Schaef, author of *When Society Becomes an*

Addict, points out that addiction is any process over which we are powerless. While alcohol and drugs may be the most readily identifiable addictions, we are plagued in our culture by many other substance addictions, like caffeine, sugar and food, as well as *process* addictions, like gambling, sex, relationships, work, worry and accumulating money.

Personally, I have struggled with workaholism, an addiction actually lauded and encouraged by our society. We think that an employee willing to consistently work overtime is a gift! But we could not be more wrong. Workaholism usually involves an addiction to adrenaline, a self-generated chemical. I have known many days when I was unable to stop working because the adrenaline was pumping so fast. I wouldn't take time, even on weekends, to be with my family. I wouldn't take a break to go outside on a beautiful day to enjoy some sunshine and fresh air. Sometimes it was hard for me to stop even for a bathroom break.

According to experts like Schaef, like any disease, addiction is progressive and will lead to death unless we actively recover from it. I have had to look hard at my disease and how it affects my family life, my health and my happiness. It has created so much pain for me, stopping me from experiencing intimacy with my loved ones, that even writing about it makes me cry.

It takes a huge commitment to oneself to face an addiction and get help to heal it. And, like all commitments, it has to be made over and over again, every day. I often wonder about the ability to really commit to something in advance. We make marriage vows, for example, to live with each other for the rest of our lives, not really understanding that commitment is something that happens over time, day by day. I am "in recovery" for my work addiction, but constantly challenged by the temptation to overschedule my activities and push beyond the level of my body's comfort and ease. I have to admit regularly that I am powerless over this disease and continue to get help in my efforts to heal it.

But there is help! No matter what you are experiencing in life, whether it is an addiction that is destroying your life, or depression, insecurity or fear, someone else has already been there and can probably help you. I firmly believe that much of the suffering we go through in our culture could be avoided if we were not afraid to show our vulnerability. As Maya Angelou wrote in her poem *Alone*, "Nobody, but nobody/Can make it out here alone."

Of course, committing to dealing with an addiction is on a different level from committing to making cookies for the church bake sale. In the case of the cookies, someone else is counting on you to keep a promise you've made. Hopefully, the consequences won't be too grave if you either stay up late making them or show up at the sale empty-handed. But in the case of marriage or a job or recovery from addiction, the potential consequences are obviously much greater. In every case, though, true commitment comes down to you and *what you are willing to do for yourself*.

Chellie Campbell's story is an inspiring example of reaching out for help, and her resulting commitment to self. She reminds me of what the poet Minnie Richard Smith said: "Diamonds are only chunks of coal that stuck to their jobs, you see." And she shows us that, far from being the prison we often associate with the word, commitment can lead to an unleashing of creative power, happiness and other riches.

CHELLIE CAMPBELL'S STORY
My Name Is Chellie C.

My name is Chellie C., and I'm an alcoholic. This is my story of what it was like, what happened and what it is like now. Some of you will recognize this beginning as the standard opening for a speaker at an Alcoholics Anonymous (AA) meeting. Others of you may not know it, but will come to know it in the future. I, too, was once blithely unaware of my deepening dependence on alcohol.

It started as a simple habit—just a glass of wine when I got home from work. It took the edge off a hard day's work, helped me relax and change pace to a quiet evening at home. Stealthily, insidiously, when the hard day became a little harder, the glass of wine became two. Then, in classic alcoholic denial, I bought *bigger* glasses so I could still say I had only two glasses of wine. I wonder whom I thought I was fooling.

I had my reasons for drinking. I was under a lot of stress. I was teaching financial stress reduction workshops, and I was the most financially stressed person in the room. I was trying to keep my small business alive after having lost a $300,000-a-year account. I was trying to pay off the $80,000 credit card debt, trying to sell the $160,000 condo that was now worth only $90,000, trying to forget the deaths of my mother, my uncle, my aunt, my cousin's six-month-old baby, and one of my best friends. I was trying to keep up appearances as a business leader in the community, president of the local chapter of the National Association of Women Business Owners, and a board member of my rotary club. I put my game face on every day and washed it off with alcohol every night.

Of course, I knew I had a problem. I even knew I had to do something about it. I knew about Alcoholics Anonymous and "one day at a time." I tried doing it by myself. Every morning, I'd get up and say, "Just for today I won't have a drink." And I'd keep that promise every day until I got home from work. And then I would have a drink. Finally, I had to face the fact that I—smart, savvy, educated businesswoman—could not go one day without a drink. Not one day.

One Saturday I went to lunch with a friend. Mexican food. Oh, how I love Mexican food. But especially the margaritas! So Sally and I cheerfully ordered our drinks and downed them pretty fast. "Do you want to have another one?" I smoothly asked Sally. "Oh, no," she replied, "it's the middle of the day." *Bitch*, I thought, as I smiled sweetly. Lunch couldn't be over fast enough.

I ran to the grocery store afterwards, bought some tequila and margarita mix and made my own margaritas at home. I drank them down and went to sleep on the couch. I got up Sunday morning, finished off the tequila and went back to sleep. Monday morning I cursed myself. Couldn't I think of anything better to do for a whole weekend than drink?

It wasn't long after that weekend that I hit bottom. Finally.

Bottom looked like this: My liquor cabinet was practically bare, so I went to the grocery store to stock up. I picked out a bottle of cabernet, a bottle of merlot, some Chardonnay, Chablis, vodka, gin, bourbon, tequila, margarita mix, Bloody Mary mix, some assorted liqueurs—altogether I had about twelve bottles in my shopping cart—and some chips. Shopping complete.

The woman at the checkout stand started ringing up each bottle, smiled and said knowingly, "Having a party?" Not understanding why she would think that, I said, "No." I will never forget the look on that woman's face. I remember with stark clarity the utter humiliation I felt as I realized that if I was buying twelve bottles of booze, I *should* be having a party! I blushed furiously and scurried from the store. I could never shop there again.

That night, I lined up the twelve bottles on the counter and stared my disease in the face. I couldn't quit on my own; I needed help. I called my friend, Barbara, who was a member of AA. She sounded pretty excited when I asked if I could go to a meeting with her. Apparently, she'd been "saving a seat" for me. When I asked her what tipped her off that I had a problem with alcohol, she said it was the weekend we went to the health spa and I took a six-pack of wine with me. Oh.

So we went to the Wednesday night AA meeting at the University synagogue. It is one of the largest meetings in the world—over 900 people were there. I was completely shocked. There I was intro-duced to a wonderful community of people who had faced their demons and were helping others, along with themselves, to live life clean and sober. Everyone I met gave me their phone number and said if I felt like having a drink, to call them instead. I made a commitment to sobriety that night, went home, and threw away every bottle of alcohol in my house.

They told me I'd have to go to ninety meetings for ninety days. "Are you crazy?" I sputtered. "Have you seen my schedule? Do you know who I am?" Impassive, they shook their heads. "Ninety meetings for ninety days. If you want what we have, you have to do what we do."

"How do you know?" I whined.

"We're sober and you're not," they answered. Well, that made sense.

So I went to their ninety meetings for ninety days. I didn't feel like it. If you wanted alcoholics to *feel* like going to a meeting before they went to one, the rooms would probably be empty. But they have a saying, "Suit up and show up." They don't care how you feel about it, just that you do it.

Old habits die hard, but if you are determined, die they do. In the next months, I had to face every defect of my character and feel all the feelings that I had used alcohol to avoid. Sometimes after meetings, I would go to my car and collapse in sobs over the steering wheel. Kindly souls knocked on the window and asked if I was all right. There were nights I cried myself to sleep, looking at the moon deep in the night sky outside my window. "One day," I vowed, "it will be six months from now and I won't hurt this bad."

And one day, it was and I didn't.

Breakdowns will lead eventually to breakthroughs, if you are committed. As they say in AA, "It works if you work it." I grew into a new life and a new self. I deepened and matured. New awareness came to consciousness, as did a deeper empathy for people. My financial stress reduction workshops prospered as I told the raw truth about my experiences. My failures and recovery gave others the courage that they, too, could rise above the past and succeed. My book *The Wealthy Spirit* found a publisher and readers around the world. I cleared away the wreckage of the past and built a better life and a bigger bank account at the same time.

However financially stressed-out you are, I have been there. However unhappy you are, I have been there. And I know that you have the power to change it because I have done it. If you get help and follow a program of recovery, it can get better. In fact, it can get great. I now have a business I love, work that doesn't feel hard, and clients who praise me and pay me. I'm not Donald Trump; I'm not Bill Gates. I can't teach you how to make billions. There are other people for that.

I'm just a middle-class, middle-aged girl who once was miserable and broke and now is living rich, inside and out. I make a six-figure income; am debt-free; have savings, investments and a retirement plan; and travel the world on exciting vacations every year. My recreational beverage of choice is Diet Coke. I have wonderful relationships with family and friends and a spiritual foundation to my life and my work that deepens every day. I'm making more money and having more fun than ever before in my life.

Consciously or unconsciously, we create our lives. We create them out of our thoughts, attitudes, beliefs, feelings and the choices we make from them. Our life story is the sum total of our decisions. We have such power, and yet so many people feel powerless. We give up our power to the things we have chosen and then think we are helpless to change it. But we are responsible for it all.

We choose where we live, who our friends are, what our work is. We choose whether or not we exercise, smoke, take drugs, donate to charity, get a degree, have pets, have spouses, have children. We pick what we read, what we think and what we believe. Our lives are testimonials to our choices. Each moment is the point of power. Each moment, we can continue to choose what we have already chosen or we can choose to choose again. A life filled with abundance—inside and out—is yours for the taking.

There is a road from poverty to prosperity, from failure to success. I know, because I have walked it myself. You know it, too, but perhaps you have forgotten. Let me remind you. The road beckons. Come. There are many who will walk it with you.

"Our lives are testimonials to our choices. Each moment is the point of power. Each moment, we can continue to choose what we have already chosen or we can choose to choose again."

—Chellie Campbell

READER/CUSTOMER CARE SURVEY

BB1

We care about your opinions. Please take a moment to fill out this Reader Survey card and mail it back to us. As a special **"thank you"** we'll send you exciting news about interesting books and a valuable **Gift Certificate.**

Please PRINT using ALL CAPS

First Name [ ] M.I. [ ] Last Name [ ]

Address [ ]

City [ ] ST [ ] Zip [ ]

Phone # ([ ]) [ ] – [ ] Fax # ([ ]) [ ] – [ ]

Email [ ]

(1) Gender:
___ Female   ___ Male

(2) Age:
___ 12 or under   ___ 40-59
___ 13-19   ___ 60+
___ 20-39

(3) Marital Status
___ Married
___ Single
___ Divorced/Widowed

(4) Did you receive this book as a gift?
___ Yes   ___ No

(5) How many Health Communications books have you bought or read?
___ 1   ___ 2-4   ___ 5+

(6) How did you find out about this book?
Please fill in ONE.
1) ___ Recommendation
2) ___ Store Display
3) ___ Bestseller List
4) ___ Online
5) ___ Advertisement
6) ___ Catalog/Mailing
7) ___ Interview/Review (TV, Radio, Print)

(7) Where do you usually buy books?
Please fill in your top TWO choices.
1) ___ Bookstore
2) ___ Religious Bookstore
3) ___ Online
4) ___ Book Club/Mail Order
5) ___ Price Club (Costco, Sam's Club, etc.)
6) ___ Retail Store (Target, Wal-Mart, etc.)

(9) What subjects do you enjoy reading about most? Rank only FIVE. Use 1 for your favorite, 2 for second favorite, etc.

	1	2	3	4	5
1) Parenting/Family	○	○	○	○	○
2) Relationships	○	○	○	○	○
3) Recovery/Addictions	○	○	○	○	○
4) Health/Nutrition	○	○	○	○	○
5) Christianity	○	○	○	○	○
6) Spirituality/Inspiration	○	○	○	○	○
7) Business Self-Help	○	○	○	○	○
8) Teen Issues	○	○	○	○	○
9) Sports	○	○	○	○	○

(14) What attracts you most to a book?
(Please rank 1-4 in order of preference.)

	1	2	3	4
1) Title	○	○	○	○
2) Cover Design	○	○	○	○
3) Author	○	○	○	○
4) Content	○	○	○	○

TAPE IN MIDDLE; DO NOT STAPLE

BUSINESS REPLY MAIL
FIRST-CLASS MAIL PERMIT NO 45 DEERFIELD BEACH, FL

POSTAGE WILL BE PAID BY ADDRESSEE

HEALTH COMMUNICATIONS, INC.
3201 SW 15TH STREET
DEERFIELD BEACH FL 33442-9875

FOLD HERE

Comments:

ii · Openness

n the first leg of a flight to Los Angeles recently, I found myself sitting next to Sgt. Karl Mohr, an Emergency Medical Technician (EMT) in the Army National Guard. He was returning from service in Iraq and had not seen his wife in eighteen months.

The experience had had a profound impact on him. Stationed in Kurdistan, he had connected deeply with the people, whom he described as happy, even among the poorest. He observed that people are the same everywhere—that these people had the same needs and hopes as most: to be treated decently, to have their kids go to school and to live in a world free from fear.

When I asked him how he had connected with the Kurds, he said, "It all comes down to listening. The Kurds love to sing and tell stories. Whenever possible, I would take off my weapon, remove the gear and sit with them. Despite my level of activity, I always tried to stop and just listen to them."

Listening, I thought, *the secret weapon.* And the openness it takes to really hear what is said.

I knew it was true. Just months before, my husband and I had reached an all-time low in our ability to communicate. It was ironic because I was a professional speaker, and he had been a technical writer who had even owned and managed a documentation company. Both of us were known for our ability to communicate!

But true communication always involves two parts: transmitting and receiving. As I would learn, my communication skills were built mainly on the ability to transmit information, rather than receive it. When it came to having a two-way conversation, I often interrupted, always thinking I had something more important to say than the other person. In fact, I could hardly hear what the other person was saying because I was so busy thinking of the next thing I would say as soon as I could jump in. And when both people in a so-called conversation are in transmitting mode, there is no opening for either to listen to the other, and communication breaks down in a big way.

Desperate to improve my ability to communicate with my husband, I prayed for a way to learn how to listen better. I was guided to a weeklong program called "Living in Process," based on the work of Anne Wilson Schaef, a leader in the addiction recovery movement. For an entire week, I attended meetings in which the group modeled how to listen. It didn't matter whether the person who had the floor talked for one minute or one hour; as long as he was speaking from the heart, rather than the head, the rest of the group remained open, listening without interrupting. If group members felt antsy or bored or irritated with what the speaker was saying—or the fact that he or she was going on for so long—they had to take responsibility for their own feelings *without interrupting.* I came away from that process with an openness that allowed me to really listen and *receive another person,* which seems to be permanently in place.

As a result, very little about the next story, from Leah Green, surprises me. But it inspires me beyond measure. That the simple act of listening to another can have such healing and profound effects is irrefutable. That the simple act of listening can be the basis of peace is a reality, demonstrated by the work that people like Leah are doing.

In every human communication there is always this play of masculine and feminine, transmitting and receiving, speaking and listening. Conflict occurs when there is only transmitting; harmony can be realized when transmitting is balanced by someone open enough to receive.

Leah Green shows us the profound depth of human experience that occurs when we become open to listening to, and receiving from, each other.

LEAH GREEN'S STORY
The Secret Weapon

It was 1991. The first Intifada, the Palestinians' uprising against the Israelis, was raging. A group of Americans and I walked quietly through the twisted alleys of the al-Fawwar refugee camp near Hebron. We could hear Israeli soldiers moving through the other side of the camp. We turned a corner and came upon a middle-aged Palestinian woman picking through rubble. Our host explained to her that we had come to listen to the people of Israel and Palestine— to see the situation firsthand and listen to their stories.

The woman turned to us and, gesturing at the pile of rubble with despair, began to speak. "This was my home," our host translated. The woman cried with rage as she told us that her youngest son had been shot and killed by the Israeli army, and her oldest son had just been sentenced to life in prison by a military court. After the sentence had been handed down, her home had been bulldozed. She and her two daughters were left with only the makeshift shed that housed their animals. The woman began to wail, and our host translated: "Why do Americans hate us? What have we done to you? We've lost everything! We are just struggling to survive." We stood in shock as she continued to give voice to her anger and her grief. For most in the group, this was their first awareness that many Palestinians believed the United States was waging war on them.

Then, to our surprise, she took out a handkerchief, wiped her eyes and invited us inside her shed for tea. We sat with her on her dirt floor, drank watered-down sweet tea and listened to one another.

My initiation into Israeli-Palestinian reconciliation had begun in 1982 when, as a young woman, I participated in a year-long training at a community in Israel called Neve Shalom/Wahat asSalaam. Although well known now, the community was new when I went there; the founders were early pioneers in reconciliation work. At the community's "School for Peace," Israelis and Palestinians came together, often for the first time in their lives, to connect with one another as human beings. I saw that when people shared the simple truth of their own stories and their own personal suffering, their adversaries could listen without blame and without debate. A bond was formed between them, and a small space of peace was created.

The experience had such an impact on me that, over the next few years, I continued to be involved in Jewish-Palestinian reconciliation work, both in Israel and the United States In 1990, I began experimenting with another approach: I started taking Americans to the Middle East to listen to the stories of Israelis and Palestinians. I felt it would be healing for those in the conflict and enlightening for the Americans. It seemed particularly important to take American Jews over to hear these stories, knowing the stereotypes I had grown up with in the Jewish community: "Palestinians just want to throw us into the sea." "They can't be trusted." "We've always been at war with them." I wanted to continue to create opportunities for Jews and Palestinians to remember that we are cousins, and that peace is possible.

By 1996, after many successful listening trips to the Middle East, my work had become known as the Compassionate Listening Project. The Project is a reconciliation effort based on the ideas of Gene Knudsen Hoffman, a Quaker peacemaker who began encouraging the peace community to practice compassionate listening twenty years ago. Hoffman's thinking, in turn, was influenced by Thich Nhat Hanh, a Buddhist monk who challenges peacemakers to stay open to all sides of a conflict. The Americans who participate in the Compassionate Listening Project are trained to listen respectfully to all sides. The goal of the Project is to build international support for peace in the Middle East, while offering a practical tool for conflict resolution among the people "on the ground" in those countries.

What differentiates us from other organizations working with Israelis and Palestinians is that we work predominantly in the Israeli-occupied West Bank, where tensions are always high. The Palestinians there live under Israeli occupation—often the only Jewish people they know are Israeli soldiers and settlers with whom they have hostile relations. We invite ordinary Palestinians to come together with ordinary Israelis and talk to each other as real people, often for the first time.

In the groups I've led over the last decade, hundreds of Americans have listened to thousands of Israelis and Palestinians with the intention of discovering the human being behind the stereotype. No one has declined a listening session with us. We've sat with people in homes, offices, streets, refugee camps, the Israeli prime minister's office, the Palestinian president's office and on military bases. We've listened to settlers, sheikhs, mayors, rabbis, students, Bedouins, peace activists and terrorists. We've learned that it is easy to listen to people with whom we agree. It's when we listen to those with whom we disagree, those whom we hold as our enemies, that listening becomes a challenge.

The fundamental premise of compassionate listening is that every party to a conflict is suffering, and every act of violence comes from an unhealed wound. Our job as peacemakers is to hear the grievances of all parties and find ways to tell each side about the humanity and the suffering of the other. We learn to listen with our "spiritual ear," to discern and acknowledge the partial truth expressed by everyone—particularly those with whom we disagree. We learn to put aside our own positions and help the speaker tell his or her story. We learn to stretch our capacity to be present to another's pain.

Let me share an example. Sitting in a room with Israelis who lost family members in Palestinian terror attacks, the grief was palpable. Tears softened our faces as we listened to a father tell us about his twelve-year-old son, kidnapped, tortured and murdered by Palestinians. Another man cried through the retelling of his wife's recent murder. They had moved to Israel from New York and had experienced a peaceful community life for the first time in a Jewish settlement in the West Bank. They felt they had finally come home, only to have their lives shattered months later.

Sitting in a Palestinian refugee camp in Gaza, we wept again as we listened to the rage of a Palestinian refugee, a member of Hamas, who saw his father and other relatives killed in front of him when he was a young boy. He was arrested many times and tortured. We felt the grief he carried from being arrested on the eve of the birth of his first child, a son he didn't hold until the child was five years old. I think of the times when I've had thoughts of revenge for incidents so trivial in comparison. I remember the times I've fallen short in forgiveness for so much less a grievance.

In 1998, we began teaching compassionate listening workshops to Israelis and Palestinians so they could continue the work themselves in their communities. One of our first workshops included Ester, an Israeli Holocaust survivor in her late seventies, and Mary, a Christian Palestinian in her early twenties. For both of them, this was their first time coming face to face to listen to the personal suffering of their adversaries.

On the second day, twenty-five of us formed a circle to listen to Ester and Mary tell their stories. Ester went first and started by telling us how she had survived World War II. She had grown up in Germany and had been sent to England when she was fifteen years old with the Kindertransport, a group in Britain that transported Jewish children out of Germany. It was extremely difficult being separated from her brother and sister and her beloved parents. All three of the children had gotten out, but her mother and father had been killed in Auschwitz. Ester eventually married and moved to what was then called Palestine, but would soon become Israel.

Ester told us what it was like raising a family in the new state of Israel and living through so many wars—how heartbroken she was that Jewish families could not live without the threat of violence after all the persecution and terror they had lived through in Europe. She talked about how sad it was for her that her children and grandchildren have all been in the army and suffered terrible effects from the war and the fighting. She described living with the constant fear of suicide bombers and her daily concern for her family and friends.

But the most moving part of her story was hearing how, in recent years, she had found forgiveness for the Germans. She told us she visits Germany each year now and talks to schoolchildren about her experiences during the Holocaust. She attributed her ability to forgive to her parents, who taught her not to hate. "Even spinach they didn't allow me to hate!" she said.

While Ester spoke, Mary, the young Palestinian woman, who

had never had personal contact with an Israeli Jew before, sat and listened to her story and cried just like the rest of us. Mary acknowledged Ester's pain and her amazing road to forgiveness for the Germans, and her heart opened to an Israeli Jew for the first time in her life.

Then it was time for Mary's story. Mary sat quietly and told us excruciating details of what it was like to grow up under Israeli military occupation in the east side of Jerusalem. She told us about schoolmates she had lost. One schoolmate was riding home from school on a bicycle and was shot in the back by Israeli soldiers. He just fell off his bike and died right in front of her and her classmates.

She told us about another time when she was surrounded and harassed by Israeli soldiers on her way home from school. She was terrified that she was going to be dragged away and killed, and that her family would never know what had happened to her. Her story was one of day-to-day harassment and humiliation. She trembled the whole time she was telling her story. By the end, her body was shaking violently.

When Mary finished, the group wiped their eyes and sat in silence, taking in these two incredible stories. Then Ester got up, walked across the room and embraced Mary as if she were her own granddaughter. Mary cried in her arms, and Ester rocked her and comforted her. We all shed tears yet again, overwhelmed to be witnessing the first loving, human contact between these former enemies.

Over the following years, Ester maintained contact with Mary. One year she even brought her friends from Germany to meet Mary at her workplace, a beautiful convent in the old city of Jerusalem. Can you imagine? Here was a Jewish woman bringing her German friends to meet her Palestinian friend! They had bonded during the workshop and made a connection that has lasted to this day, despite the ongoing conflict. When I saw Ester not long ago, she told me, "You should have seen the sparkle in

Mary's eyes when I walked in the door that first time!"

In March 2003, Ester's grandson was killed by Palestinians during a military operation while he was serving in the Israeli army. Ester was attending a memorial ceremony at the Holocaust Museum in Jerusalem when she received the news. Still, she remains committed to the path of reconciliation—now more than ever, she says.

Once people have humanizing contact with one person from the other side, anything and everything becomes possible. All of a sudden, the spell is broken that "Palestinians are all terrorists," or "You can't trust any Jews," or "Jews have never shown sympathy for our story." Acknowledgment of one another's suffering is the key.

Once the divide is crossed and there's humanizing contact, the process of creating peace can begin. You've set the stage between those two individuals to be able to envision peace. And I think this is the most important thing. If we can't envision peace, if we don't have an experience of it in our hearts, we're not going to believe that it's possible. Even if a peace agreement is made at the political level, it will take people on the ground like Mary and Ester to build real peace between people. When we sit with Israelis and Palestinians and hear their stories, regardless of where they fall on the political spectrum, it becomes possible to affirm their humanity at the deepest level. Personally, I've found that I can have compassion even for extremists on both sides of the conflict. That doesn't mean I condone their actions, just that when I hear their stories, I can sometimes imagine myself making the same choices. And what a difference that makes in my perspective.

This is the work we do. It's slow and it's laborious, but it transforms people at the deepest level. Once a heart opens to the other side, it can never completely shut again. This is how I believe real change occurs—one person, one heart, at a time.

Leah with Gene Knudson Hoffman

"We've learned that it is easy to listen to people with whom we agree. It's when we listen to those with whom we disagree, those whom we hold as our enemies, that listening becomes a challenge."

—Leah Green

12 · Acceptance

I was in the eleventh grade the year that public schools in Baton Rouge were integrated. Racial tensions were running high in the Deep South at that time in the early sixties. An example close to home was that my father, a news reporter, was attempting to film police brutality towards a group of demonstrating African-Americans, when a policeman on horseback actually prodded him with an electric cattle prodder to try to stop him from showing the world what was going on.

Robert E. Lee High, the all-white school I attended, was one of three that had been selected for the huge event of desegregation. Students and faculty alike stood outside that first day of school before class, both curious and anxious as they awaited the arrival of the African-American students who would make history in our area, breaking the tradition of more than a hundred years of racial segregation.

Escorted to the school grounds by police, the five boys and girls looked scared and alone. I felt sorry for them and silently wished for their integration into this white world to be easy. I worried about the behavior of some of my friends and fellow students. Although the first day passed without incident, we had, after all, grown up in a black and white world, where the only real mixing of races occurred when an African-American woman worked as a maid in a white woman's home.

In my grandparents' generation, African-American women had often looked after the children in white homes. My grandmother, for example, was literally raised on a plantation in Mississippi by an African-American woman who was her wet nurse—arguably as much a part of her family as any blood relative. Although she spoke fondly of her early years and her nanny, her conditioning about African-Americans in general was so deep that I couldn't take her out for a cup of coffee, so loud were her derogatory remarks toward any African-American within earshot.

Despite my own conditioning by this culture, I was fortunate that my father had an innate sense of the equality of all human life, and my mother had grown up in a completely different environment. Born and raised in England, she had no preconceived ideas at all about differences between the races.

My mother, in fact, had a close and cherished relationship with our maid, Katie. She was our housekeeper and nanny whenever my mother went out, leaving my little sisters and me at home. I always noticed how my mother took care of her as much as she took care of us. In her later years, long after she worked for my family, Katie could always count on my mother for help of any kind. We were the only white people at her funeral.

I thank my lucky stars that I was raised by parents who advocated tolerance and preached against prejudice. One of the most precious moments of my life occurred when I was working as a Peace Corps volunteer in West Africa, living in the minority for the first time in my life. One day I suddenly realized that I no longer noticed whether a person's skin was brown or white. I remember being keenly aware of the freedom such acceptance had given me.

But my experience of acceptance was only a taste of what my friend Catherine Carter would eventually model for me. I had not seen Catherine, a Southern friend also raised in Louisiana, for many years when I heard that she was in town. So I tracked her down to have dinner with me and catch up on the years since we had last met. I was totally unprepared for the story she shared with me that evening.

Catherine could not have been prepared for what would happen to her in this story either. I share it with you now because it helped reinforce for me the understanding that acceptance is often the first step in healing—and always a move in the direction of love.

CATHERINE CARTER'S STORY
What Would Love Do?

One day while I was working away at my desk amidst deadlines and car pools and computers, a message flashed into my mind, clear, strong and unmistakable. It knocked me back into my chair and announced: "You are going to have to disengage from all this, because soon you will need all your time and attention for something else."

"All this" was quite a lot. I was mom to a lively nine-year-old boy, president of a publishing company, and editor and associate publisher of a regional travel magazine. I wrote a weekly column for the local newspaper and was a Junior League volunteer and

Sunday school teacher. I also taught meditation and traveled to meditation courses and retreats as often as I could. I sat on various community boards and barely a week went by that either my husband, Richard, or I or our business *didn't* appear in the local news. We were hot stuff in our little corner of the cosmos.

The message didn't specify exactly what that "something else" might be. But it had an absolute and authoritative feel to it. And then came the postscript, which rang true: "And if you don't take time to spend more time with your son, you are going to miss his childhood."

So I began to dismantle and simplify my life. Not one to walk away from a responsibility, I had to disengage gradually. I finished jobs that I'd agreed to do and stopped taking on new commitments. I practiced saying "No." I also began to spend more time with my son. I relished being able to be the one to pick him up at school and take him to his violin lesson. I realized how much I had been missing and was grateful for the message that changed my life.

It took about a year to get to a place where my day-timer was not already filled before the month began. I prayed that someday I would not even need a day-timer. Specifically I asked that God become my secretary and day-timer, and just let me know day by day when and where I needed to show up, and with whom.

One night toward the end of that year, Richard and I were enjoying a weekend away at the country plantation home of friends. After a gracious dinner, we were all clearing the table and getting ready to pitch in and wash the dishes. Unexpectedly, Richard asked the hostess, "Would you mind if Catherine and I went out for a walk? We haven't had much of a chance to be together for a long time." She said, "Sure, that's fine." I was surprised but pleased that we'd have some time alone together. Richard had opened an out-of-town office during the previous year and was away a lot of the time these days.

We strolled off into the piney wood that surrounded the big, white-columned home. After we had walked for a while in silence, Richard said, "I haven't been able to look you in the eyes for a long time, and after I tell you what I have to say, you may never want to speak to me again. You may want to get a lawyer first thing in the morning."

I froze inside. I had no idea what he had to say. We found a spot to sit down. Richard stared at the ground for a few moments, then he said, "I've fallen in love with a man."

I went blank. I couldn't think. He said that it was a person I had introduced him to. He told me he'd been spending a lot of time with gay friends in New Orleans and felt that he was bisexual. He went on for a long time, probably an hour or more, but I was oblivious of the time. As I listened, my whole world was silently blasting apart, like my own private version of the Big Bang.

In the following months, I was disoriented to a degree I had never known possible. Many times I woke up in the middle of the night and didn't know where I was, or even what year it was. I looked back on that conversation in the woods as the moment when my life was put into a giant blender and the button was pushed.

But I was also surrounded by loving helpers, both seen and unseen. Although I was often confused and terribly sad, I also felt a sort of grace. For about six months I felt the support of angelic presences literally holding me up, especially when I had to go out in public. I mostly stayed at home or out in nature, feeling so fragile that the thought of running into people I knew was unnerving. Our Southern town was conservative—it was sometimes called "the buckle of the Bible Belt"—and I couldn't face the reactions I thought even my good friends might have if they knew.

My son was my lifeline. I focused on helping him with his homework, dealing with a challenging situation he had in school that year and driving him to those violin lessons. I poured all the love from my broken heart into caring for him. Richard and I talked to a counselor who specialized in gay issues, and he advised us that it was enough for Stephen to know that there were difficulties between his dad and me. He recommended that we wait until after puberty before telling him that his father was gay.

Richard was a rock, staying with me and wanting to help me through this trauma. For months I thought we could keep our family together and somehow make it work. I loved my family dearly. We had shared joyous times and laughed often, and the thought of losing that was devastating. And so, we went to counselors, and I read books and asked a thousand questions about what being gay was all about. Richard sat and talked with me for hours, helping me to grasp this new piece of information.

This was just one indication of the profound change he had undergone. Richard was a much kinder person now that the "monster" was out of the box. He had been a bit of a tyrant at work before, setting strict standards and requiring sacrifices of himself and all of us in the company. For years he had insisted that everyone be at work by 7:30 in the morning. Even a hardworking single mother who was sometimes a little late from dealing with a sick child got no slack. This kind of behavior made sense when I came to understand the pain he had been concealing.

Richard told me he had known he was gay since he was five years old. Growing up in a small farming community, he had never imagined that he could live his life the way he wanted to. He assumed he'd have to deny his natural feelings and find happiness as much as he could in a conventional way of life. For years he managed pretty well. Then, when he fell in love and could no longer deny his feelings, he couldn't face either alternative: continuing to live a lie, or coming out with the truth. He told me that not long before our talk in the woods, he had stood for a long time on a balcony in New Orleans, thinking that the only solution was suicide and trying to muster the courage for it.

Sometimes I felt compassion for his pain, and sometimes I felt very betrayed. He should have told me! I never would have married him! How could he have made such a terrible mistake? But I couldn't help seeing that Richard had always tried to be the best person he could be. And I knew he loved me. I never doubted that. In all my confusion, the one thing I knew for sure was that I desperately didn't want to have to start my life over without him.

One night about four months after that walk in the woods, Richard and I went to bed together, as we still did. In the middle of the night I awakened with a deep feeling of despair. It was dark and painful beyond any emotional strain I'd ever experienced. Over the next few hours, a seeming eternity, I went through a period of terrible pain. After hours of agony, all I could think of was that death would be better than this torture, and many ways of killing myself flashed through my mind.

Just before dawn, as I lay there in a pool of sweat in utter exhaustion, I called out in a silent scream, "Help me, help me, oh God, help me." Seven times I called out for help and then I finally fell into a numb sleep.

When Richard got up to dress for work, I stirred and sat up in bed. I said something about having had a rough night, but from his expression I knew that was obvious. I'm sure I looked like hell, since it seemed to me that that's exactly where I'd been most of the night.

At eight o'clock that morning, the phone began to ring. A parade of my dearest friends and family members called to say, "Are you okay?" and "I was just thinking about you and wondering how you are doing." Only one of them had been contacted by my concerned husband. The rest had just felt the urge to reach out. Several of them were people I rarely spoke to since they lived far away.

By the early afternoon I was shaking my head and laughing at the response. There had been seven calls—one for each of my cries for help. Clearly, I had never been alone and without help, even in that dark pit of torment.

I had hit my bottom point. And from that day onward, though I was still quite tender and wounded, I began to feel more and more centered. Slowly I began to pull myself together and move forward into the unknown adventure of my new life. After a while, my unseen helpers gently let me know that it was time for me to walk on my own. For a while I felt more wobbly, but gradually I regained my balance.

As I grew stronger, I began to seriously doubt that my idea to stay together was workable. One evening, standing in my kitchen pantry, I heard another message. This one was decidedly more lighthearted than the one that had come so many months before. It said, "Catherine, you can stay married, but it will be much more difficult than is necessary." And then with a playful tone, almost a chuckle, it said, "Honey, you're gonna have your cake and eat it too." At that point I knew that I could keep all the love that we had and still move on to find a partner who wanted to be with a woman, someone who could receive my love on all levels.

When I told Richard about this experience, he agreed, but he still wasn't in a hurry to leave. One evening as we sat together deciding how to handle the details of the divorce, he showed me a flyer he'd received in the mail that day. It was from the current owners of our first home—a duplex we had totally renovated. When we had first seen it, I had said, "I can't live here! This is a dump!" Richard had said, "I promise you'll love it when it's renovated." And sure enough, it was a work of art when he was done. We had sold it years ago. The flyer said it was being torn down to make way for a hospital parking lot, but they wanted to preserve the "beautiful architectural elements." Anyone who wanted them was invited to come and get them. Richard looked up after reading it and said, "We built this marriage lovingly, one piece at a time, and we're going to take it apart that way too."

The toughest test came when we had to deal with the lawyers. To my surprise we ran into some of our worse challenges yet over purely legalistic matters. But I found the best way to deal with this and other tough issues was always the same: Whenever I had to make a decision, I asked myself, "What would love do?"

In time Richard moved to a charming gatehouse apartment nearby that I found for him. Stephen could ride over on his bicycle and we all stayed very close. Our divorce was finalized exactly two years after that walk in the woods. Soon after, I moved away to go back to school and Richard moved to the Northwest, where attitudes about gays are decidedly more tolerant than in our hometown. Stephen went to live with him when he was fourteen. Richard had no partner at that time, and it wasn't until a year later that he sat down with Stephen and told him he was gay. Although it must not have been easy for Stephen, he accepted it and never let it stop the flow of love between them.

I thought at the time that my "piece of cake" perfect new man might be just around the corner. It didn't happen. For over fifteen years I looked and watched and waited and tried to make something happen. Finally, I let go of that desire. And from that place of letting go I felt the most glorious freedom. Soon after that, sure enough, a beautiful, loving relationship opened up to me and continues to unfold.

Looking back, I can see the perfection. Those fifteen years, while longer than I would have chosen, gave me the opportunity to heal from the trauma and begin my life anew, a life based on honesty as well as love. I outgrew the last stabs of resentment at how my picture-perfect life had been blasted apart. I saw the deeper wisdom that provided Richard, Stephen, my new love and me with just the right opportunities at just the right moments. We all grew, and our love grew too.

We still get together for holidays, birthdays and family trips. Our loving family has expanded to include a man who shares Richard's life. I call him my husband-in-law! And this Christmas, sixteen years since it all began, my new life partner will join our family gathering. Love was there in the beginning, the middle and the end of this great shift in my life. I'm just glad I had the heads-up warning, and had already turned my day-timer over to God. He made all the appointments for me. I just had to show up.

"I found the best way to deal with this and other tough issues was always the same: Whenever I had to make a decision, I asked myself, 'What would love do?'"

—Catherine Carter

13 · Harmony

 omen are the managers of their relationships," said expert Justin Sterling on a weekend-long seminar I once took. Frankly, the idea scared me; I already had enough to manage.

But the concept became clearer to me when I later saw the results of some research by a team that included Dr. Deborah Tannen, renowned author and gender expert. The video I saw showed certain differences between males and females at various grade levels ranging from second grade through university.

Put in a room together, boys constantly moved about, always looking for something to do. When they did sit down, it was usually at angles—in one case, almost parallel to each other—and they rarely looked at each other directly. However, they did interact. Mostly, they directly disagreed with each other, put each other down, initiated mock assaults on each other and implied that the other was doing things wrong.

Girls, on the other hand, even in the second grade, typically sat down facing each other immediately, looked directly at each other's faces and began talking. They did not look for anything else to do, as they were satisfied that they were already doing something: talking with each other. They supported each other by agreeing with and adding to what the other said and reassured each other that they were doing things right.

Dr. Tannen pointed out to me that the boys were definitely *relating* with each other, just differently from the girls. But I found the differences, which she summarizes in her book *You Just Don't Understand: Women and Men in Conversation*, to be telling.

It just seems to be the nature of women to harmonize. How many times have we heard it said: If women ruled the world, there would be no war. Of course there are exceptions, but I believe with all my heart that women do not want or need war as men seem to. I don't think it's generalizing too much to say that our tendency is to cherish life more than commodities or political power. We believe in win-win and the possibility of no one ever needing to lose. And, in general, we believe that killing is rarely the answer to anything.

In the movie *Troy*, Agamemnon, king of the Mycenaeans, expressed this view in the line, "Peace is for women." He practically spat it out, as if the desire for peace were a weakness, something to be pitied. And yet, I heard it as a ringing tribute to the talent and innate tendency of our gender to keep sight of deeper values in times of conflict and to strive, as the Grecian women did, to preserve life, home and harmony.

In the less dramatic but also deeply stirring story that comes next, Yaniyah Pearson struggles with her own inner war of judgments about the group of teens she worked with. Circumstances presented the perfect opportunity for her to transcend those judgments and find the deeper universal love that connects all humans—and furthers harmony between the generations.

Her story reminds me of one of my favorite Mother Teresa quotes: "If we have no peace, it is because we have forgotten that we belong to one another." It is clear in Yaniyah's story that she has remembered.

YANIYAH PEARSON'S STORY
The Beat

I t was a perfect day for a long drive. The sky was clear and the air crisp. I was grateful for the accommodating weather conditions as I packed four young adults and their belongings into my Pontiac Bonneville. We were heading to Washington, D.C., to join 125 young people from across the country at the YouthBuild and AmeriCorp National Young Leaders Conference.

After five years as director of the YouthBuild program in Brooklyn, New York, I was thrilled that the four students in our Policy Committee and I were finally able to make this trip. YouthBuild is a national program that provides high school dropouts with on-the-job training in the construction and renovation of housing in their communities. The bigger goal is leadership training—and what better opportunity than a trip to the national convention to try to get our delegate elected to the National Young Leaders Council?

But my enthusiasm was tempered by some anxiety. I had to spend five hours in a car with four young adults. What would we talk about? What kind of music would we listen to? I knew they would prefer rap and hip-hop, which were definitely not to my taste. I love classical, soul and New Age music, music that speaks to the heart and awakens the spirit. I often go to drumming circles, where we move to the beat of powerful drummers. But like most people in my generation, I find rap and hip-hop to be materialistic, crude and downright offensive. Still, I was in the minority, so I prepared myself to surrender to their choices.

Half an hour into the trip, as we cruised along the highway listening to the rap and hip-hop station, I was struggling with a growing sense of isolation. I felt trapped in the car and battered by the sounds and rhymes, the "N" word, the derogatory names for women, the glorification of violence and greed in the music. With no way to escape, I took a deep breath and thought about the gap between us.

I generally got along well with young people. I liked to think of myself as approachable, caring and even funny at times. Meetings with the Policy Committee were usually relaxed and upbeat, and we operated well as a team. The cultural differences between the YouthBuild teens and me were obvious, but until now I hadn't felt the weight of them. We were all African-Americans, but I had been blessed with opportunities. I grew up in Massachusetts, in a neighborhood safe enough to navigate without the protection of an adult or a gang. My working-class parents expected their children to succeed, and I went to a private high school and graduated from college.

My YouthBuild teens had none of these advantages. They were high school dropouts, living in the most economically devastated communities of Brooklyn, New York. They were struggling with poverty, gangs and substance abuse, and subject to indignities such as random drug testing. At my college, the student council had given away free drugs like marijuana and acid once a year. For my teens, getting busted with one joint could end any chance of a job at Home Depot or getting federal financial aid. I was as dedicated to their success in life as I had ever been to any cause, but I was under no illusions about the gulf between our realities and subsequent worldviews. And sometimes, like now, that gulf limited my ability to connect on a deeper level.

As I mulled it over, it struck me that I didn't usually concern myself with how I could bridge this gap with my students. My approach had always been that I was the authority, and they had to learn to do things my way if they wanted doors to open to a better future. They had to reach for me, not the other way around. I didn't change my language patterns; they had to change theirs. I didn't subject my value system to criticism, but we had daylong workshops cutting theirs to pieces. My "policy" weighed heavily on me as I chauffeured my committee to D.C.

So did my discomfort, which was close to becoming intolerable by now. But I told myself that no matter how long five hours might seem, it was really only a short period of time. I took a few deep breaths and surrendered, finding my center again and preparing to continue to suffer the music in silence.

Just then, one of the boys asked if he could play a cassette tape. I said sure, then held my breath as he loaded the cassette and hit the play button. To my surprise, some of my favorite soul music filled the car. I smiled to myself and relaxed. And from that moment on, we had a great time, singing along with the tunes, telling jokes and sharing our strategies for getting our delegate elected.

We arrived at the hotel that night, tired but excited and full of anticipation. I immediately offered my assistance to the national staff but found that all the major responsibilities for running the program were covered. My role would be simply to support the young leaders who were in charge of the event. This was a rare treat. As the first day passed, I realized that I was on pure love duty. I only needed to listen and show compassion to the tense staff and the young leaders who were carrying everything on their shoulders.

During the next day, I found that I had a greater ability to love. The bonding I had experienced with my students during our trip just kept expanding to include more people. By the end of the day,

I was elated. I felt more deeply connected with others than ever before. When conflicts between staff and the youth leaders emerged, I was able to stay focused and nonreactionary. Usually their anger would have triggered the same in me. Young people sought me out to express their discontent and occasional disillusionment with their roles as leaders. Staff sought me out when they just needed to relax. I felt that I had become a sacred witness and a healing balm.

As the excitement swirled around me, I realized that I was responding to life in a profoundly different way. It felt as if concentric circles of love were being generated by this incredible gathering of 125 young people of all races from all corners of the country, who had emerged out of poverty and deprivation and were now connecting through YouthBuild. It was like being under an enchanted spell, where angels were sprinkling me with tenderness and joy. I was in love with everyone.

My heart grew fuller with every exchange until I felt I as if I could explode. I needed a way to release some of this emotion. Music! I needed music! For two days we had all just been talking. There had been no background music, no singing. I hadn't even had enough time in my room to turn on the radio.

It wasn't until the last night that my wish came true. Another group at our hotel was having an Up With People! concert at their final banquet, and they kindly invited some of us to the show. The young Up With People! performers were from various countries, and nearly every musical selection was a fusion of their national/traditional songs and modern American music. The influence of African-American hip-hop culture was indisputable. Imagine the jubilation of young people listening to the music they hear in the streets of the inner city—music despised and condemned by much of America—being performed by young people from all over the world in this beautiful banquet hall. It brought tears to my eyes, and the young folks just got happy.

When the performance was over, we flowed out into the lobby, telling everyone we saw about our experience. What to do with all this energy in a suburban Washington, D.C., hotel! I decided to go out for a short walk.

As soon as I stepped onto the sidewalk, I discovered an ethnically diverse group of ten young men from the conference huddled in a circle. They were freestyling, an improvisational rhyming contest, and a central component of hip-hop/rap musical culture. Suddenly I wanted to experience their world from their perspective—not like an observer or researcher, but as one of them, without a sense of separation.

I slowly inched my way into the circle. Standing shoulder to shoulder, they were enthralled by a current of indisputable force. Before long, I found myself swaying in unison to the "beats," which were vocal sounds created by two of the young men. Their guttural sounds imitating percussion instruments held down the rhythm. Whenever one of the rappers was inspired to rhyme, he would step into the center of the circle. For the most part it was synchronized so that just when one was done, another would jump in and take his place.

The vibration of the circle pulsated throughout my body. I started to feel light and became unaware of the ground supporting me. It was as if I were suspended in midair, completely connected, safe and secure. I listened to the lyrics, but it was the beats that held my attention and moved me into this trancelike state. Some of the lyrics were positive and uplifting messages. Some were more "gangsta," with cursing and boasting about thugs and shootings. But oddly enough, the negative messages didn't feel any different from the positive ones. They all exuded a high quality of love. *It's like building a fire of dogwood and cedar,* I thought; *the flame is still beautiful when you add some leftover newspapers. The beauty of the fire prevails.*

The greatest expression of love came from the men making the beats. Always in the background, never taking center stage, they provided the foundation of the music. It's the beat that inspires the rapper. He or she is completely dependent on that constant pulse upon which every word flows. And keeping the beat is not easy. It requires a lot of breath control, stamina and focused attention.

As I swayed to the beat, I was reminded of my drumming circles, where we would lose ourselves in the rhythms. For the first time I could relate the spirituality of our music and that of the music of the young people I had come to love and respect. Both had the power of the beat. But this young group also had the power of the language they used and the way they flowed in harmony with each other, made room for each other and collectively intuited the space between a beginning and an ending.

As the curfew hour approached, the circle broke up with smiles, back slaps and high fives. I felt both embraced and invisible, which, ironically, seemed appropriate. I had done nothing to earn entrance into their circle except surrender myself to the same currents that moved their spirits.

Alone in my hotel room, I couldn't think of sleeping. I was still reeling from the excitement of the evening. I wanted to write. Although I hadn't had the nerve to rhyme in the circle, a kaleidoscope of words was circling in my mind. Lyrics came as one more gift from those young men. I sat up and wrote some verses.

The next morning when the group facilitators called for us to share some reflections from the previous day, I couldn't resist. I rushed to the front of the room and recited my verses in dedication to the freestyling brothers. As I spoke, they began to accompany me with the beats, the truest sign of recognition they could have given me.

Looking back on that night, I am grateful for that beautiful opportunity to cross cultural barriers, removing the illusion of separation. The very music I had hated on the trip to the conference had become a vehicle to connect in love. We all have the ability to love each other and find the deeper place where our spirits unite. We can do it through the universal language of music, or in countless other ways. Because the truth is, we all come from the same creative source. As I said in my verses:

Truth is—that we share rhythms, vibrations,
connections to a beat. A universal beat that ain't even old,
because it has always been here.
There has always been a beat here, in my heart,
in the heart of the ancestors,
in the heart of the Mother, our Mother Earth,
and even before Her birth, there was the beat—
like the breath of God—permeating all the universes.

"We all have the ability to love each other and find the deeper place where our spirits unite."

—Yaniyah Pearson

14 · Freedom

 hated college. Although I loved to read and learn new things, at that point in my life, I also felt lost. I went into journalism by default, having a journalist father and no clue what else to major in. I couldn't bear the deadlines and constant pressure to produce for the university's daily newspaper, or being assigned to report on endless, boring meetings. To make things worse, I joined a social sorority, going through the arduous and pressure-filled process of getting invited to join it, only to discover that my social and political interests and conscience clashed with the never-ending planning of parties with South Sea Island themes. And I felt oppressed by classes I took to help me make a living that didn't even come close to stirring my soul.

So I will never forget the day I walked out of my last final exam of my senior year. I stood in the quadrangle of my university's beautiful grounds and vowed I would never set foot in a classroom again. I was twenty years old—and I was free!

So often, we associate freedom with externals. I once heard Jack Canfield, my mentor and coauthor, say he agreed with Tony Robbin's idea that success is the freedom to do whatever we want, whenever we want and with whomever we want. For many, freedom is very much related to survival issues. For women in Afghanistan, freedom means now being able to go to school. For most prisoners, it means being on the "outside" again. For endless numbers of people throughout the world, the right to speak freely or to express emotions openly and honestly are at stake daily.

But over the years, I have learned that true freedom has far more to do with an inner state than with a lack of external restrictions. Victor Frankl was a living model of this when he survived the concentration camps of WWII by constantly seeking the good in everyone around him, including his captors and guards. "Everything can be taken from a man but one thing, the last of the human freedoms: to choose one's attitude in any given set of circumstances, to choose one's own way," he said. True freedom!

And a popular folktale goes like this: A wise woman who was traveling in the mountains found a precious stone in a stream. The next day she met another traveler who was hungry, and the wise woman opened her bag to share her food. The hungry traveler saw the precious stone and asked the woman to give it to him. She did so without hesitation. The traveler left rejoicing in his good fortune. He knew the stone was worth enough to give him security for a lifetime.

But, a few days later, he came back to return the stone to the wise woman. "I've been thinking," he said. "I know how valuable this stone is, but I give it back in the hope that you can give me something even more precious. Give me what you have within you that enabled you to give me this stone."

Freedom from material needs and desires is one of the deepest, truest freedoms, especially in a materialistic culture like ours. The accumulation of wealth and possessions is highly prized in our society, often accompanied by the feeling that only when we have enough money can we be truly happy. While wealth can certainly give us opportunities we might not have otherwise—in terms of travel, philanthropy or study, for example—we hear countless stories of people who have it and yet are lonely and unfulfilled at their deepest core. It is a curious quirk of fate that life lessons related to money can be the result of having too little of it—or too much!

In the next story, Despina Gurlides was forced to take a deep look at what freedom meant in her own life and how it related to success. Despina's story reminds me of one I read about women executives at a leading high-tech corporation. Their average age was thirty six, and their average net worth was $10 million. They rarely saw their families and for most, their lives centered around their computers. They took little time to enjoy their material possessions and experienced very little satisfaction from their money. In fact, using their wealth to buy child-care and home-care services mainly enabled them to work longer and harder. They hoped that someday their success would bring them freedom, but, by their own admission, they were not living the lives they wanted, and as a result, they were not free.

Clearly, material abundance isn't the automatic ticket to freedom that many expect. I have heard that most people in the United States are wealthier than 99 percent of the world's population and 99.9 percent of all the people who have ever walked this earth. And yet, the stress and isolation of our lives can sometimes make us less free than our ancestors who lived in simpler times.

Perhaps we need to look at freedom from a different angle. Perhaps the greatest truth is that we are free when we recognize that what we have is enough, and that the experience of sufficiency is true abundance. As Nina Wise says in *A Big New Free Happy Unusual Life*, "Our longing for freedom cannot be satisfied by cars or houses or diamonds; by private jets or offshore bank accounts

or caviar; by miniature computers or mighty weapons. Our longing for freedom can only be satisfied by recognizing that we are
each sufficient as we are, and that what feeds us has nothing to do
with what we buy and everything to do with an inherent vitality of
soul."

When we know this, I believe we are truly free.

DESPINA GURLIDES'S STORY
What Do You Really Want?

All my life I had wanted to be successful, accomplished,
respected and wealthy—and by the age of thirty-seven it
looked as if I had achieved my goals. A Greek girl, born of
immigrant parents in Astoria, the Greek town of New York City, I
had been the first in my family to go to college. While I enjoyed
teaching, I decided not to pursue it as a career because it wasn't
lucrative enough. Instead, I obtained my MBA on a scholarship
and proceeded to work my way up the corporate ranks, becoming
a vice president of a billion-dollar entertainment company by the
time I was in my early thirties. I married a man, not because I was
in love with him, but because I knew he would be even more successful than I was. And I was right. In his early thirties, Michael
became one of the youngest managing directors of an investment
bank, and we were able to live very well, with a beautiful prewar
co-op apartment in Manhattan, as well as a weekend house with a
tennis court and swimming pool in the Hamptons. I should have
been happy, but I wasn't.

On the outside my life looked wonderful. Our marriage was
perfect—I thought. Michael and I were the best of friends. We

loved going shopping together, picking out clothes for each other or furniture for the house, dining at beautiful restaurants, having friends over. Well, actually, we didn't have that many close friends; they were more like business acquaintances. Most of the entertaining that we did was for business. Come to think of it, our marriage was more like a business partnership as well. There was no fighting—that was true. But there was also no passion. I didn't see that as a big problem at the time. *After all,* I thought, *we're in our thirties, sex shouldn't be that important. We have common interests and goals; that's what's important.*

My job was great too. I was a vice president of an entertainment company, managing three departments. I was well respected, and it was reflected in my salary and bonus, not to mention all the other perks: ten-day ski trips to Aspen every February for a "planning meeting" (the chairman liked to ski), fall meetings at beautiful resorts, a large expense account, hosting lunch at the company's private dining room (Sophie, the French chef, always made my favorite chocolate desserts), all the free music and videos I wanted—and the list went on.

Okay, maybe the job wasn't that great. My boss, Nathan, a large, scary man, could be—and often was—abusive. He believed that we were paid well enough to withstand his rudeness. He often yelled and shouted, criticizing my work. The first week that I started working for him, he came into my office yelling that I had destroyed his department with my incompetence. When I pointed out to him that I wasn't talented enough to destroy a department in one week, and that I was merely trying to fix the mess he created, he smiled at me for the first time. I realized he was testing me. Nathan couldn't stand wimps, and if he thought you were one, he would walk all over you. I was determined to stand my ground with him, and I did. But it took its toll on me. During the five years that I worked for him, I was sick to my stomach every morning before work. Throwing up became a normal part of my morning routine. It didn't occur to me that this was unusual. At least I didn't have an ulcer, as Michael did.

So I continued working and spending most of my money on doctors, trying to figure out why I was always tired. Surely the building I worked in—one of those skyscrapers on Sixth Avenue, with windows that hadn't been opened in thirty years—couldn't be the only reason. I was getting bored with the work, tired of the politics and fed up with my boss. At home I was bored as well in the passionless marriage I had created. Most weekends I would stay at home, sleep late, then spend the rest of my time on the couch reading a novel. In the beginning Michael was sympathetic, trying to cheer me up by cooking one of my favorite dishes. Later, he was too busy to notice. He flew to London weekly on the Concorde, sometimes just for a day meeting. He was exhausted, but I was cheering him on. How else could we afford to live the way we were?

Money was definitely needed because shopping was now my main escape from my life. When Michael worked late, which in the later years was most of the time, I went shopping. Sometimes I bought three pairs of shoes for $1,000, only to forget them in a closet somewhere. Sometimes I splurged on a whole new wardrobe, all beautiful suits for work, of course. What else was there to do but work?

I didn't seem to have friends anymore. Somewhere along the way I had lost them all. I was too busy working late, shopping or being with Michael to have other relationships. When I wasn't too busy, I was too tired. I dreaded the phone ringing on the weekend, as I had no energy to speak to anyone. Michael would pick it up, or the machine would get it. No wonder people had stopped calling me.

This life of "luxury" took its toll on my physical appearance as well. While I have never had a weight problem, all the rich food I was eating without exercising made me lose my form and tone. I looked good in my suits, but I didn't look sexy. My hair was cut very short, probably an inch long. It was a sophisticated look, a look that said I was competent, but it didn't make me feel feminine. I couldn't remember the last time a man had looked at me on the street as they did when I was younger. But then again, I was in my thirties, married and busy. Being sexy wasn't part of the package.

My life had settled into what seemed to be the routine I would have the rest of my life. But, thank God, a power higher than me was writing the script. This higher power suddenly pulled the rug out from under me. Events during a six-month period when I was thirty-seven years old served as louder and louder wake-up calls: A man pulled a gun in the subway car I was in. Someone threw a rock at our car while we were driving, shattering the windshield. I flew to San Francisco on business on October 17, 1989, just in time to experience the terror of the earthquake.

I had heard that bad things happen in threes, so I hoped this was the end. It wasn't. A few months later my husband asked for a divorce. In our seven years of marriage, he had stored up a great deal of resentment, which he was finally releasing. He didn't tell me at the time that he also was having an affair with the secretary of a client, and that he wanted to marry her.

On the day he was packing to move out, I was in a taxi accident. Bleeding, but not seriously hurt, I got home and fell on the floor, crying. There wasn't anything I could do but surrender: my life was falling apart. I entered a "dark night of the soul" that felt like a kind of death. For months I cried, my arrogant bubble burst, the life that I had created gone forever.

Gradually, I began to make some choices that later transformed me and my life. I could have played the victim role; there were plenty of people who were happy to commiserate with me, telling me how horrible Michael was, how I deserved better. But the truth was that for years Michael had been a good husband to me, doing his best. He had loved me with passion in the beginning, a passion that I did not reciprocate. Most men in a sexless marriage would have had many affairs, but he had been faithful for a long time. I felt gratitude toward him for taking care of me during the seven years that we were married and for having the courage to leave.

A sexless, passionless marriage was not okay, I realized. Thirty-seven was too young to live the way I was living. I joined a gym, and after a couple of months of working out, I saw my body beginning to tone up. Hmmm . . . I started to remember my youth. I let my hair grow out and started paying more attention to my makeup. One day I was putting on my coat at my new hairdresser's when a handsome man looked my way and smiled. I turned around to see whom he was smiling at, but there was no one behind me. He was smiling at me! I was so flustered that I couldn't put my hand through the sleeve of my coat. For the first time in years, I felt alive—and beautiful. I started to date, and I loved feeling my emotions and my body begin to wake up.

I connected with my friends again. The great thing about true friends is they keep loving you, even if you go away. Friends whom I hadn't seen in years, from different parts of the country, came to spend time with me and offered the nurturing I needed. People from work invited me out. The discussions were personal, not about business. I was feeling very vulnerable, and people were responding with open hearts.

However, the most important change related to my spiritual growth. I started asking questions about the purpose of life and began finding answers. I read books containing truths that I knew on some level, but had forgotten. *We create our own reality.* Of course, I knew that. I had created my life. I had set out with the intention to obtain all the material goods that I could think of. How lucky that I had been able to do this, and how lucky that I had found out that was not where happiness lies.

I realized that I had many more choices than I thought. I didn't have to work for an abusive boss. For the first time the idea occurred to me that I could actually quit my job, and I did, much to Nathan's surprise. He thought that he had placed "golden handcuffs" on me. But I had realized that I was free, free to recreate my life.

I took time off and spent months by myself, sleeping in, going to movies, walking through Central Park, letting each day flow with no agenda. My intention was to take a few months off, then start working again, but I found I couldn't go back to the corporate world. To my surprise, I realized that I didn't want to stay in New York either. The beautiful city where I had been born and had lived most of my life now seemed abusive to me. *Wouldn't it be nice,* I thought, *to live near nature, where the people and weather are friendlier?* The Upper West Side co-op was worth a lot of money; I could sell it and start a new life.

I found that the Bay Area was calling me. So I sold my co-op, moved to Marin County, learned how to drive and started a new life, thinking that now I would be happier. But things didn't work out the way I expected. I couldn't find work, especially after the Internet industry crashed, and I wound up going through my savings faster than I could believe. After some time, I found myself in a desperate financial situation, living off my credit cards, and wondering if I had made a terrible mistake.

Then one night I turned on the local access TV station. A man was lecturing, and I was stopped in my tracks by what he was saying. He talked about not betraying yourself, not taking a job that you hate out of fear of survival. Was he talking to me? I really didn't want to work in the corporate world, even in a milder environment like San Francisco. No wonder I couldn't find work; my heart wasn't in it. He talked about most people living the lives of donkeys, running away from the stick (their fears) and running toward the carrot (their desires).

Was I being a donkey? He talked about the possibility of ending this life of "donkeyhood" by telling the truth and being willing to give whatever it takes to find true freedom and happiness—a happiness that comes from within, not from material possessions, power or relationships. He spoke to my heart, and I was thrilled to learn that he was holding meetings in the area. I went to the next one and, as I listened to him speak, my heart opened up even more; I felt as if I had come home.

My life, however, was *not* magically transformed. I still couldn't find work, and now I was up to my eyeballs in credit card debt. Bankruptcy followed, and I sold all my belongings and downsized, moving in with a roommate. This was the start of a second and even more terrifying dark night of the soul. The sense of failure I experienced because I was unable to pay my bills, and the terror that I felt because I thought I would be homeless, felt like death at the time. Actually, dying seemed as if it would have been a relief!

But as I went through these trials, I began regularly attending meetings to learn more from this teacher, who was proving to be an important support and guide for me. I heard him say that the gate to freedom is guarded by death and terror. I was willing to meet them if it meant gaining my freedom.

And I did! The more willing I became to follow my heart instead of my beliefs, the happier I became. Over and over, I asked myself, *What do you really want?* The more honest I was, the easier it got to let go of all the externals that had made up my picture of success and a happy life.

Now, three years later, I can say that I am truly happy for the first time in my life. I have downsized my life enough that I no longer have to work at a job I hate just to pay the bills. At the same time, I've begun choosing work that brings me joy, putting my happiness ahead of making money.

For example, I always wanted to be a teacher, but instead I chose to go into the business world because I didn't want to be poor. As soon as I decided to try supporting myself by tutoring high school and college students in math, I discovered that tutoring is surprisingly lucrative in my area. Who knew that you could actually get paid well doing something easy that you love? I have helped students go from failing a class to getting A's, and I have seen their self-esteem improve as a result. I was never very connected with young people, but now I have six or seven students whom I am very fond of. They often share their aspirations with me, and I get to pass on to them some of the wisdom I am gaining.

I have also always loved writing, but it comes so naturally to me that I never even considered that I might be paid for it. Working part-time for the foundation dedicated to world peace established by my teacher, I started out using some of my MBA skills to help with financial budgeting. Then I began editing his books and articles—sheer bliss!—and working in a sweet office, with true friends, and going to the beach on my lunch break.

This work led to other writing jobs, and now I am able to support myself as a freelance editor, sitting on my sunny porch reading manuscripts and making corrections. And I get to choose the jobs and authors I work with. Work is no longer a painful way to make money, but a way to express my love through the talents that I have been given.

At a gathering a few weeks ago, friends were talking about what they would do if they won the lottery. Most of them said they would quit their jobs and either rest or travel around the world. I realized that I wouldn't change a thing. I would continue working for the foundation, editing books and tutoring my students. I'd just do it for free!

I used to think that freedom could be achieved if you had enough money. I now know that freedom is achieved when you no longer desire things that you don't have, and when you don't let fear motivate your choices. The heart is trustworthy, and only choices made from love can lead to joy.

*"I used to think that freedom could
be achieved if you had enough money.
I now know that freedom is achieved
when you no longer desire things that
you don't have."*

—Despina Gurlides

15 · Self-Acceptance

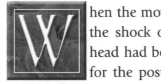

When the movie *Pretty Woman* came out, I remember the shock of hearing that Julia Roberts' gorgeous head had been placed atop another woman's body for the posters advertising the movie. Even Julia's body wasn't deemed "perfect" enough.

For many women, identity is a lifelong struggle focused around the desire to be somebody other than who we are. Nowhere is this more obvious than in our efforts to achieve a certain standard of physical beauty handed to us by advertising and the media. We long to be impossibly thin (most models are thinner than 95 percent of the population), and we spend $1 million an hour on skin-care products and cosmetics in this country!

Let's face it, the standards of perfection we're given defy attainment.

I have personally struggled with this issue my whole life. As I entered my teen years, I was stricken with a terrible case of acne

that lasted for many years, well into adulthood. I felt hideous—
and terrified that not being attractive made me unworthy of love,
or anything else, for that matter. My fears were constantly vali-
dated. I remember the day I came home from school and found a
pale blue strapless organza prom dress covered in ruffles, which
my mother had bought for me to wear to my junior high prom. I
never got to wear it, though, because I wasn't asked to go (girls
didn't ask boys in those days). In high school, I didn't date either.
I was friends with the popular girls—all cheerleaders with football
player boyfriends—but not pretty enough to really be one of
them. I longed to fit in, to be like them.

I still have scars from that period, literally and figuratively. For
forty-two years I wore makeup every day of my life—foundation,
mascara, lipstick, the works—even on days when I wasn't planning to leave the house or see anyone. Otherwise, I couldn't stand
to see myself, even in passing, in a mirror. I couldn't bear my ugli-
ness, and I wanted to hide it. It didn't matter that others didn't
even notice my skin most of the time.

Then one day, while working on this book, I just stopped. I
looked at myself in the mirror, noticed that I wasn't wearing any
makeup, and just could not be concerned about it. I no longer
identified "who I was" with "what I looked like." It seemed that,
along with my growing authenticity, self-acceptance had suddenly
become a natural experience. I had become passionate about my
vision as it related to this book and the simultaneous emergence
of my own "soul" discoveries. I see now that when we are in touch
with our own soul-knowing, not only can we accept ourselves, but
also find the deepest love imaginable within ourselves. *Not* accepting ourselves then becomes impossible.

I was struck by something I read about Bette Midler, who said
she had always been bothered by the feeling that she didn't belong
as a kid: "If only I'd known that one day my differentness would
be an asset, then my early life would have been much easier." In

my own case, my "differentness" also became an asset, because overcoming my own self-doubts forced me to go deeper than my body to find my value.

When I heard this next story about Wanda Roth, I was immediately captivated by how different she was. Not many of us can boast a lioness as a best friend! But Wanda, too, struggled as a child because of her differentness, and ultimately it was her friend, the lioness, who showed her she could be who she was and still be happy.

I think the quote from Masha Mikulinsky in my book *Diamonds, Pearls & Stones* says it all: "The person you are trying to be is probably not nearly as interesting as the person you are."

WANDA ROTH'S STORY
Lying Down with the Lioness

I n my long experience with animals, both domestic and exotic, I recall only one occasion when, in a single moment, an animal "remembered" who and what she was—what nature had hardwired her to be. When Peaches, the African lioness I raised, experienced just such a moment, I was watching. Witnessing that miraculous transformation changed me as well.

My story begins with my own childhood. I was raised in New York City, in the Bronx. From a very early age, I could sense whether people were telling the truth, and I could feel a dissonance if the way they were acting didn't match how they truly felt inside. With a child's innocence and forthrightness, I might, for example, ask my uncle, "Why are you angry?" Or say to my aunt, "What are you afraid of?" And it was common for me to say to adults, "Why aren't you telling the truth?"

I could always tell when people were sad. "You're so sad," I'd say, and they'd either start crying or yelling at me. It made people scared and uneasy to feel so exposed. I had so much compassion that I made people feel vulnerable. They called me disrespectful and would say things like, "How dare you talk to me like that? You don't know what you're talking about. You're only a child!" Their harsh responses shocked and confused me.

Although my parents loved me, their only child, they didn't understand me either. Family friends and relatives called me a brat; they'd complain to my mother and ask how she could let me talk to them like that. As time passed, they made it clear that they wanted me to stay away from them. I felt so alone.

And so I began to withdraw into my own world. Since I'd been born with a deep sense of connection with all animals—my first word was "horse"—I turned to them for companionship, feeling they were more my family than humans. From the age of four, I brought home anything I could get my hands on—fur, feathers, scales, it didn't matter, I loved them all. I had no fear of any animal. I went into our basement and caught mice and rats. My mother screamed when I brought them into the house. Next, I brought in a garter snake from the field near our house. Again, my poor mother was horrified. I had a baby chick that would hide his head between my arm and my body. But when he turned out to be a rooster, he had to go. I begged my mother not to get rid of him, as we were friends, but she didn't listen; she just wanted something that would lay eggs.

I fed and played with every stray cat that came into our yard, and finally my mother relented and let me have a puppy. I was thrilled. It was the first time I looked into eyes that were unafraid and true. But when we moved to a new house, I had to find another home for my dog. This parade of pets that didn't work out for one reason or another added to the pain and loneliness I felt for so much of my childhood.

High school was even worse. It was the fifties and I lived in a rough urban neighborhood. I never dated and continued to keep to myself. I didn't like what kids did to other kids. There were gangs in my school, and every day I felt as if I were in a war zone.

One day when I was about sixteen, I saw a girl my age wearing riding clothes: jodhpurs and boots. I found out where she took riding lessons and persuaded my mother to let me take the bus to the stable. It was an hour-and-a-half bus ride each way, but it was worth every minute. I was in heaven. Although I had no money, I arranged with the owner of the stable to walk and brush the horses in exchange for riding time. For the next two years, I lived for my Saturdays, when I could ride the bus and be with the horses. I remember running into the kitchen every Saturday night and putting my hands up to my mother's nose. "Smell this beautiful smell," I'd say. And she would smile to see me so happy.

When I graduated from high school, I found a job on Wall Street. I was completely alienated by the materialism and dishonesty. Almost breaking from the loneliness, I decided to follow a dream I had had all my life to travel to Africa. For a whole month in 1968, I visited the game preserves of East Africa and took a photographic safari, immersing myself in the world of African wildlife.

Once back in the United States, I used my Wall Street connections to get a job with a company in California that dealt with exotic animals. I was happy to be working with animals, and even made a few friends who appreciated animals as much as I did. The job was like a deep breath in my life; I could connect so easily with the zebras and the baby elephants, and revel in their simple love, unclouded by ego.

But my happiness was short-lived when the company unexpectedly went bankrupt. I was devastated. My job and the contact with all the animals I loved were gone. Jobs working with these kinds of animals were rare. I couldn't bear the thought of living and working with people who, it seemed to me, did not live in integrity, rarely took responsibility for themselves, and didn't want to explore or discover their deeper feelings. It was so much easier to be with animals!

I needed a retreat. I hid away on a large ranch by myself for six months, even cutting off the telephone. Every night I walked with Stormy, a wild appaloosa gelding with striking markings, and King, a wise and gentle German shepherd. The three of us would fall asleep under the stars out in the hills. King was always lying by my side, watching over and protecting me. In the morning, I'd wake to see Stormy standing right above me, a mischievous glint in his eyes, as he dropped wet grass from his mouth onto my face.

During that period, I spent a lot of time examining why I wasn't able to function in the world like everyone else. Clearly, I saw things others didn't and cared deeply about things others seemed to dismiss. I was the proverbial square peg in a world of round holes. I had no one to talk to about it and lived a very lonely life. I spent many nights in the stall with Stormy, my arms around his neck. Using his head to pull me in close to him, he would nicker softly as I cried.

I soon found work at a compound that was used for the "affection" training of exotic animals for studio work, movies and commercials. I felt alive and free working once again with the animals I loved so deeply. It was at this compound that three African lion cubs were born, a female and her two brothers.

My ranch home was an eight-by-fifty-foot mobile home tucked under large trees, where I could watch Stormy run to his heart's content. I begged my employers to let me take the little female cub home with me. She needed to be socialized, so they agreed.

I named her Peaches. From the beginning, she was magical, different from any lion I had ever been around. Her eyes were soft and open, and her walk was loping and puppylike. She had a look of total innocence, unlike her brothers or the other "large cats" I had known. Most of them, even at an early age, have a predatory look in their eyes and a low-slung, stalking gait. Peaches didn't seem to know that she was a lioness. She shared her food with the dog and played around with the horse.

I felt a profound connection with her soul and felt that we communicated deeply with each other. Every day, we played together and napped side by side in the fields; we ate together and slept in the same bed. There were even times when she would start sucking on my thumb in her sleep. Her most comfortable resting position was lying on top of me. As she started to fall asleep, this eighty-pound lion cub would start leaning to one side and then both of us would tumble out of bed, wide awake. Living with Peaches brought back my playfulness and my spirit.

As Peaches grew, she and Stormy loved playing together too. The love and trust between them was very apparent. They would run in the fields kicking and swatting at each other. Stormy would play-kick at Peaches, skillfully missing by only an inch at times. Peaches, older and heavier by then, about 275 pounds, had a powerful swing and she would run, jump and swipe at Stormy's legs, also purposely missing by just an inch.

Watching these two day after day, I began to reflect on my own life. Although Peaches and Stormy were so different from each other, they seemed to have found a deeper bond that made their differences irrelevant. And although their playing style was rough, they never once hurt each other. I asked myself: *Is there a way that I can be myself and not scare others away? Or hurt them?* I knew the answer lay in what I was seeing but wasn't sure how to make it happen in my own life.

Over two years passed. One day I was sitting under a tree watching Stormy and Peaches play. Although Peaches was close to full-grown, at about 375 pounds she still acted like a playful cub. Suddenly, I saw Peaches stop and stand totally still. She was completely motionless and silent. I sat up straight, alert to the scene before me. This was not her usual manner. I noticed that she was standing with all of her paws rooted firmly in the grass. I could tell that she was grounding herself—feeling the earth's energy. The experience of it was palpable. I felt the power of it inside my own body.

At that moment, it was as if Peaches awoke to who she was: an African lioness. Immediately her whole bearing changed, became regal. She turned towards me in a majestic way, head held high over her shoulder and looked directly into my eyes. *I see you, too,* she seemed to say, *I see who you are.*

In that instant, it felt as if a lightning bolt went through my body, and I felt something shift inside me. *It was time.* I was finally ready to be open to life and to be bold—to be that innocent and truthful child now grown into a woman. I remembered how I had once been: never doubting what I saw or felt—accepting the truth as I knew it. Now I was ready to live that way. Peaches had taken me with her in her moment of transformation. Like her, I saw I could be who I was and be an adult in the world.

On that day, I lost the fear that had directed my life, and I stopped isolating myself from other people. Over the next few weeks and months, I became a realtor, went dancing and began successfully communicating with people—maintaining my integrity without worrying about their reactions. My new acceptance of myself enabled me to accept others, and I had even greater understanding and compassion for what others were experiencing—without feeling I had to confront them or bring anything to their attention. Soon after that, I began a relationship that eventually led to marriage.

More than twenty years have gone by since Peaches and I shared our wonderful epiphany. Today I live every day in the way I see fit. My intuition is clear and I feel freer than ever before. I know that I can never hide myself again.

Although my life at present doesn't allow me a permanent

animal companion, wherever I go, when I encounter an animal, I still experience the communication and communion that kept my heart alive for so many years—the bond that eventually allowed me to love and accept myself just as I am.

"Today I live every day in the way I see fit. I know that I can never hide myself again."

—Wanda Roth

Wanda Roth and Peaches

16 · Accountability

efore a recent trip to Toronto, I called AT&T to see if my wireless plan included making calls from Canada. I had to go through the normal punching in of endless numbers, but when I finally got a real person on the other end, I was taken aback by what she said. After thanking me for my patience (how did she know?), she said, "My name is Angie. I care about your issue and will take ownership to resolve it today."

Now, I am usually put off by people who answer the phone with more than three words. But ownership? I couldn't remember the last time I had found someone willing to be accountable for what they were *supposed* to be doing. I found it refreshing and asked her about it after we had taken care of my business. It was a policy that had been instituted by the local manager of the Bothell, Washington, call center; customer response to it had been so favorable that Angie told me she wouldn't be surprised if it caught on within the company nationally.

What made my exchange with Angie noteworthy is that the need to blame others and avoid taking personal responsibility of any kind has become pervasive in our culture. In the world of business it can be annoying, time-consuming and downright scary at times. For example, if we call a large company to discuss a problem or request a change of service, we're likely to have to listen to endless automated menus, sometimes never hearing an option that covers our need and often being unable to reach a live person. Or we get passed from one person to another, often hanging up in frustration without having resolved anything.

In other areas of life, we point fingers at people in authority, wanting to hold them responsible for our personal and collective woes and problems. We deflect ownership of our own issues by finding fault with others or pointing out their shortcomings. We feel jealous of those who have more than we do, even when it's clear they've earned what they have. And we take a position *in opposition* to another, not wanting to acknowledge the possibility that another's belief may be true—and right—for him or her, even if it's not for us.

Bill Clinton spoke at Book Expo of America when his book, *My Life*, was about to be released. What impressed me most was his suggestion that, when you don't agree with someone, instead of blaming or attacking, you simply say, "I think you're wrong, and here's why." He modeled this during his speech (referring to a particular person or the government), always speaking the words evenly, with thoughtfulness and intelligence. He helped me to see the connection between accountability and authority: when we take ownership of our thoughts, beliefs and ideals, we assume an authority that cannot possibly be present otherwise.

Alexis Quinlan, author of the next story, was a perfect example of the desire to blame others and make them responsible for her unhappiness. She wanted to be a writer, but she didn't want to put in the time to learn how to write well. She perceived that all the ills of her life were somebody else's fault, yet she still looked to others to "fix" her. Her story is a humorous yet poignant account of her life when "attitude" ruled, and how life unfolded when she started to become accountable for herself.

ALEXIS QUINLAN'S STORY
Moon in Capricorn

I n 1986, three years after graduating from an Ivy League university, the best I could manage was a couple of part-time jobs and a shared apartment in Manhattan's East Village. I had wanted full-time work, but I'd been let go from a two-month tryout in a public relations firm and fired from a real job in advertising for insubordination—an attitude I did not recognize in myself. I worked a lot of temp jobs before taking a job in marketing that I felt was beneath me—a feeling I didn't connect to the insubordination charge—and then promptly quit it when offered a more glam job at an art magazine. Actually, the job itself wasn't glam—it was in sales—but I was still disappointed when, the day after I began, the owner decided to cut costs and make my position part-time. I stayed on, picking up another part-time job at a downtown wine shop. I considered myself an oenophile back then, though I rarely paid five bucks for a bottle of red. The way I saw it, I was in the wine trade and the art business.

As such a resume hints, I had other problems—dilemmas unrelated to work. To begin with, I didn't get along with my boyfriend with whom I'd lived off and on since college, and I couldn't stand my mother (generally a decent yardstick for a woman's peace of mind). Too, I couldn't control my temper (just ask the boyfriend) or stop eating or stop drinking or even bear my reflection in the mirror each morning.

Then there was the matter of my attitude. (By the bye, why was the world run by a bunch of idiots?) Rather than letting on how delighted I was to be at the magazine, I scorned everyone from receptionist to publisher. They were tacky, loud (or suspiciously quiet), had horrible accents, dressed badly. It's no fun keeping such venom to oneself, so I was lucky to find an ally in misanthropy. Anthony stole toilet paper from the supply closet out of plain spite and was wildly handsome. So what if everyone said he was gay? My crush was on. Though he was something of an office star—he'd begun as a mail clerk and was shooting through editorial—Anthony maligned everyone, with blistering asides for the UPS guy and the office décor. A sharper gal might've figured out his sexual preference by this alone.

And Anthony was the only man who could tease me. I often arrived for work—if staring at a list of numbers I was too scared to dial was indeed work—wearing the tee I'd slept in and a black knit skirt I must have thought was flattering, since I wore it constantly. When Anthony spotted me, he'd cry, "Dress for the job you want!" We helped each other get through many a slow afternoon, mocking what was actually a great group of bright young New Yorkers.

There was one we loathed above all the rest: "Gina." The publisher's wife, she didn't work for the magazine but shared our office space. Anthony dubbed her the Freeloader, but that wasn't what had us going. It was her laugh. Or laughs, for there were long belly laughs, pretty giggles and wild yahoos all bragging for her: nothing came her way that did not bring more joy. Her howls of delight carried through the whole loft, but her office was just behind my cubicle, so I heard every gurgle and guffaw.

Stopping by my desk for a cigarette, Anthony would ask in mock despair, "Can't that hyena be stopped?"

I'd hiss, "It's like an insane asylum around here."

It didn't stop. Why would it? The woman was married to the most powerful guy in the loft and could do whatever she wanted. She wanted to laugh. She had a couple of beautiful kids when I arrived, had a couple more while I was there, and she was a writer. In fact, she was so prolific that she couldn't have laughed as much as I recall. In my three years there she published two books, including a charming one for children, and began a biography of a nun. Gina was a Catholic convert, which sort of tortured this lapsed-Catholic-adamant-atheist. Occasionally, when Anthony and I huddled to bemoan an especially long fit of hilarity, I'd bring it up. How could a woman who'd been to college believe such hogwash? Hadn't she heard about Darwin? For Anthony it was beneath discussion. "That's the least of her problems."

In the end, as in the beginning, the laughter was her chief offense. Anthony stopped by my cubicle almost daily, stirring Sweet'n Low into his coffee and muttering about how only bird-brains are so damned cheerful all the time. I'd shake my head rue-fully at the terrible weight of it. And I had to sit so near! A crazy lady! He'd extend his sympathies and return to his cubicle, wafting cigarette smoke as he went.

As for my actual job? My sales were as bad as my attitude. I didn't believe in advertising, didn't know anything about art, and I hated asking people to buy things. Once in a while I'd be given a special project and would make a tidy sum, then return to my standard doldrums. Once I overheard the publisher scolding the sales director for not motivating me. I felt sorry for my boss, since it wasn't her fault. As a mystery to myself, I was unsolvable by mere managers.

In lieu of working, I kept watching Gina. Secretly I didn't believe the rap Anthony and I had. I knew what I was hearing: Gina was happy. I knew the reason it bothered me: I wasn't. And she was no birdbrain, but a writer.

Writing was what I wanted—it was all I wanted—but I couldn't have it. I had a slew of reasons for this. For one, I wasn't a great genius. And I was lazy, for I wasn't writing much, unless you counted the stack of wire-bound notebooks beneath my bed. Though no longer an adolescent, I'd filled these poor little journals with dozens, no, hundreds of bad poems on (what else?) despair. Writing was so hard, I think I'd have preferred to have already written than to actually sit down and do the job. But my main hindrance to writing was more mysterious, almost magical, and even now it's hard to explain. It was as if I didn't have the special permission a "real" writer had. I can't say who or what I thought was dispensing this permission. Despite claiming to be an atheist, I had faith that I was cursed, that I could never have what I wanted.

Looking back, I was more miserable than even I knew.

And one day something happened. It was another New York–office afternoon, humming with fluorescent lights and bulky PCs and smelly copy machines and ringing phones. Kitchen chat in the background. A name called from the lobby. And Gina laughing hard, then trailing off in chuckles. I'd been waiting for this moment, though not quite consciously. I rose from my desk and walked toward her office. She'd just gotten off the phone—I knew because of the quiet—and was rubbing her hands together and turning toward her Selectric when she glimpsed me hovering at the door and stopped.

Gina was a natural beauty, with pretty, girlish features, shiny black hair and a great smile. Her only makeup was lip gloss. I'd guess she was about ten years older than me—thirty-five or so. I knew her Japanese mother and grandparents had been put in WWII internment camps, but the Asian was hard to spot aside from her hair. A little dazzled, and certainly surprised to be there at all, I finally squeaked out, "Hi."

She responded, friendly as ever. Still squeaking, I asked, "How's it going?"

"Good," she said with enthusiasm. She added something else I don't recall, probably about her work. She was always wide open about it, making great tales of her progress on the chapters. I remember when she was nine months pregnant and at work on the nun book, she joked about writing the chapter on lust. She had no secrets, it seemed then. No shame, I think now.

Then, the reason I'd come, whether or not I knew it: "It seems so cool," I said, "how you get to write your books all day, do stuff you're really interested in."

I don't know what I was expecting here. Maybe I imagined that she would sit me down and whisper how to get the special permission. Perhaps teach me to write a book. Could I have hoped she would befriend me and make me laugh, too? That she would find me a husband and an editor and an office and a world that comforted-cradled me?

"Well," she said, pausing to flash a sympathetic smile that seemed to say she knew what I wanted and she could help. I hadn't even known I was asking for help, but in that moment I knew it and believed that she would tell me the truth. Outside, the office went on: Her husband was bellowing on the phone, the sales manager was calling the top sales rep into her office, the photo editor was complaining to the office manager. Gina's phone lit up—my eyes darted to it, then to her, but she shook her head slightly as if to say my question was important and she would concentrate only on it. "Well," she said, "God gave me a few talents, and I'm just happy I can use them."

God! At first I was puzzled. Was she cuckoo after all? *Happy I can use them!* What the hell did that mean? Then I knew: She didn't want to help me at all. She wanted to hurt me. I was angry; I was embarrassed; I was resentful. In short, I was myself. I wonder how I got out of the office.

Life went on, but I didn't approve of it. I craved change, wanted it so badly that I'd catch myself muttering, "Change, change,

change change change." I went to therapists and learned to blame everything on my father's early death, my mother's ensuing depression. When that didn't help, I went to psychics, acupuncturists and astrologers to lift the curse. I even learned astrology. Yet I never sought out help with my writing, and I somehow remained unable to change myself. Meanwhile, change was happening all around, some of it to me. The college boyfriend moved across the country, and it dawned on me that I'd loved him, that I'd behaved badly (a lot), and he was gone for good. The wine store I worked for closed. Anthony left the magazine to dance full time. (That's when I admitted he might be gay.)

Maybe it's a good thing I didn't change, or understand the changes around me. Staying in one place for so long, I began to write something besides the sad poems. Little bits at first. Less sad poems. Essays on life in the East Village. Tentative stories full of high-flying vocabulary and low-blow sentimentality that I sent straight to *The New Yorker*. Which promptly rejected them. I finally enrolled in a writing class, spending Monday nights watching and listening to the other writers and sharing my stories. It took a while to hear anything but cruel criticism from them, but, amazingly, I stuck it out. I boldly sent a few pieces to several women's magazines. They were rejected, but a young editor named Lisa called and said she wanted to learn more about me and promised she'd be in touch.

On my twenty-sixth birthday, I left the magazine to become a writer. I patched together a bunch of freelance jobs, even writing two pieces for Lisa. Then at twenty-nine I finally admitted that I needed help. I enrolled in grad school in Houston and left New York.

I had some direction at last, but life remained difficult, and I still figured I was cursed. Overall, thanks to my Ivy League expectations, I considered myself a bitter disappointment. One day, on the way to a fiction workshop, I rifled through a stack of English

Department giveaway books. I was scanning an Edna O'Brien novel when a top-selling spiritual self-help book caught my eye. I sneered at it—I was engaged in high art, after all—but grabbed it as a joke. I told my classmates we should all write self-help-God-talk if we wanted to make rent. I got a few laughs and tucked the book away. That night I tossed it onto my bedside table and forgot about it.

Six months later, in the middle of a sleepless night, I opened the book. It was just the sort of New Age drivel I'd expected. It talked about love. Love was stronger than might. Love was redemptive. The love of a higher power was the most redemptive of all. Just what I'd expected, but different.

I finished it that night, then read it again. And again.

It was a conversion, but it was hardly perfect. I told no one about it. I was a bit less arrogant, but I didn't want people knowing I'd gotten so desperate that I'd turned to God. Still, that Easter Sunday morning I woke early and, wholly unplanned, drove to one of the churches the book had mentioned, a Unity Church of Christianity. The minister said we were here not to suffer but to have full, happy lives. It sounded almost obscene. I liked it.

I drove out to spy on the church's Wednesday "Empowerment Nights." Designed to broaden and enrich your life, they opened with a lecture—part sermon, part pep rally—about harnessing the power of the spirit with prayer. After the minister spoke, members of the audience raised their hands to tell what had happened the previous week. Jobs obtained, love found, lost bikes returned, couples reunited. Much laughing, clapping and smiling—more pep rally. Finally, the congregation split up into groups of five or six, in which members shared their problems and their goals and then promised to pray for each other for six weeks, meeting on Wednesdays to report results.

There was only one hitch. I could share my problems: the increasingly nutty romance I was in, the drinking and drugging, the self-loathing. But my hopes? I didn't want six people to know what I secretly longed for. I was in grad school for writing, but it wasn't quite okay to want it. It still wasn't okay to be me.

After much hesitation, I told one of those small groups about my writing dreams. Actually, at this point I wanted to be paid for the fiction I wrote. They thought nothing of it, only jotted it in their journals and made sure I wrote down their goals too so I could pray in turn for them. And I did. I prayed with them in the group and prayed for them all week. I returned the next Wednesday, though the first week brought no change, because I wondered what had happened to them. A couple of members of my prayer team had experienced small shifts, which was hopeful. We shared petitions—mine stayed the same—prayed once, and left to pray for one another for another week.

A few days later I was home poring over a short story when the phone rang. Before I could manage hello, I heard, "Teresa! Teresa! I need that copy!"

What? The voice sounded like my old editor at the women's magazine. "Lisa?"

"I need it yesterday, Teresa."

It took awhile to tell her who I was, to ask what was going on.

"Alexis?" She paused. "I thought I was calling Copy."

"You thought you were dialing four numbers but dialed ten— *my* ten?"

We laughed and she explained that she was editing an old story of mine that was finally running, that my number was right there on the article. "Maybe that's why I dialed you," she concluded, though she didn't sound convinced.

We spoke briefly, inquiring after each other's love life and talking about the article, a tale of an eighties East Village party girl, which I hadn't quite been, though I knew the ropes. (In other words, it was fiction.) I asked about the last article I'd begun for her. A "spec" assignment, I'd written half and sent it in for her okay. When she never called me back, I figured she didn't like it and dropped it.

"Oh, yeah," she said. "Why didn't you ever send that to me?"

You can probably guess the rest. I faxed the half-done article and Lisa insisted I write an ending. Then she loved the finished piece, as did her boss. I reported this to the group, who were happy if not terribly surprised—they'd been hanging out at Empowerment Nights longer than I. To top it off, Lisa told me I was their new favorite writer and asked what the magazine could do for me. Huh?

Actually, I had an idea. I would be leaving grad school in a few months and needed steady money as a base for the writer's life. I needed a column. There weren't many options, for the magazine's advice column was penned by a longtime employee, as were its book and movie review columns. I knew I couldn't manage a finance column. But there was one thing. Way back I'd learned astrology. I wanted the astrology column.

So, under the pseudonym of Allegra Quince, I wrote the column for three years and worked for the publisher for another three. I was briefly devastated not to find a top New York publisher for my stories, but I liked astrology. I still think there is something to it; my story, for example, is pure Moon in Capricorn: an ambitious gal doing everything the hard way. I moved to L.A., where I drew out the horoscopes each month (I enjoyed the geometry) and concentrated on "empowering" the readers. In truth, my columns were full of all I'd learned at the church in Houston. I began writing for other magazines and then got a teaching job at a great college nearby. Teaching was a skill I'd learned in grad school and I loved it. As the years passed, my peace of mind increased with my gratitude. And, though I'd imagined none of this, my prayers and the prayers of those five kind souls in Houston were still being answered.

I still freelance and teach and recently began to publish poetry, my first love, which—of course—I had never been good enough for. I came to love my Mother not long before she died, and I even learned to love the men I love. At forty-two, I'm engaged to be married. Though I often fear it won't happen, I try to enjoy being engaged today. I sometimes attend Catholic mass, where I hear enormous praise and love, though I'm sure it wasn't there when I was young.

Often, in my new, largely grateful, mostly peaceful life, I remember Gina. Gina, to whom God had given a few talents. Gina, who liked what she had and who worked with whatever came along. How insulted I'd been by her words, how confused by her happiness. And how grateful I was that I could hear her now. For I finally knew that I, too, had been given a few talents by God—whatever that means, wherever She is—and I'm happy I can use them.

"As the years passed, my peace of mind increased with my gratitude. I finally knew that I, too, had been given a few talents by God."

—Alexis Quinlan

17 · Self-Expression

y late father used to tell me that my career as a professional speaker began when I was about seven years old. I'd gather all the children in the neighborhood and make them sit in rows in our driveway so that I could speak to them!

Later, in the eighth grade, I heard that the local 4-H Club had a speaking contest along with its annual livestock-grading and sewing competitions. You had to prepare and deliver a four-minute speech on the 4-H pledge. I thought, *How fun! How easy!* So I joined—and won the contest the first time I entered. The following year I won the state competition on the first try. It seemed that speaking in front of groups of people came as naturally to me as breathing.

I'm sorry to say that I did not realize at the time that I was living my passion. As Deva Premal, the author of the next story, says about recognizing our gifts, ". . . it's usually right in front of our eyes—that's why we miss it!" Premal also points out that society teaches us to appreciate only the things we have achieved through effort and hard work, so it can be easy to ignore the value of what comes naturally to us. So easy, in fact, that for most people, child-hood passions never get the chance to become part of their adult-hood reality.

In my case, for example, although I majored in journalism with a minor in speech and broadcasting, I very quickly got off track. I got so far away from what I do naturally that I actually spent ten years in the field of accounting. Oh, yes, there were aspects of it that I loved: an accounting system demands accountability, order-liness and balance, all of which I enjoy. But one day I woke up and thought, *What am I doing?* I wasn't having fun.

I began to reflect on the things I had loved doing when I was younger. I remembered the contests. I remembered being the only student who took speech *as an elective* every semester for four years in high school. One step at a time, I made my way back into the world of communication, eventually forming my own speaking company. I've been speaking happily ever since.

But I'm one of the lucky ones. Eighty percent of Americans do not like what they do for a living. If you are one of them, you are probably spending almost a third of your life doing something that does not bring you joy or satisfaction. So many of us don't seem to realize that we are each born with our own unique nature, drawn naturally to express ourselves in certain ways. We all have something to express in the world that literally cannot be repli-cated by another person. As Vicky Edmonds says in this book, your "very presence is a gift waiting to be opened."

Deva Premal's presence is, indeed, a present! I love to fill my home and car with the exquisite music of Premal and her partner, Miten. To hear them in concert, as I have in New York and San Francisco, is to experience absolute stillness through sound.

This is the story of how Premal discovered her own "voice." In it, Premal affirms what dancer and choreographer Martha Graham so beautifully said, "There is a vitality, a life force, an energy that is translated through you; and because there is only one of you in all of time, this expression is unique."

DEVA PREMAL'S STORY
Finding My Voice

I grew up with music. My mother taught viola da gamba and piano, and our home in Germany was often filled with the sound of a young student's best efforts. My mother was at home with classical music. Through her influence I learned to play classical violin and piano, but it never really nourished me. Playing those instruments felt a little stiff and awkward to me, and having to stick to the musical score was like walking with crutches.

My father was and is the free spirit in the family. He's an artist by profession and a passionate drummer in his spare time. He even makes the drums he plays. He's been on a spiritual path since he was young, studying yoga, reading spiritual scriptures and books, and meditating every morning between 3:00 A.M. and 5:00 A.M. He taught himself Sanskrit and loved to chant mantras when I was a child. Mantras are verses containing sounds that have deep effects on human consciousness. He believed they could help us open our hearts and have greater awareness.

Most precious to my father was the Gayatri mantra, which he sang to me in my mother's womb and taught me at a young age. The oldest and most powerful of mantras, it purifies the person chanting it as well as the listener. Translated, it means "May all beings on earth reach enlightenment," but as with all mantras, the meaning of the Sanskrit words isn't as important as the effect of their vibrations on the body's energy centers. Every night, we sang the Gayatri mantra and other mantras, as well as verses from the great Indian scripture *The Bhagavad Gita*. Although I did enjoy singing them, I had no real connection to them of my own.

Looking back, it was a childhood of rare opportunities, but in those years all I wanted was to be "normal." My parents were considerably older than my friends' parents; when I was born my mother was thirty-eight and my father forty-nine. We were vegetarians, didn't own a TV, and instead of comfy couches, we sat on wooden meditation chairs my father had made. They were beautiful, but all I wanted was to be able to bring friends home to a house with leather couches, a TV and parents like everyone else's.

Basically, I felt I didn't fit into either world—my parents' or the so-called normal world—and I didn't know what, if anything, I had to offer. My mother had her gifts and abilities, and my father had his. But although my mother said I had talent and a good ear, practicing every day was a chore; I didn't find much joy in it. I loved music, but I didn't expect to make it my life. I just had to trust that I would find my calling eventually.

Then everything changed. My mother and I found a spiritual teacher we loved, and when I finished high school my parents gave me their blessing to go and live in the community he had created in India. As soon as I arrived, I felt at home in the world, perhaps for the first time. I was still living a life that was out of the ordinary, but now it was through my own choice. I quickly discovered the bliss of participating in the sacred music that was central to the nightly meetings in our community. I especially loved singing the devotional songs that graced our meditations. Just to sing among a group of people in a meditative way gave me great joy.

Eventually I developed a very special friendship with an Englishman named Miten, who was in the group of musicians that led our nightly singing. Although I was twenty years old and he was forty-two, our hearts immediately connected. I wanted to sing with the group, but when I asked Miten to listen to my voice, he said it wasn't his style, too classical. I was disappointed, but as I had no ambition to be a singer, there was no problem. I just kept singing with the larger group and let myself melt more and more into the music.

A few months passed, and one day Miten heard me sing again. This time he smiled and nodded. From that day on he began including me in the meditations, where I sang harmony with him and played keyboards.

My education in music theory and my trained ear served me well. I discovered that I was a natural harmony singer, inventing my own lines and surprising myself and even my mentor. From Miten, I learned about improvising. It freed me and allowed me to be purely in the moment, without any thought of what would come next. For the first time in my life I had no musical score to follow, no rigid classical rules to obey. I could be as adventurous as I dared. I began to relish the freedom of expression and rejoiced in my free-floating voice.

In our nightly meditations, we were not performing so much as leading the singing. There were two thousand people in the hall every night, and we were all facing in the same direction, with the musicians in the rear. I could make mistakes and not be embarrassed, which was perfect. I needed to develop the courage to be wrong in order to find my voice. My voice was changing, but not due to "practicing" or technical training; the growth all came from inside me. When something opened up in my heart or some other aspect of my awareness, my voice would change.

For a few years I was Miten's apprentice. We began to travel in Europe, playing concerts and offering voice workshops, using devotional music from different cultures to open the voice. I still played a supporting role, singing second voice, playing keyboards and co-leading the workshops. I was too shy to sing alone.

Whenever I tried, I sounded weak and insecure, no matter how much Miten encouraged me. But in my heart of hearts, I was waiting for the time when I would be able to contribute equally to our musical partnership.

As years passed, I began to think it would never happen. Then one day in England, I heard a woman's voice singing my favorite childhood song, the Gayatri mantra. I had drifted away from the mantras during my teenage years. As I listened to the simple, haunting melody, I felt tears come into my eyes. I softly began to sing along, remembering the words and the melody. From that day on, I started to sing it in our concerts with my voice in the lead. As soon as I began to sing, I felt as if I'd arrived home. I felt no trace of shyness or self-consciousness, and my voice simply sounded right.

At last I had found my song! I had found something that felt like "mine." We began featuring the Gayatri mantra in our concerts, and I watched as it touched people night after night. I began searching out more mantras, and one by one the other mantras came back into my life. People knew I loved them, so they'd come up to me and say, "Hey, I have a mantra for you," and they would sing it to me. At first I sang only the traditional melodies, but after some time, Miten and some of our musician friends began to create their own melodies, and I realized they carried the same power as the traditional melodies. So we had begun to create a new music, equal parts traditional and contemporary.

Now that I was finally singing lead, Miten suggested I make my own CD. By now he and I had been friends and life partners for many years. Our plan was to make an album for people who attended our workshops. We came back to Germany, and all the arrangements fell into place as if by magic. We recorded it in my mother's flat—the same one I was born in, where the Gayatri mantra had been sung to me all those years before. I sang all of my favorite mantras on the CD, which we called *The Essence*.

It was received with an enthusiasm beyond our wildest dreams. We were soon receiving floods of orders and had to continually replenish stock! It went to the top of the New Age charts in Europe and America, and in Germany still remains in the top 10 after five years. We later recorded other CDs, and again, they were received with love and appreciation—and became best-sellers in their own right throughout the world.

Miten and I love to give concerts and share the mantras. We both sing, and Miten plays guitar. Our concerts are like meditations. We encourage everyone to sing with us and journey deep inside. The nature of the mantras is to bring us into silence, and so we ask people not to clap after we sing. We sit with hundreds of people in pin-drop silence. Our feeling is, the deeper the silence, the stronger the appreciation. People feel nourished and then they take that feeling home. In silence, the music is still inside you, and you can carry it with you.

Sometimes, in the midst of the deep happiness I feel when I sing, an inner voice pipes up and says, "If I can do this so easily, it isn't worthwhile." I know it's the ego, always so ready to acknowledge only the difficult tasks as valuable. It's always ready to whisper in our ears: "It's nothing. Anyone can do that." I have to laugh when I realize that, even now, after I've received so much loving feedback from so many people, my ego can still try to devalue my gift. I'm learning to smile at this little monster and just keep singing.

I feel deeply blessed that spirituality, creativity, work and love all mean the same thing in my life. This is what happens when you find your own song—your own unique gift to the world. It comes down to doing what comes most naturally to you, as naturally as breathing, with no mind trips or "shoulds" about it. The animals and plants give us such a great example. Each one seems perfectly content with its own particular gift. I've never seen a bird striving to be more beautiful or trying to sing a song more challenging than the one it's been blessed with.

As human souls, we need the courage to find our song and the trust to own it and honor it. My whole life took flight when I discovered mine.

"I've never seen a bird striving to be more beautiful or trying to sing a song more challenging than the one it's been blessed with."

—Deval Premal

18 · Humility

 aster magician Doug Henning once lived down the street from me. In fact, I attended his wedding to a beautiful woman named Debbie. It was a delightful and magical affair filled with beauty, love—and white doves appearing right out of the folds of Debbie's very full wedding dress, as the magician laughingly wove together the wondrous and the sacred.

Doug always seemed to be filled with wonder, and he loved to evoke it in others through his magic. But he had almost forgotten why he became a magician when an amazing encounter reminded him. While on tour, he was invited to do a show for a group of Inuits (Eskimos). He told the story of what happened in the following interview with *MAGIC, The Magazine for Magicians:*

> We were on the edge of this little town in the wilderness, 400 miles from the North Pole, and about 60 below zero. I set up my show in a little building, and the Inuits came in to

watch. They sat on the floor in their parkas, and I did what I thought was some pretty good stuff. They just sat there, didn't smile, didn't say a word and, at the end, nobody applauded. But they were completely focused on me, like I was some sort of phenomenon. Only one of them spoke English, so I asked him, "Did you like the show?"

"Yes, we like show," he said.

Then I asked, "Did everybody like the magic?"

He said, "The magic?"

I explained that I was trying to entertain people.

He said, "Entertainment is good, but why are you doing magic? The whole world is magical." We sat down on the floor and he told me, "It's magic that snow falls; all those little crystals are completely different. That's magic."

I said, "But what about when I made the rabbit and doves appear?"

"Why do you do those things?" he said. "It's magic when the walrus appears each spring; he comes from nowhere. That's magic."

Now I was grasping, trying to explain magic to him. I thought of my Zombie, which I thought was my best thing. I said, "I made that beautiful silver ball float in the air; that's magic."

"But there's a ball of fire floating through the sky every day. It keeps us warm, gives us light; that's magic."

Then the Inuits started talking among themselves. The man came to me with a big smile on his face, and said, "Now we know why you are doing that. It's because your people have forgotten the magic. You're doing it to remind them of the magic. Well done!"

I cried right then. I said, "Thank you for teaching me about the magic. I didn't know."

That was really the first time I knew what wonder was. It

was the most memorable thing that has ever happened to me. I never forgot that, inside.

If you ever saw Doug perform, you saw his awe at the wonder of life. One of the greatest magicians in history, Doug performed *The Magic Show* on Broadway for four years, then turned it into an annual TV spectacular, *The World of Magic*, which attracted millions of viewers. Yet, he was humbled by his experience with the Inuits and affected by it for the rest of his life. In his case, humility was the result of a simple exchange with someone who perceived life in a different and deeper way than he previously had seen it.

But so often in our culture, it takes failure or tragedy to bring about humility. We hear of people being humbled by a life-threatening disease or event, the threat of financial ruin, or not winning something they expected to win. Humility does not seem to be invited or cultivated in our society, because it's perceived as weakness. If we're humble, we ask, how can we have enough power to win or be successful?

But true humility is not weakness; it is knowing that we are part of a bigger picture. It is often accompanied by feelings of gratitude and the awareness that success of any kind comes more from the grace of God than from anything we did ourselves. It is the feeling that we are flowing in the river of life.

People who know Eileen Danneman, the author of the next story, may laugh to see her name linked to humility. Eileen is an aggressive social and political activist who fights with tenacity for causes she believes in. But the experience of powerlessness that she experienced on a mountainside in the south of France brought her to her knees, literally and figuratively. Humbled by her circumstances and the revelations given to her while trapped, she has been forever marked by a sense of gratitude for life.

EILEEN DANNEMAN'S STORY
The Quest

As the bright red helicopter and the yellow-suited man suspended from it descended into the valley, they looked much like the brightly colored Lego toys my children played with when they were young. But this was no game; the man and the helicopter had come to rescue me from my small cave in the slick granite face of a mountain in the south of France.

I had been invited to join a tour in the south of France with a mystery school whose adventure it was to follow the path of the Holy Grail. This was the legendary cup that Christ was said to have drunk from at the Last Supper and that Joseph of Arimathea had used to catch his blood at the crucifixion. The story is that a group of Christ's followers carried the Holy Grail with them for safekeeping when they were exiled by the ruling class from Israel to France after the crucifixion. A thousand years later many knights of medieval Europe, including those of King Arthur's roundtable, made the search for this vessel their holy quest.

Whether this is the stuff of legend or literally true is disputed by scholars. But historical documents chart the path of the group that carried the grail to Europe, and I was glad to be able to walk in their ancient footsteps. I related to the medieval knights' quest for a deeper connection with the divine. I had been on my own quest to know God for many years. This trip seemed to be a tangible way to make more progress. I was hoping for deeper insights, even—why not?—a revelation.

We had already been to Israel and Turkey on earlier trips. Now, here in the south of France, we were following the route Mary

Magdalen and her entourage had taken as they journeyed through the country on a small raft. I had just arrived from New York without much sleep when we began our ascent of Mt. Baum, where it was said that Mary and her brother Lazarus, sister Martha and maid Sara had lived for many years.

As the group ascended the mountain, I soon separated from them, carrying nothing but a staff and a bottle of water. I was drawn to the east side of the mountain, knowing that Mary must have watched the sunrise there.

As I climbed, I came to many bends in the trail. Every time I reached what seemed like a dead end, I felt compelled to go beyond it one more time—just one more bend to see what was on the other side. There were no warnings against climbing in this area, and the terrain was well within my ability, so I wasn't concerned about going too far on my own. It was late in the afternoon when I finally reached a summit crowned by a pile of stones and a simple crucifix made out of wood. Many travelers had reached this point, but you could tell it had been only those who had their heart in the journey, for the marker was handmade and nothing official.

I was moved by this primitive outpost of faith and took a few moments to appreciate the profound stillness of the spot. Then a breeze picked up and my attention shifted from the sublime to the physical. I realized the light would fade soon and I should hurry back to the hotel where I was supposed to rendezvous with the group. I started back but soon became aware that there were no trail markings—at least none that made sense to me. There were only goat paths down the mountain, so I followed them. After a while, with growing anxiety, I realized that perhaps the goats weren't going back to the hotel.

As I searched for a better trail, the terrain changed and became increasingly difficult. Finally, I stopped. I looked down the vast granite mountain, then far off to the left and to the right. As far as

I could see, it was becoming like sheer glass without the usual jagged edges and outcroppings. A long way down, I thought I saw the big trail we had started out on. Anxious to reach the group on time, I figured that the shortest distance between two points would be a straight line.

I began descending the mountain in the only way I could see possible—straight down a dried-up waterfall declivity. The incline of this long granite mountain slope was about 80 percent. As I slid down and around the huge boulders and hung onto the occasional tree that rooted itself between the stones, I became increasingly aware of the seriousness of what I was doing.

When I finally arrived at what I had thought was the big trail, it turned out to be nothing at all. There I was, hanging from my last tree. Leaning out a bit, I saw that I was suspended on a small ledge sticking out of the sheer granite mountain face. I was at the end of my journey but there was no ground in sight. Somehow, the illusion of a trail had appeared where there was nothing but thin air. I thought to myself, *Eileen, my dear, you have really done it this time.*

I turned back to face the mountain. I was half-standing, half-lying, my front flat against the mountain, hugging it like a toy doll with suction cups on her knees and hands. I looked like something you'd put on your refrigerator door. Looking up, I assessed that I could not climb back up the way I had come, as the roots of the grasses were not strong enough to hold my weight. The boulders were of no use either, having no edges I could grasp to pull myself up. To my right and left, there was nothing but sheer, gray-glass granite. I turned again to face the valley. Horrified, I saw the forest I had come from some thousands of feet below. This was no joke. I was in serious trouble.

I spied a small jagged ledge the size of a two-foot triangle jutting out of the granite near my left foot. I reached over with my foot, stepped onto the ledge, and sat down for about ten seconds. The ledge was so small and the height was so astounding that I immediately became dizzy. I got up quickly and faced the mountain, hugging it once again.

Now, I consider myself an adventurous person. For years, I have been a world-class activist, capable of strategizing my way out of enigmatic situations. I do it all the time. But this time there was no chance of my getting out of here without help. No chance. I closed my eyes and humbly asked God to guide me and protect me.

As I looked around for some lifesaving possibilities, I noticed a small cavity in the side of the mountain on my right. A small oak tree was growing out from it. Leaning over, I was able to take hold of the tree and pull myself over into the miniscule cave. With a little effort, I was able to curl my body into a ball and fit myself into the cramped space.

There I remained, wedged into this small cavity in the side of Mary's mountain. As the hours went by, I thought about the possibility of dying here. Perhaps this wasn't a bad way to go after all. *Better than dying in Bloomingdale's,* I mused.

Then it occurred to me that my group would notice I was missing and call for a search party. And indeed they did. Off in the distance, I began to hear the whirling noise of a helicopter. Leaning out of my cave, I saw it appear on the horizon. It drew nearer and I waved my white Ann Taylor jacket, desperately trying to get their attention. But to no avail. To them, I was probably the size of a fly on the wall. My heart sank as my steel-bladed savior whopped its way off into the sunset.

The sky soon darkened and I nestled in for the night, trying to find a comfortable way to remain curled up on the hard rock. I was exhausted, but I hesitated to sleep, fearing I might fall off the mountain. I tried to keep my spirits up as I struggled to stay alert throughout the long night. Alone in Mary's place, I had plenty of time to think about life. The words of Jesus, *"And I shall send a comforter,"* filled my thoughts. I thought of the people dying of cancer and of all those that Mother Teresa had ministered to. Everyone must necessarily endure life's trials, but ah, to be comforted—that was the key. How grateful I was to sense the presence of angelic beings, comforting me through my ordeal. At last I could see the light of dawn and, as I watched, the same sun rose in the sky as it had for Mary two thousand years before.

Several hours later I heard voices a long way below me. The relief was indescribable. I could see little men and little cars scurrying around in the forest. I guessed that the French police had given up their search on top of the mountain and were now scouring the base, perhaps thinking I had fallen. I quickly wriggled out of my lavender overalls and hooked them onto a stick I'd found in the cave. When I turned toward the clear blue sky to wave my flag, I gasped in astonishment.

Above me, a dense cloud hovered in the unmistakable shape of an elegant knight with his right hand raised and his left hand pointing downward. And there was more. Below his raised hand was another cloud, this one in the shape of a huge goblet, a wineglass. It looked much like the drawing of the Holy Grail in our guidebook.

For a moment I stared in shock, too amazed to believe what I was seeing. Then with a jolt I came back to my present occupation. I began to wave my lavender flag and yell out to the little men below. At first they couldn't see me, but finally my flapping overalls caught their attention and they waved back and signaled that the helicopter would come.

I fell back into my cave with relief and then turned my full attention to the amazing cloud shapes, now slowly dissipating into mist. With profound humility I relaxed into the moment of grace. I understood the message.

The goblet was the same size as the knight. Indeed, it was the size of the human body. Here on this desolate mountain, confirmed for me in the clouds, was the understanding that *the Holy Grail is the human body, the temple in which and through which we can know God. The body is the vessel that contains his love . . . no, that is his love.* The quest we were all on was not to find something outside ourselves, but to find *ourselves*. To know that this exquisite vessel, the human body, is the sacred cup of God. I felt this as a deep knowingness in the very cells of my body, and I felt that I now understood the purpose of all life.

A short time later, I began to hear the familiar sound of the helicopter. Flying overhead, the pilot couldn't locate me the first time around. Then he saw me and came directly at me. The helicopter was bright red and looked brand spanking new. I could see a man inside all dressed up in a bright yellow jumpsuit with a matching helmet. It was a beautiful sight. The yellow-suited man was soon suspended on a cable and flying toward me.

The whirling blades of the helicopter created such a wind that it nearly blew me off the side of the mountain. That would have been an ironic ending to the ordeal, I thought, after surviving on my own all this time. The man in yellow reached me and grabbed my arm. He stepped onto the ledge and, staring intensely into my eyes, wrapped the cable around my waist and motioned to the helicopter to haul me up. As I flew through the air, he stayed behind on the ledge.

I was placed down safely amidst a throng of perhaps thirty French policemen. Each one looked more wonderful to me than the next. I thanked them profusely for saving my life. I felt a rush of gratitude and relief at having my feet once again on firm ground. I was safe and sound. I felt my legs and stretched out my arms, and looked at them with love. I was filled with a new respect for the human body I call my own. After all, it is the vessel of God's love, and I cherish it as I pursue my life's purpose—to fill it to the brim.

"The quest we were all on was not to find something outside ourselves, but to find ourselves."

—Eileen Danneman

19 · Grace

race is a mysterious and unexpected experience of understanding, acceptance, surrender, recognition or resolution. It is a gift of exceeding worth.

When I traveled around the world for a year after leaving West Africa, I had hundreds of memorable encounters with people, places and animals. But two stand out as moments of the purest grace imaginable. Both had to do with the natural world.

I was in Nepal, planning to go "trekking" in the Himalayas. I had my government-issued trekking permit, required for any tourist who wants to go into the mountains there, already in hand. The day before I was to go, an earthquake shook the room I was renting in Katmandu. A mere tremor, it only lasted a few seconds. But fearless as I was in those days, I sensed that heading into the Himalayas by myself was not a great idea. I did not have a travel partner at the moment, I would be among people who spoke no

English and I had heard stories about problems with food. Hepatitis was not uncommon among travelers. And there were no hotels where I was going.

So I decided to go, instead, to a beautiful valley called Pokara, just a few hours away from Katmandu by bus. It was cloudy and hard to see much until we got to the valley itself. But the next day the skies cleared, and I rented a small rowboat from the camp I was staying in and paddled out to the middle of Lake Pokara. Then I lay on my back in the boat, looking up at the entire front range of the Himalayas, the magnificent Annapurna mountains. I stayed there all day, watching the light change on the face of the mountains as the sun moved across the sky.

On the return trip to Katmandu, as I sat squashed in the center of the backseat of a taxi between two Nepalese, the hairs on the back of my neck suddenly rose, and my spine started tingling. Something made me turn around—and I found myself looking directly at Mt. Everest for the first time. My mind stopped for a moment, and then I cried. The beauty and the majesty of the world's highest peak literally transmitted to me an experience of the divine, touching a place within me that I had not known before.

The second experience happened soon after that. I left Katmandu on a bus headed for India. After many months on the road in other countries, I was finally returning to India, where I had gone after leaving Africa. I was on my way to Benares, or Varanasi, the holiest city of India. I was looking forward to seeing the famous Ganges River for the first time.

Our bus traveled all day and night, arriving in Benares well before dawn. In the darkness, I made my way toward the river, asking directions of people already awake in the streets. I found a *ghat,* a series of steps leading down to the river. Sensing I was close, I set my bags on one of the steps and sat down, settling in to wait for the sun to rise.

I could hear the sounds of the river lapping at the steps. As dawn approached, I could hear other sounds of water being poured; I would eventually see a man standing in the water in his *dhoti*, performing morning prayers and ablutions. Around 5:00 A.M., the first rays of the morning unveiled the river Ganges. As I watched the light on the rippling, gold and black water before me, my mind and body settled into a state of perfect stillness. I felt the greatest peace I had ever known. It was another moment of grace, in which the experience of what is holy is revealed.

Another beautiful image of grace was given to me by musician, author and counselor Janet Sussman, who says that grace goes to the very heart of what God is. When she thinks of grace, she told me, the image that comes to her is that familiar sight in autumn, when a leaf falls and floats a little at a time, and there is a grace, an effortless dance towards resolution. She describes grace as a unifying process where you're able to understand something or resolve issues that were previously causing pain or suffering, and come to a state of peace—a deep level of comfort that's more than just pacification.

Even the everyday sense of the word implies an element of the divine. A graceful dancer or athlete expresses an adeptness, a finesse, that evokes wonder and awe and that can't be explained by talent alone. We sense that the person has been touched by a divine presence. The same thing is true when we see a great piece of art or hear the music of a composer like Beethoven. Surely, we think, divine inspiration has graced the lives of such artists.

But grace takes many forms. The ability to make sense out of tragedy is a certain kind of grace. To be given love, especially consistent, unconditional love, is grace. And anything that allows us to have some measure of peace is a form of grace. We cannot claim it or demand it. And we must be awake to notice it when it happens.

I believe that grace is always present; we just have to notice it.

And the next story, by Nancy Bellmer, is an example not only of noticing grace, but also of how to receive it and use it fully in the way we live our lives.

I am reminded of the scene from Thornton Wilder's *Our Town*, in which Emily, looking back at her life after she has died, says, "Oh, earth, you're too wonderful for anybody to realize you." She then turns and asks the Stage Manager, "Do any human beings ever realize life while they live it?—every, every minute?" The Stage Manger replies, "No," but upon reflection adds, "The saints and poets, maybe—they do some."

I think Nancy Bellmer—and her husband, Rick—may be saints.

NANCY BELLMER'S STORY
Bathed in Light

We almost lost him before he was born.

In 1982, seven months into my pregnancy with my son Braden, I was taken to the hospital in Reno, Nevada. My husband, Rick, and I learned that I had an amniotic leak and a baby who weighed only three pounds.

The doctors told us that I needed to carry Braden as long as possible, and that if I could make it to thirty-seven weeks—just three weeks short of full-term—he could be born in our own Lake Tahoe birthing room, rather than at the hospital in Reno. But they felt the chance of his being born within one or two weeks was so great that they urged us to stay in Reno, which we did for a couple of weeks.

During those two weeks, I began focusing on keeping my baby inside me. Rick and I had been practicing meditation for several years, but this was the first time I had ever attempted applying my consciousness in a focused way to achieve a specific outcome. And we made it—at least until midnight the night before my doctor's "three-week rule" would have set in.

Happily, it was close enough for my doctor, and after a short, four-hour labor in our local hospital, my son was born. He weighed four pounds, eight ounces—so small! But the doctors rated him a "10." He was totally vibrant, and certainly his lungs were fine. To us, everything about him was perfect. We went home later that same day, feeling extremely blessed and cherishing every moment, appreciating how fortunately things had turned out.

As Braden grew, people often commented that he was different. Our friends described him as blissful, and someone once told me that he looked as if he "walked on air." When he was one-and-a-half years old, we moved to a small community in the Midwest, where he started attending child care a few hours a week and loved it, even at that age. His constant joy and delight with the world affected everyone he met, including Rick and me. Our family life was exceptionally close and loving.

In June 1984, Braden was a little over two years old. That month a close friend from Tahoe came to visit. She brought her son, whom she had given birth to in our Lake Tahoe home. He was just a year older than Braden, and the boys loved playing together. I was working at the time; I had my own business, a cottage industry making food that was distributed locally. I loved it because it was something I could do in my home.

One night during our friend's visit, Braden began crying from a bad dream. I went into his room to comfort and massage him. He was still coughing a little from a cold he'd had. "Owie, owie, hurt head," he cried, repeating this phrase over and over to tell me about his nightmare.

The next morning Rick remarked about a dream he'd had. In the dream he was driving a white Mercedes and hit and killed a teenaged boy. He then saw the boy's twin on the side of the road, which he interpreted as the boy's soul. Rick thought the dream was weird, and wondered out loud to me why he would have dreamed such a thing.

Then we both got ready for work. Rick sat in the driveway for several minutes in the seat of the huge delivery-sized van he was using for work, going over some paperwork, the engine idling. I got started in the kitchen, while my friend stood in the doorway talking to me and at the same time, keeping an eye on the boys, who were playing outside on their big plastic tricycles. When Rick was ready to leave, he glanced over and noticed the boys were eating watermelon on the porch. He turned back to his paperwork, put it away, then looking in both rearview mirrors, backed out.

But every parent knows how quickly children can move. In one of those irretrievable flashes of time, Braden had gotten back on his tricycle, pedaled along the side of the truck and was behind it when Rick backed out of the driveway.

I heard Braden's cry and ran to him. His soul waited just long enough for me to get to him and take his hand in mine before he slipped away.

At that instant, I experienced a deep stillness and felt my identity vastly expand. I was filled with an enormous light that seemed to come from above, which enveloped me, completely bathing me in light, inside and out. The light encompassed not only me, but the entire situation. I had always believed in God, but when I experienced this all-pervasive light, I knew that my longstanding desire for a direct experience of God had been fulfilled—though at an unexpected moment. The light was so overpowering, so huge, that it dwarfed the shock and the loss that were also there. I felt supported and protected, as the size and nature of the light allowed me to feel only the light. The pain was there, but it was only a very small part of my experience. The light also gave me the experience of complete acceptance and surrender—and compassion for Rick, who was in unspeakable agony.

When Rick realized what had happened, he had run inside the house crying and screaming. A few minutes later he'd come out, and together we had held our little boy. All through the next hour, in the midst of the physical and emotional shock and the arrival of emergency vehicles, I remained completely enveloped by the light.

After Braden's body was taken away, Rick and I went into Braden's room to meditate. Afterwards we discovered that we'd both had the experience of Braden's spirit in the form of a pinkish light, and the knowledge of these words being spoken: "I'm fine; I'm free." It comforted us greatly. During that time, while we were in a reflective state, we also remembered the two dreams. It gave us a strong sense of prophecy, the feeling that this was beyond our control and our limited understanding.

That evening, when our kind neighbors brought over dinner for us, I had my first experience of the huge contrast between what was happening inside me and the mundane details of "getting on" with life. I felt physically hollow from the loss, but was unable to eat. I had the thought: *If I eat this, this is what I will be filling my emptiness and loss with.* At the same time, I felt buoyant, blissful, light-filled— it was the most powerful spiritual experience I have ever had.

In the weeks that followed, even in my deep sadness, I felt expanded and open and filled with love. At times I felt I even had to limit my bliss, because it seemed so incongruous to others' tears and grief. When friends came to visit, I found myself comforting them. Although they had walked into our home tentatively, unsure of what to say in the face of such a loss, and with tears in their eyes, something of our expanded internal state seemed to touch them and they left feeling transformed. People remarked that the upliftment they felt offered a new and liberating perspective about death and tragedy.

I definitely had questions, especially that very human question: *Why?* At times I felt confused, as well as sad. But I never felt angry, either with Rick or God, who had given me such a huge, incredible blessing.

Over the next six weeks, Rick and I took turns, it seemed, having clear and powerful experiences of Braden. One was of an angelic child. Another image was of him growing into a princely young adult. The last experience was a clear visual picture of Braden as an old soul, complete with flowing beard and robes, floating in the air, leading a group of heavenly beings. This was the last "visit" we would have, and through it all, the message was clear: Our lives and our souls were not separate; Braden was—and always would be—with us.

Yet when the visits ceased, we began to feel the physical loss. We recognized how much we missed being parents and deeply wanted to have another child, not to replace Braden, but to give us the opportunity to parent again. We later realized that it was right at the six-week point, when our visits from Braden stopped, that I became pregnant with our second child, Shane. Clearly, it was time to shift our attention.

As we looked towards the birth of a new child, our previous loss became easier to accept. Pregnancies and deliveries became easier, too. My pregnancy with Shane was smooth; this time my baby arrived within two hours. And when I later gave birth to our third child, Saralyn, she rushed out in forty-five minutes!

When I reflect on what happened to us in June of 1984, I see many things now that were less clear then. Most importantly, I feel that the grace that I experienced as Braden died was a gift that is often given, but not always perceived. Losing Braden revealed to us what could be called the "Big Picture." On the surface, there was the tragedy of our child's death, but that wasn't the whole story; there was also the light, the grace of God, surrounding the whole experience.

This made me aware that there is always more than what

appears on the surface. And that experience has remained with me to this day. It's easier for me to accept the daily happenings when I know that there's a bigger purpose, a larger context for all the things that happen in life. I now believe that grace is always available to us, in spite of tragedy or struggle or stress—it's just a matter of choosing. Seeing the big picture makes it easier to choose.

Another important choice I made was about my husband. People have often asked how Rick and I stayed together through all this. I got a clearer picture about what happened to us as a couple one day as I was talking to a close friend of ours, talking to him for the first time about Braden. He wanted answers to the same questions that had come up so many times before: *How did you forgive Rick? How did he forgive himself?*

In the presence of this friend's compassion, I was finally able to see that my own compassion for Rick had never allowed me to blame him. Like the light, the compassion I felt had made any resentment seem so small. I had chosen to follow the compassion. From the first moment, I knew that anger and blame were irrelevant; Rick and I were in this together and needed each other to survive. There was never even a question of divorce.

This year, Rick and I will celebrate our twenty-fifth wedding anniversary, nineteen years after Braden's passing. A couple of years ago I attended the graduation of the class that would have been Braden's. I wanted to see how far his buddies had come. It was very sweet—I felt as if I were their mother too. I wept, not from sadness at Braden's absence, but with the tears that come from such poignant moments and the knowledge that Braden had already shared his own special graduation with us so many years ago.

For me it has become evident that there are two sides to our experience as humans. On one side, there's the humanness—the part that goes through the sorting out and the healing of the issues we face in our lives. On the other side, there's the divine. When we are truly awake to the divine, it is so big that the grace dissolves every challenge we face. It's not about avoiding the issues in life— it's just a question of which you make your priority. This wisdom about life is a part of that enormous light that has remained with me. I consider it Braden's greatest gift.

"When we are truly awake to the divine, it is so big that the grace dissolves every challenge we face."

—Nancy Bellmer

20 · Compassion

 had the great blessing of meeting Mother Teresa in India when I was traveling around the world in the early seventies. I was staying at the home of a Christian family in Bangalore, when my hostess invited me to accompany her to the church she attended to meet "Sister Teresa," as she was still called then. Already world-renowned, Sister Teresa was coming to visit the children in the church's attached orphanage and speak to the women of the church.

I followed Sister Teresa closely around the orphanage, watching her touch and hold the children close, caressing them and speaking to them so lovingly. I tried to follow her example, noticing that it did not come easily to me. Afterwards, she lectured to the group, then stood at the doorway greeting each person.

Suddenly, she was holding my hands in hers and looking into my eyes. I have no memory of what she said to me. All I can

217

remember is the feeling of compassion that swept over me and the understanding that I was in the presence of greatness. From that moment on, I longed to become a living example of compassion and kindness.

Actress Jennifer Moyer says that compassion is not something you do. It's a feeling that arises when you realize that "this river of life that flows through me is the same river of life that flows through everybody and everything that exists." On the other hand, the Dalai Lama talks about *practicing compassion.* "If you want others to be happy, practice compassion. If *you* want to be happy, practice compassion," he says.

Compassion to me means having a deep awareness of another's suffering without overidentifying with it or being overwhelmed by it ourselves. I don't know if you can go to a seminar and learn how to practice compassion. I try to bring compassion to every action and every relationship, whether personal or professional. Sometimes I'm successful, sometimes I'm not. But although my personality may momentarily forget, my soul does not. And when I am in the presence of compassion, the transmission goes deep into my psyche and my soul, and once again, I become more compassionate.

Mother Teresa often reminded people that we cannot do great things, only small things with great love. Lynne Twist, author of the next story, shows how those small things can have great results, as she works for human rights globally, while remaining committed to spiritual authenticity in everyday life. An activist and fundraiser, she grounds her work in the principles of sufficiency and reciprocity and tries to live her own life based on them as well.

Reciprocity, she says, is like the breath we breathe in and out. We take in no more than we need, and let out exactly the amount that must be released. This process is sufficient, precise and life affirming. "To recognize, lift up, and shine a light on the beauty of reciprocal relationships and interactions in our lives is to uncover vast reservoirs of existing wealth that we have taken for granted. In reciprocity, there is nourishment and joy: I am there for you and you are there for me." Surely, she could not have imagined how dramatically this truth would be tested, as she shares in the following story.

This story took place just after Lynne had returned from Africa, where she had been working with the Hunger Project, an international organization she helped found, dedicated to ending hunger worldwide. At their New York office, she attended a meeting on the accomplishments of the region of West Africa where she had been. Feeling deeply related to Africa, especially the women with whom she had worked, she felt proud, thrilled and fulfilled by the success they had experienced together.

From there she went to Park Avenue for another meeting of a foundation whose board she was also on. It was about the results of their work taking place in the Middle East, which she described as spectacular and moving. She left the meeting feeling blessed and light enough to walk on water. It is at this point that she picks up the story of what happened next.

I believe Mother Teresa would have been proud.

LYNNE TWIST'S STORY
The New York City Cabdriver

t was a typical hot summer night in New York City. I had just been at a meeting celebrating some successes in humanitarian work I had been involved with in Africa. I was full of inspiration and fulfillment with the experience of making a difference. It was about 9:30 P.M. when I hailed a cab, which screeched to the curb to pick me up.

Almost as soon as I got into the cab, I realized that I was in the presence of a very angry young African-American man, full of enormous rage and hatred. He didn't need to say anything—I could feel it. He drove as if he wanted to kill someone. He honked at every moving object. From Park Avenue over to Broadway, he cut people off, jammed his cab into small spaces and was both rude and reckless. I sat frozen in the backseat; I felt I was in the grip of a raging monster.

Suddenly, an Indian taxi driver, a Sikh man with a turban, cut us off, and my driver went into a rage that was deep, horrible and frightening. He screamed expletives at this guy, who drove away as fast as he could. But when we came to the next red light on Broadway, the same driver was next to us. My angry, monstrous cabdriver opened the door of our cab, went over to the Indian driver and started pounding on the hood of the car. He started screaming at him: "Racist! You Indian drivers! You Pakistanis!" Then he went around to the open window, pulled out a knife and tried to stab the Indian driver. The Indian driver ducked the knife, the light turned green and he drove away.

My cabdriver then came back to the car, where I was still sitting in the back seat, unable to move. The knife was still in his hands. My heart was pounding. I was sweating profusely, and blood was coursing through my veins. I thought, *Do I scream for the police? Do I try to get out? What do I do?* I had a million thoughts going through my mind, but perhaps the loudest was, *I can be effective in Bangladesh or Africa in empowering people to begin to turn their situation around, but can I walk my talk with this man?*

So I stayed in the cab. There was no chance of getting out anyway, because he pulled away abruptly, as the light turned green, at eight zillion miles an hour. He was still screaming and yelling, so I said to him, "Maybe you should pull over and calm down a little bit, and I'll get out." He turned around with the same rage and started yelling at me: "You white honky, you bitch, you rich, white woman, you have no idea what I've been through in my life. You're just a bunch of . . ." Focused on me now, he hardly looked at the road as he drove. I was frozen with fear as he went on and on.

And then suddenly, I stopped listening from my head, and I moved into a place of compassion in my heart. Somewhere along 42nd Street and Broadway, I just leapt from my head to my heart. I could hear the rage and anger, and also the terror and hurt in his voice. When we got to our destination, which was in Greenwich Village where I was staying, he turned around and screamed the cab fare that I owed him.

Now I don't know if we could scientifically prove this, but when you're in your heart, it seems you have access to courage. I think there's no fear, because love is devoid of fear. I have often heard my mother say that when you drop into your heart, no matter what the situation is, you'll handle it with compassion and wisdom.

I said to him, "You know what? I don't have anywhere else to go now; my day is over. Would you like to talk?"

He looked at me as if I was completely crazy. He stopped yelling. He stared at me for a moment and then, slowly, started talking. He started telling me the tragic and brutal story of his life. He talked about his mother, who was a drug addict on crack, and his father, who had beaten him and kicked him in his stomach when he was three years old, which had given him problems with his back ever since. He talked about the horrors of his neighborhood.

Suddenly, I realized that I could no longer separate myself from this man. I realized, *He and I are just the same. His world is the world I live in, too.*

And I got out of the back seat and into the front seat, and I took his hand. Right beneath my hand and his hand was the knife. The switchblade was still open. Then he started to cry. He started weeping about the horrors of his life, and the Pakistani cabdrivers, and Indian cabdrivers—he insulted every single group completely and totally. But this time it was in communication with me, rather than yelling at someone.

By the time he finished his story, he was sobbing. I took his other hand and looked at him. I told him my name was Lynne, and he told me his name was Robert. I said thank you; he said thank you. I paid him and got out of the cab.

Again, in that moment, I realized that we are all part of the same human condition. I saw that even in this angry man, the yearning to love and be loved was at the heart of who he was. In going through that experience with him, I had been given a deep understanding of how the human spirit can be crushed and moved to rage. I could actually feel it in my heart.

I don't know if it made a difference in this man's life. I don't know if he went on to murder the next person he picked up. But I maintained my own integrity. I walked my talk and it wasn't in Bangladesh or sub-Sahara Africa, where I'm supposed to walk my talk. It was in New York, where the norm would have been to get out of there as fast as possible and report the guy. I don't know what came over me, but somehow I brought love and compassion and myself to him.

I feel that this man is a part of my life forever. To this day, I have love for him—and I believe that makes a difference. I can't prove it, and I have no evidence. I'll probably never see him again. But I really believe that because I've taken a stand to give my life in a way that makes a difference, every action I take can, in fact, make a difference and generate a more compassionate and loving world.

Gandhi said, "The unadulterated love of one person can nullify the hatred of millions." I think that is true. I believe that when you take a stand with your life—powerful enough, grand enough, blessed enough—you will always find the way to your heart and moments of truth.

"We are all part of the same human condition. The yearning to love and be loved is at the heart of who we are."

—Lynne Twist

21 · Receptivity

ooking at her life from the outside, you might have thought Catherine Oxenberg had it all. What more could a person want? Royal ancestry? Catherine is a direct descendant of Catherine the Great of Russia and was named after her. Her mother is Her Royal Highness Princess Elizabeth of Yugoslavia, her grandfather was the Regent King of Yugoslavia and her grandmother was Her Royal Highness Princess Olga of Yugoslavia. In fact, she is related to all of the European royal families, including Spain, England and Italy, through blood or marriage.

And what about fabulous friends? At thirteen she was making up crossword puzzles with Richard Burton; at seventeen she had food fights with Prince Albert of Monaco and her cousin Prince Charles. She partied on Mick Jagger's boat, was proposed to by Prince Andrew and hung out with many of Hollywood's elite.

Youth and beauty? When she went to *Vogue* to apply for a

modeling position, the top editor, Polly Mellon, said, "Look at that face," and signed her on the spot for a ten-page photo spread. Intelligence? She graduated at the top of her class from St. Paul's, one of the most prestigious preparatory schools in America, and was accepted at Harvard, though she ended up choosing a modeling and acting career instead.

A successful acting career? Soon after starting acting classes, Catherine was picked to play Princess Diana in the television movie *A Royal Romance* (and later in another called *Charles and Diana: A Palace Divided*). A short while later, she landed the plum role of Amanda on *Dynasty*, the nighttime soap opera hit that became the No. 1 television show in the world in the eighties, watched weekly by a hundred million people around the globe.

Eventually, she also had other things that brought her deep happiness: self-love, forgiveness, gratitude, a husband she loved and three beautiful children. But before then, this fairy tale life had a very dark side. All that she had couldn't save her from the pain of a deep self-loathing. Despite all she was blessed with, she felt empty. She could not see any beauty in herself and felt only shame and hatred for her body. By her midtwenties she was experiencing chronic depression and a crushing hopelessness. It is at this point that Catherine begins the following story, an expression of one of the feminine's most beautiful principles: receptivity.

I listened in amazement when Catherine first told me her story. Because a dream was at the heart of it, I might have been quick to dismiss it had it been anybody else. So many books have been written about dreams—their meanings, how to interpret them, how to make use of them for understanding yourself and your life. But I've never had much success in using them for anything, especially since I usually can't even remember them long enough to write them down. I tend to regard them as insignificant.

Because it was Catherine, I listened carefully. And she confirmed for me something I have thought for a long time: Messages can come to us in the most unlikely ways, and support is everywhere, if we are open to receiving it.

Listening, the focus of the story in the chapter on openness, is an aspect of receptivity. What I love about Catherine's story is that she models for us the ability to listen to *everything*, knowing that guidance can come from anyone, anywhere, in any way. In her case, her ability to receive it affected her life in the deepest and best possible ways.

By the way, since "receiving" Catherine's dream experience, I have had a number of dreams in which I found meaning, significance, consolation or inspiration. My ability to receive is improving, and the result is ever deepening and enriching knowledge of myself and the world.

CATHERINE OXENBERG'S STORY
The Crowning of the Princess

By my midtwenties, depression was taking over my life, and I was desperate for help. I began therapy and started unraveling the parts of my life that had been suppressed. As I learned more about myself, I began to seriously explore many forms of healing. I was willing to try anything that seemed to be helping people. I started attending 12-Step meetings for overeaters, codependents and adult children of alcoholics. I practiced yoga daily and learned meditation techniques, including Transcendental Meditation. I even did a ropes course—three times—the first time alone in a blizzard.

Through all this work, I began to unearth a lot of the issues of childhood that I had repressed. I realized that I had been denying my feelings about my parents' divorce when I was five years old. Through deep breathing practices, I relived and released from my subconscious memories of the abuse that I had suffered as a child. I had vivid memories of being sexually abused, including orally, as a baby by a family member (not either of my parents). This discovery was devastating, but knowing also felt like a relief on some levels.

And it helped explain the eating disorder, bulimia, which had plagued me in cycles of bingeing and throwing up ever since my first sexual experience at age eighteen. I was able to identify the purging as a form of acting out related to the original abuse. It was a way of trying to get the "poison" out of my body.

I went through long periods of celibacy, as I couldn't deal with the feelings that came up in relationships. I now believe that I stored memories in my body, particularly in those areas that were abused, and any sexual relationship threatened to trigger those dormant memories. But I became pregnant, and, with no desire to be married, I gave birth to a beautiful baby girl on my own.

As my child reached the age of nine months, the age I had been when first molested, I began having stronger and clearer memories of my abuse. By the time she was one, I reached the point where I was no longer able to eat. I knew that I was going to die if I didn't get help.

I checked myself into a rehab clinic for six weeks and found it gave me solitude and the strength to stay with my arduous inner journey. I continued to have many sessions of a process called "soul retrieval" and did a great deal of "inner child" work using a technique called "self-parenting." But despite periods of abstinence, the bulimia was triggered any time I was in a relationship.

Little did I know that the death of my beloved grandmother would be the turning point for me. It was October 1997. I was unable to attend her funeral and, feeling sad and distant from my family, longed to connect with her in some way. I had been raised a

Christian, but I had become very eclectic in my spirituality. I didn't know any Christian rituals I could perform on my own, so I took a ceremony from E. J. Gold's *American Book of the Dead,* an American adaptation of *The Tibetan Book of the Dead.* I put my grandmother's picture on a small table with a bowl of rice and some holy water. I lit a candle, read some passages from the book and prayed with all my heart for her soul to be guided into the light.

That night I went to bed and had a deeply prophetic dream. It was what I call a "God dream," a completely lucid dream in which you are guided from a source of greater intelligence, and in which you are literally "blinded by the light." I knew I was dreaming and also knew I was receiving important knowledge.

In this dream I was in a place I somehow knew was Jerusalem, although I'd never been there. I was standing in a garden with two beautiful beings I recognized as Joseph and Mary, the parents of Jesus. Joseph talked to me about my life, and his words rang true. I felt I was being shown a picture of my life and certain patterns in it. Then he said the hardship in my life was over, and that I would soon be experiencing serene anchoredness.

The part of me that was watching the dream said, "Make note of that." The term "serene anchoredness" was unfamiliar to me, but I knew it was important. It was a quality that had certainly eluded me thus far in my life.

I was then guided down a cobblestone road past an ancient cemetery. All of a sudden I knew I was in the presence of the Holy Spirit. I fell to my knees, and I saw before me a column of crystal white light that was somehow also water. It came toward me, and I bowed my head and was bathed in the pillar of liquid light. I felt I was being washed clean. My mouth opened, and tears came out of it. It seemed to me that the trauma from the abuse I had sustained as an infant was being healed, and a darkness that I had been trying to purge from my body for years was being washed away.

I felt electricity running up my spine; my impression was that my nervous system was being rewired as that column of light. I asked the Holy Spirit why I kept relapsing with bulimia, and why it was so hard to overcome. I was told it was so that people would see the transformation. I didn't really understand what that meant. But I was also told that the most important thing for me in my life was to remember to pray, and I deeply understood that.

At that moment I woke up. The room was filled with light. I remembered each part of the dream: the garden in Jerusalem, the "serene anchoredness," the pillar of light and water. I thought of my prayer for my grandmother and realized with profound gratitude that I was the one who had been guided into the light. I prayed it had happened for her, too.

Over the next three weeks, a deep shift occurred in my life. I was inspired by Napoleon Hill's book *Think and Grow Rich* to write out a statement of what I wanted to manifest in my life and speak it out, twice a day, morning and evening. I wanted to impact the change on a physical level, so I made sure to involve my body as I spoke. I wanted to show the universe that I was serious, so I stood in an empowered way and made my statements with conviction and commitment. I learned that it takes at least three weeks to break an old habit and make a lasting change, so I embraced this exercise diligently, practicing daily without fail. It was another discipline to add to meditation, yoga, prayer and everything else I was doing. But it was different in that I kept having the idea that it was "anchoring" me. The phrase from the dream kept coming to my mind. I felt I was imprinting a different pattern of behavior in my life.

Then, one night, exactly twenty-one days after starting this practice, I was lying in my bathtub when I suddenly saw the crystal pillar of light and water above me. I started to cry. It was exactly what I had experienced in my dream, but somehow I now knew that it was nothing but myself, my higher self. Again, I felt baptized in healing light and water. I had a deep sense of self-love as I merged with my higher self. I cried and cried with relief and joy. I understood that the pain that most of us live with comes from feeling separate from our true self, and I felt that pain fade away.

There's only one phrase that really captures how I felt after that second baptism: yes, "serene anchoredness." I felt the beautiful, settled, solid bliss of meeting my self, of being reunited with myself.

And, after that day, I never threw up again, never once. The weight was lifted.

The day after what I call my "bathtub baptism," I got a call to audition for a Lexus commercial in which I'd play the part of Hera, the wife of Zeus, the Greek god over all the other gods. And I got it! I had such a good laugh. I took it as a humorous hint from God that I had glimpsed the divinity of my soul—I got to play his wife in a commercial!

And exactly one year after my dream, I met my future husband when we both got roles in the same movie. We went to Jerusalem to film it, and I was amazed one day when we filmed in front of an ancient cemetery, identical to the one I had seen in my dream!

Looking back, I think the turning point in my struggle for healing and self-love was my desire to pray, not for myself, but for my grandmother. The act of selflessness in prayer was one of the keys that opened my heart and allowed a space for my soul to enter. Prayer brought me God's grace, as I believe it always does. Today, I'm so grateful to feel the continuum of grace in my life. With this, I can enjoy everything else I have. And this fairy tale can have a real-world happy ending—which is really an ongoing beginning.

"The act of selflessness in prayer was one of the keys that opened my heart and allowed a space for my soul to enter."

—Catherine Oxenberg

22 · Forgiveness

 headline on the front of a *Reader's Digest* caught my eye: "The Power of Forgiving." Turning to the article, I read about the latest research that shows the profound benefits of forgiving those who hurt us. The article said that forgiveness has become "a hot new way to manage anger, cut stress, and maybe, most important, improve health."

I was already aware that if I needed help forgiving someone, I could choose from a large, and growing, number of books devoted to the topic. Many contain inspiring stories, such as the famous one of Nelson Mandela, who, after serving twenty-seven years in prison for his political beliefs, invited his prison guards to his inauguration as President of South Africa!

Countless others who have been deeply wronged have reported that they could find no peace until they found forgiveness. And author Catherine Ponder says it can even be a technique for becoming rich. All in all, forgiveness has such far-reaching benefits that it seems we would all want to practice it every day!

So when I started working on this chapter, I decided to give it a try. I asked myself if there was anybody I needed to forgive. Two people with whom I had invested a significant amount of money came to mind immediately. They had not paid me back as they had agreed, and I resented it. But as I thought about releasing my resentment and anger toward them, I was faced with a surprising and somewhat embarrassing realization: I wasn't sure whether I *wanted* to forgive them! The question of justice was big for me: Did they deserve to be forgiven? I watched as my ego struggled with itself.

But deep down I knew that forgiving someone doesn't mean that what they did was okay or that we should let ourselves be treated unfairly. It means letting go of our own feelings of victimization and the blame we assign when we try to make someone else responsible for our own lives. In blaming the couple with whom I had invested money, I was sidestepping my own responsibility. I had not done due diligence regarding the investment, and I had entered into the agreement knowing there was no collateral. I had given them my money, and now I was giving them the power to determine my happiness!

I realized it was myself I needed to forgive—first for making a big mistake, then for trying to blame someone else for my risk taking. I stopped focusing on them and started looking to myself, telling myself, as Catherine Ponder recommends, "I forgive you," even when, at first, I didn't really mean it. Over time, I've come to feel at peace with what happened and committed to not making the same mistake again. And I fully believe that the more I release *them* from being the focal point of my resentment, the greater the possibility to free up the energy around the situation—and the more likely I'll even be paid back.

The words "for giving" suggest releasing into the flow of life, "giving" ourselves into the stream of life's events. The good health of the soul depends on this ability to be yielding, flexible and flowing. I have noticed in my own life that not to flow, or forgive, is to try to stay fixed in one position and to remain more committed to anger and hurt than to my own peace.

In situations where we feel powerless, sometimes forgiveness is the only way out. And we may be asked to do it over and over again, each time letting go at a deeper level.

But it's worth it. Research has found that forgiveness can reduce chronic back pain, decrease stress by up to 50 percent, increase energy, and improve mood, sleep and overall physical vitality.

Perhaps even more striking are the divine revelations resulting from forgiveness. One such remarkable example is the story of writer and Christian evangelist Corrie ten Boom. Corrie, her father and her sister were imprisoned in Nazi concentration camps during WWII for harboring Jews in their home in Holland. Though her father and sister died in the camps, Corrie survived. She wrote of her experiences in her book *The Hiding Place* and spent the latter years of her life traveling the world, speaking of her life and her faith.

Late in her life, Corrie met face-to-face with one of the cruelest German guards she had encountered in the camps. He had humiliated and degraded her sister and her on a regular basis, frequently jeering at them as they stood in the delousing shower. Now he stood before her with hand outstretched and said, "Will you forgive me?"

She writes, "I stood there with coldness clutching at my heart, but I know that the will can function regardless of the temperature of the heart. I prayed, 'Jesus, help me!' Woodenly, mechanically, I thrust my hand into the one stretched out to me and I experienced an incredible thing. The current started in my shoulder, raced down into my arms and sprang into our clutched hands. Then this warm reconciliation seemed to flood my whole being, bringing tears to my eyes. 'I forgive you, brother,' I cried with my whole heart. For a long moment we grasped each other's hands, the former guard, the former prisoner. I have never known the love of God so intensely as I did in that moment."

For Susan Brandis Slavin, the author of the next story, forgiveness was also about something deeper than relief from physical symptoms. As with all stories about forgiveness, her story illustrates the truth often attributed to Corrie ten Boom: "To forgive is to set a prisoner free and to discover the prisoner was you."

SUSAN BRANDIS SLAVIN'S STORY
My Sweet Revenge

I sometimes joke that my family would have aspired just to be dysfunctional. Being in show business, I've learned to make light of a background that seemed to place boulders in front of me at every turn. Thank heavens I was born with the belief that anything is possible! That helped me get through the suffocating poverty of my childhood and the turbulence of a family dealing with mental illness.

They were good people who tried, but they couldn't overcome their disabilities—and my younger sister's problems were severe. Dolly had been an adorable but hyperactive little girl. As she got older, she got progressively sick, eventually becoming paranoid schizophrenic. Given to violent outbursts, she was obsessed with my mother, which made me her enemy. If I even tried to be in the same room with my mother, Dolly would scream and threaten both of us. My mother could never spend any time with me alone, because the fear of Dolly's violent outbursts was always present. Dolly constantly taunted me with the suggestion that I should leave home.

Dealing with their own emotional problems, my parents gave in to her every whim, order and demand. My father suffered from a nervous disorder that made him shake all the time, as if he were shell-shocked, constantly in a state of alarm. My mother, a song-writer who had shown real promise as a child, had never been allowed by her own mother to pursue her talents; she spent her time either berating my father or retreating into a fantasy world. Neither was present enough to parent, and we lived in an environment of hysterical, nonstop screaming.

I was thirteen when our family moved to Los Angeles, where my father hoped to find a better job. I was thrilled, as I had always known I wanted to be an actress. But Dolly immediately insisted that she and my mother move back to Chicago—and she got her way. With almost no money to live on, we were being kicked out of one apartment after another because Dolly was overbearing, loud and violent. My parents were afraid of her, so they somehow managed to get enough money together for my mother and Dolly's train fare home.

That left me alone with my mentally unstable father, far from my mother as I entered my teen years, when she had provided the only shred of safety in my world despite my sister's efforts to destroy my relationship with her.

But that year the dream I'd had my whole life started to take shape. In Los Angeles, even junior high schools have excellent theater departments. I threw myself into the one at my school, and it became my lifeline. My ability showed, and in my first year, a well-known Hollywood casting director saw me in a play and cast me as Anne in a local production of *The Diary of Anne Frank*. By the time I finished junior high, I was already "in the business" as a professional actress.

When my mother and sister returned from Chicago a couple of years later, I hoped this would win me some of my mother's attention. But she was so distracted and overwrought most of the time that she hardly seemed to know I existed. I was heartbroken and lonely, and the only outlet for all my feelings was acting.

This made me a deep actress for my age, and I was noticed. By the time I was in the twelfth grade, I had amassed a large collection of trophies for acting. They were precious to me because, seeing myself through my family's eyes, I had felt I had no value at all. But now I had my trophies! They gave me a glimmer of hope that I might be worth something.

One day I walked in the door after school and sensed something was wrong. Both my mother and sister seemed to be avoiding my eyes. I looked around the dimly lit room; the shades were drawn, as usual. I glanced at the TV and suddenly realized that my trophies were no longer on top. A few pieces of bent metal were scattered around the floor, but my trophies were gone! I couldn't breathe. My mind raced. Where were they? What had my sister done to them? And why had my mother let her? Suddenly, I snapped. I started screaming wildly as I fell to the floor and lay there sobbing.

I don't know how long I was there. I cried until there were no more tears. Totally spent, I finally looked up at Dolly, standing silently beside my mother. She looked at me with a faint smile on her face, and I realized she had won. I couldn't fight her for a piece of my mother any longer. I gave up. It was over. *She's yours!* I cried inside. *Who cares about any of you, anyway?*

I stood up, and for the first time in my young life, I felt the power of cold rage. I would close my heart to them and become a success. Someday I would get even. I would prove myself to the world, become famous—and never speak to them again. I would make them sorry they had not seen me for who I was.

A few months later, I graduated from high school and immediately moved to New York City. I was frightened and fragile, but fueled by rage and revenge. I worked fervently on building a new life and blocked out my family as much as I could. With no net of parental support to fall back on, I found resources within me I hadn't known I had. As I experimented with my abilities, I developed a strong belief in my own talent. This was tested again and again as I built a successful career as an actress. The more I learned to value myself and my talent, the more I put into my craft and the better I felt about my work and myself. My self-esteem and my success grew hand in hand.

I made many new friends, most of them performers as well, and was always sharing my ideas with them about the many ways in which self-worth and success are intimately linked. Over time they started asking me to coach them for auditions, and soon my acting school at Carnegie Hall was born. Without realizing it, while figuring out a way to thrive in the business myself, I had formulated my own technique!

When I had first studied acting in New York City with the legends of my time, I had been taught that an actor had to submerge himself in the character he was portraying. This was, and is, the conventional approach to acting. However, I found the opposite to be true. The more expanded my sense of self became, and the more I got in touch with the core of my being, the more I was able to invite the characters I played into the center of my soul, and the more full and authentic they became. Through my own passion for my art, I was then able to help others commit to their art and create a rock-solid craft that would enable them to build an unshakable, invisible bridge from themselves to the characters they played.

I also taught them how to market their talents in the industry. I began writing plays, directing and producing as well. My school blossomed into a vibrant artistic community.

As my life continued to evolve and flourish, in the back of my mind—much as I tried to push it away and pretend I didn't care—I was haunted by my sister's fate. She was still living with my mother and, after many years of erratic behavior, she had totally retreated. For the past twelve years, she had not left her spot on the couch except for one daily trip to the bathroom. My mother indulged her by serving her trays of junk food day and night. Dolly would not speak to anyone and had not seen the sky in all that time. I couldn't imagine what would happen to her when my mother died, and I secretly feared it.

As events showed that that time could be drawing near, my mother and Dolly wound up in an assisted living facility with cruel managers who kept telling my sister they would "send her away" when my mother died. Over time, their living situation became intolerable, both for them and for the management, and they were about to be evicted from their tiny room for not paying their rent. Under the stress of the situation, my mother's health failed. When she was taken by ambulance to the hospital, Dolly bolted into the streets, alone in the world for the first time. I spoke with my mother in the hospital and tried to locate Dolly from New York, but to no avail. I had no clue where she might be or if she was okay. She had vanished.

Then one day, the phone rang and, to my astonishment, it was Dolly. Ironically, she was reaching out to me for comfort—me, whom she had wanted to get rid of so long ago! She told me her story, which was heart-wrenching. She was terrified of my mother dying, and she was now homeless with no identification and no ability to communicate with anyone as a credible person. I ached for her vulnerability, and at the same time feared being left with the responsibility of taking care of her for the rest of her life. I didn't let myself think about it though.

When Dolly called again a few days later with the news of my mother's death, I made a quick, visceral decision to go back to L.A. to bury my mother and help Dolly. The people closest to me were protective and questioned my decision. But I followed my heart and deepest intuition.

I felt a surprising depth of loss at my mother's death—I thought

I had done all my grieving for her long ago. I organized her funeral from New York and then, mustering up all my courage, flew to L.A. to attend it. Dolly wasn't strong enough to go, so I didn't see her until afterwards. Driving away from the cemetery, I was emotionally depleted but forced myself to focus on the coming meeting with Dolly. By this time, she had figured out a way to get a motel room, but she had only a few days before her meager funds ran out. I knew I had to work very fast. But I had already researched every possible avenue of housing for her and had a game plan ready.

I felt nervous as I drove up to the motel. When Dolly opened the door, I was shocked at the sight of her. All those years of eating junk food had taken their toll—she was obese and toothless. It seemed like a lifetime since I had seen her. But I was touched by her brave dignity as she invited me in and offered me a chair. To my surprise, I noticed a Bible open at the foot of her bed. I didn't know this spiritual side of her, but learned later she had been on her knees praying for courage to get through this time of darkest despair. She still wasn't comfortable talking, so it was hard to have much of a conversation. I tried to draw her out and comfort her, but soon just turned to the task ahead.

I needed to get Dolly to go with me to see housing. However, this turned out to be impossible, as she was too frightened to leave her room. She didn't seem to grasp the urgency of her situation and, despite her pain, was as stubborn as ever. So I went without her and spent most of the day looking at every possible available apartment. When I described them to her that night, for one reason or another, she rejected every one. The same scenario was repeated for the next five days, and by my last night I was growing desperate.

It was almost midnight. I had continued to look at places until late in the evening and was now too worried to try to sleep. Suddenly, I remembered an assisted living place I had researched earlier but then forgotten about. It was too late to call, so I asked Dolly to go with me to see it. Not surprisingly, she refused, so I went by myself.

As I pulled up to the building in the wee hours of the morning, it actually glowed. I entered the building and spoke to the night guard at the door. He was very kind and said that, though it was very unusual, a room happened to be available right now. I got chills as he said it.

The next morning I literally dragged my sister to see the place. The manager kindly welcomed us onto the immaculate premises and then into the vacant room. It was perfect. It had its own entrance and was like a tiny, unique bungalow. It was not only clean, it was charming. The sun was shining through its three windows, framed with delicate lace curtains, making the freshly painted walls sparkle. I knew that Dolly could afford it with her disability check and my monthly help. She sat down on the bed and looked around, and I sensed that she liked it. Then, before leaving us, the manager said, ". . . and your bathroom will be down the hall. You'll be sharing it with a very nice lady across the way."

Dolly shook her head and muttered, "No." She wouldn't share a bathroom. Period. I froze. She just kept shaking her head. My throat tightened as I saw her last option slipping away. Feeling helpless, I looked directly at her and said, "Dolly, I'm leaving for New York City tonight and then you're going to be on your own."

Suddenly, images of her living in a dangerous homeless shelter or wandering the streets flashed across my mind. In an unexpected burst of tears, I started crying uncontrollably. "My worst fear has always been what would happen to you when Mother died!" Sobbing, I said, "I just want you to be safe and okay." I slid to the floor beside her and bowed my head against her legs as I cried and cried. I couldn't stop.

Finally, I took my hands from my face and lifted my head up. Dolly was looking at me in a way I'd never seen before. She looked bewildered and kept staring at me. With difficulty, she said, "It's . . . hard . . . to absorb . . . that you care about me . . . that much." She kept searching my face. Then, with a tenderness I'd never known in her, she very gently patted my arm. She took a deep breath and settled back onto the pillow on the bed. Although I never heard her utter the word "yes," I knew she'd stay.

We met with the manager again, and then, pulling Dolly every inch of the way, I practically ran with her to the nearby K-Mart. In a couple of hours I got her everything she would need. In a whirlwind of flying packages and swirling activity, we went back to her room, and I organized and decorated her new life. I made everything as beautiful as I could, finishing it off with one red rose and a picture of me by her bedside so she wouldn't feel alone.

She seemed dazed but slowly said, "I appreciate . . . your touch . . . on everything." Then we both braced ourselves against the size of the next moment, not knowing what to say. I hugged her, and she hugged me back. And I left her to begin again.

Now, over three years later, Dolly has her own life. She's still terrified, still suffering from anxiety attacks and phobias about everything, but less so. She might call me twenty-five times and hang up before I can pick up the phone. But when she's ready, our conversations are wonderful.

"Susan," she said recently, in one of our regular phone calls, "I chose safety over the world." But these days, in her very limited way, she's definitely back in it. She goes into the lobby of her building daily and "observes" her neighbors. She takes long walks all over the city and has found a true source of delight—her beloved 99-cent shops! I glory in the fact that she's getting outside and has a safe home.

I wept twice at my sister's feet. The first time, it was for me, but the second time, it was for her. Something had grown inside me while I wasn't looking—love. And along with that has come a feeling of liberation I never imagined possible.

I got my revenge after all! I just never expected it to be so sweet.

"Something had grown inside me while I wasn't looking—love. And along with that has come a feeling of liberation I never imagined possible."

—Susan Brandis Slavin

23 · Attention

I was going through one of the darkest periods of my life. The man I thought I was going to marry—my soul mate—had just ended our relationship. To make matters worse, I worked for him! And since his office was separated from the rest of us by a wall with a huge window, there was no escaping the expressions and body language that told me whenever he was on the phone with another woman.

I was devastated. I could hardly breathe at moments, my heart felt so crushed. I implored him to let me take my office computer home to work, so that I wouldn't be faced with the pain of seeing him every day. He agreed, and the change of venue definitely helped.

But what helped me the most was the advice that my dear friend Marci reminded me of. First, if I was going to survive, the most important thing I had to do was go to bed every night before 10:00. I knew from my study of health that every hour of sleep we get before midnight is worth two hours after that time. I also knew that staying rested is by far the most effective way to deal with stress. Anyone who's ever gotten up in the morning without having had enough sleep knows how hard life can be when we're tired. When challenges are accompanied by fatigue, we can feel hopeless.

The second thing I needed to do was to focus on the things I had to be grateful for. Every night before falling asleep, I started writing down at least five good things that had happened to me that day. The principle is simple: When we focus on darkness, we usually allow ourselves to be taken deeper and deeper into darkness. When we focus on light—all the good that's in our lives—we attract more and more light.

It is a powerful truth: *Whatever you put your attention on grows stronger in your life.* It's no surprise that when we focus on the negative, that's all we can see. How often have you had ten great things happen to you in your day, but when a friend asks you how it's going, you immediately tell her about the one thing that didn't go so well? As Rob Robb, one of my favorite personal development coaches, says, "The more you believe something *matters*, the more solid and tangible it becomes. When you believe it doesn't matter, it dissolves."

This is what happened to Ellen Greene in the next story. A classics professor who reads ancient Greek, she has had a long-standing love affair with Greece—which makes the struggle she experienced in the first part of her story surprising. But fortunately, one of her beloved Greek poets got through to her! He effected a change in perspective and a shift in the focus of her attention that allowed Ellen to re-perceive her circumstances and transform a miserable reality into a glorious one.

The result is a story that reads like literature.

One of my favorite sayings is the following Japanese poem: "My barn having burned to the ground, I can now see the moon." What freedom! Ellen's story inspires me in this direction as well. It prompts me to ask myself, *Is there anything I'm suffering over right now? And if there is, is there a different way to look at my situation, a different context in which to hold it, which in itself will relieve the suffering?*

The ability to shift our attention and see small concerns in a larger context is a powerful tool in the creation of a happy, productive life—surely among the greatest of blessings.

By the way, I did end up marrying my boss.

ELLEN GREENE'S STORY
My Odyssey

I sat at the bus station in Nafplion wishing I'd never gone to Greece in the first place. For three days I had wandered through the city's crooked streets, taking in its Venetian-style buildings, busy markets and colorful wharf, a curious mixture of foreign tourists and local fishermen fixing their tangled nets. Newly divorced, I was proud to have been bold enough to travel by myself outside the United States for the first time in my life. I had thought that going to Greece for five weeks would be a natural for me. In fact, I had thought it would be the perfect antidote to the sense of alienation I felt.

In retrospect, it seems downright crazy to think that traveling alone to a country I'd never seen, only imagined, would give me any solace. But for years I'd studied the ancient texts of Greek literature, first as an undergraduate and then as a graduate student at Berkeley. The visual images of the ruins of Greek temples and the sounds and smells of the poetic landscapes of Sappho's poetry had evoked a powerful longing in me. These places, I imagined, could offer the safe haven I was looking for.

But my stay in Nafplion hadn't worked out that way. Since I had arrived in the busy harbor town, all I could see were couples walking hand in hand, arm in arm. They were all happy, I thought. I had felt so far from them as I sat in the town square, writing in my journal, trying to look like a writer perhaps, and, of course, utterly immune to such ordinary emotions as loneliness, or even the fear of loneliness.

Now, as I waited for a bus to take me back to Athens where I would catch a boat to the island of Paros, I felt utterly defeated. Although I sensed the beauty of this place, I seemed to be impervious to its effects. Being here only made me feel worse, not better. All I could see was a parade of happy couples passing in front of me. The sunshine sparkling on the splashing waters of the fountain across the way did nothing to ease the ache I felt; it was all just light, noise and color. I just wanted to get out of there.

In desperation, I reached into my bag for my copy of C. P. Cavafy's poems. In those days I carried several books of poetry with me everywhere I went, and this modern Greek was one of my favorites. I immediately came upon his poem *Ithaca*. It uses Odysseus's long journey home to Ithaca from the battlefields of Troy to convey that all of life is a journey full of adventure, if we are open to it. Something in me shifted as I read:

Ithaca

When you set out on your journey to Ithaca,
pray that the road is long,
full of adventure, full of knowledge.
The Lastrygonians and the Cyclops,
the angry Poseidon—do not fear them:
You will never find such as these on your path,
if your thoughts remain lofty, if a fine
emotion touches your spirit and your body.

The Lastrygonians and the Cyclops,
the fierce Poseidon you will never encounter,
if you do not carry them within your soul,
if your soul does not set them up before you.

Pray that the road is long.
That the summer mornings are many, when,
with such pleasure, with such joy
you will enter ports seen for the first time;
stop at Phoenician markets,
and purchase fine merchandise,
mother-of-pearl and coral, amber and ebony,
and sensual perfumes of all kinds,
as many sensual perfumes as you can;
visit many Egyptian cities,
to learn and learn from scholars.

Always keep Ithaca in your mind.
To arrive there is your ultimate goal.
But do not hurry the voyage at all.
It is better to let it last for many years;
and to anchor at the island when you are old,
rich with all you have gained on the way,
not expecting that Ithaca will offer you riches.

Ithaca has given you the beautiful voyage.
Without her you would have never set out on the road.
She has nothing more to give you.

And if you find her poor, Ithaca has not deceived you.
Wise as you have become, with so much experience,
you must already have understood what Ithacas mean.

I was stunned. This poem evoked with such immediacy the exhilaration of Odysseus's voyage of discovery. I realized with a visceral certainty that this was *my* voyage, *my* adventure. To marvel with joy at the multitude of life's experiences as "ports seen for the first time"—that is what had eluded me. Instead of shutting out the world around me in anguish, I needed to embrace the idea that life is an opportunity to be enriched by new experiences—to become "rich with all you have gained on the way." I put the book down, feeling that now I could go forward, alone, to welcome whatever came.

And, indeed, life became magical. Feeling like an ancient Greek myself, I boarded the ship and sailed deck class to the island of Paros. That night I lay sleepless, dazzled by the conjunction of stars, sea air and the odd assortment of people trying to sleep on deck under the blaze of bright lights. I heard my fellow passengers say that Paros was the place of white marble and brightly colored fishing boats. When we approached the island the next morning, I felt a thrill as these fabled sights came into view. In the harbor town of Parikia I asked for directions to the most remote fishing village on the island. After several hours on bumpy roads with Greek music blaring from the bus driver's tape player, we arrived at Aliki. I could see right away that there was only one hotel in the village, and when I inquired I found that it was full. Undismayed, I convinced the hotel manager to let me sleep in a tiny, window-less room on the roof. I was so happy with my new room. It hugged me like a glove, and the roof was all mine. From there I could see the boats bobbing in the water and the children playing Frisbee on the beach below. In the distance I could see the glow-ing sign on a disco called "Romantika."

For a week I prowled Aliki's dusty streets, tested out my new swimming skills in the crystal clear water, and talked with Greeks over muddy Greek coffee and ouzo. My year of learning modern Greek was paying off. There were no Americans here and only a few foreign tourists. I quickly learned that Aliki draws Athenians looking for a secluded place to spend August vacations with their families. Every afternoon, after hours of talking, swimming and walking along the harbor, I went up to my roof, a cup of thick Greek coffee in hand. There I sat while the wind came up, snapping the towels and sheets on the line, even knocking flowers off their stems. I had never felt a wind like that. It was relentless. But I sat content, happy to be in its path. The sun blazed overhead, spreading out over the salt sea. The light was palpable, penetrating, and I lingered in it like a lizard on naked granite. Everything was exposed, brilliant—my hair blowing back from my face, my golden earrings sparkling around my head, the red and blue of the boats in the distance, and the cloudless sky. I was filled with the beauty and the richness of the world.

Nearly every night I danced like a Sufi at Romantika, happy to find a partner or dance on my own. Time washed over me in the steady rhythms of daily life. At sunset the fishermen returned. The men sitting in the tavernas were called in for dinner. The widows, heavy in the garments of grief, went home to their dusty white bungalows. I would go in to my tiny room and listen to the wind and the clinking of ouzo glasses in the bar downstairs. I felt a part of it all, connected to this intricate web of life.

After a week on Paros I sailed to Crete, hungry for my next adventure. At dawn I arrived at Iraklion, Crete's capital, and the next day I traveled to nearby Knossos to see the ancient temples and palaces, remains of the earliest known western civilization.

The reconstructed ruins of one of the palaces at Knossos drew me into its ancient secrets. I wasn't prepared for the brilliant reds, blues and golds of their wall paintings, for the faces that seemed to stare out at me from those walls. As I stood in the queen's bedroom, the remnants of her bathtub sitting there, a monument to the intimacies shared by women through time, my mind came alive with images of these people as they carried on the business of life. I walked past rows and rows of pottery shards, pieces of lives, of spilt wine and olive oil, of sumptuous feasts and the hard grinding of flour. Here and there lay broken columns and fragments of stone, potent with life. I felt connected to these people, to these fragments of their lives.

I walked outdoors and stood amid the olive trees, the cicadas shrieking from their unseen places, and I knew I was home. I could see the water of the ancient Mediterranean in the distance, glistening in the late afternoon sun. I was comforted to know that Homer's wine-dark sea was still here. And I was here too—fully present and able to receive the many gifts of my "beautiful voyage."

"Instead of shutting out the world around me in anguish, I needed to embrace the idea that life is an opportunity to be enriched by new experiences."

—Ellen Greene

24 · Self-Nurturing

are giving is natural to women—in fact, we've mastered it. We look after partners, children, friends, employees, coworkers, clients and pets—and now, many of us are facing the significant task of caring for aging parents. It's no surprise, then, that one of the biggest issues facing women today is balance.

What is surprising, however, is that we have been so cultured to put the needs of others first that most of us don't have a clue about how to take care of ourselves. In fact, we're taught that it's selfish to do so!

But making our partners the center of our lives is an aspect of social conditioning that can have devastating effects on a woman's health and well-being. Don't get me wrong: I adore my husband! And I have no problem with a woman serving others, especially her partner or her children. I see service to others as one of the highest acts a human being can offer in this life. But *not* when it is done at the cost of a woman's own soul needs and direction. As Dr. Joyce Brothers says, "The most important advice I can give a woman when it comes to juggling career and marriage is to put herself first. Selfish? Not at all. After all, whose life is it?"

Putting ourselves last on the to-do list, says Joan Borysenko in *A Woman's Journey to God*, is one of the hardest things about being a woman in a busy world. "While both genders can fall into the doing trap, women have a harder time getting out. . . . The big question becomes, 'How can I get what I need without being selfish to others?' As long as we think that spending time on ourselves is selfish, the vicious jaws of the doing trap will stay locked around our ankles."

It's the oxygen mask theory. At the beginning of a flight, the flight attendant tells us that, in the event of loss of pressure in the cabin, oxygen masks will drop down from above our heads. We are told to put our masks on first, before tending to children or anyone else. If we are dying, literally or figuratively, how can we help others?

In the following story by Christina Sukkal, discovering what taking care of herself really meant impacted her personally and professionally. It also impacted me, revealing the therapeutic value of taking time for myself and finding the things that feed my soul, like yoga and dancing. I have learned that when my body hurts from sitting over a computer too long, it feels a lot better if I take the time to do a couple of stretches. And the longer I practice yoga, the more time I can spend at the computer or on a long drive without my body hurting.

And if I'm feeling out of sorts for any reason at all, the fastest way I've found to get out of misery is to take a short break and put on some music. As Gabrielle Roth, creator of "The Five Rhythms," says, "Put the psyche in motion, and it will heal itself." I have discovered that even five minutes of dancing to music I love can shift my mood, release stuck emotions, energize me and make me a nicer person.

Thanks to Christina, I am learning how to feed my feminine first.

CHRISTINA SUKKAL'S STORY
Feeding the Feminine

The year was 1990. My children were young preschoolers, and my marriage was nine years old. I was in some ways unconventional and in other ways an absolutely ordinary woman, concerned with being a wife and mother, serving my business forms customers and decorating our home.

At forty-one, I was a dancer who wasn't dancing—a woman without dance training, leotards or tights, yet someone whose inner nature was deeply connected to dance. I had danced with a wild passion as a little girl and a young woman, though I never stayed with any class for long. But I married a man who wasn't a dancer and then became a mother, and dance fell away.

Still, there was always the impulse—the knowing that who I was at my core was a dancer divine. I had made a few attempts to take dance classes as an adult, but the music and movements fit someone younger and more flexible than me, and they hadn't taken root. So I was living with a slightly overweight body, a feeling of frustration and no awareness of how I could make a change.

Then, one night my dancer emerged. It happened unexpectedly. My husband Michael was in San Francisco and I was home alone. I had recently been introduced to the practice of sitting on a small meditation pillow called a zafu and doing deep breathing. This night, with my children soundly sleeping, I turned off the lights, lit candles, put on music and sat down to breathe. I noticed immediately that the shape of the pillow caused my spine to be aligned in a way I had never experienced before.

The next thing I knew, I was deep inside my body in a way that was totally new to me. I felt its motion from the inside out. I felt the exquisite, minute, individual movements in my muscles. I listened to my neck and heard bone and muscle in motion for the first time. From there I got lost in my body. For the next sixty, maybe ninety minutes, I remained deep inside myself as I moved fluidly, using every part of my body and feeling its individual components for the very first time.

It was delicious. I actually dropped out of my mind and knew only my body. I wasn't thinking any more about my husband, our life, our relationship, our kids or our money. I was focused inside myself, carried away by the pleasures of exploring my body in motion, discovering its strength and its muscular terrain.

When the music was over, I realized that I had been dancing. For the first time, I had danced the dance that lived inside me, without thinking about what that looked like. It was free and real, and I knew it was beautiful. It was an artistic expression in that every move was connected to its source. The music and the movement unfolded together, every note evoking from my body its poetic response. This was dance as I'd been born to experience it— dance that was not for the world, but for me. And although I didn't yet know it, what I call my *goddess*—the deepest part of my feminine being—was waking.

I began to relish the evenings that Michael was gone. When he was around, I noticed that I was self-conscious and "other oriented." My attention was always on him, and I couldn't focus on me. So I began to see his frequent trips to the city as a gift. For the first time I saw the value in taking time apart. I realized that I had always been in orbit around him and the children and hadn't taken the time to do the things I needed to do to feed my feminine spirit. And now I wasn't lonely on my own, I was blissful.

As I continued to dance, my pelvis, shoulders and arms found a natural undulation that was as familiar to me as it must have been to women five thousand years ago. It seemed as if an ancient knowledge was coursing through my body. The movement felt sacred, and the bliss felt like a spiritual gift.

But the movement wasn't just in my body—it was in my whole life. After that first night, many profound changes occurred. A business that Michael and I had created together failed, and our finances became unstable. We weren't sure what direction to pursue. Then Michael shared with me that a new woman had entered his life, that despite his deep love for me and commitment to our marriage, he was also in love with a woman he hadn't sought out but to whom his connection could not be denied.

Suddenly our lives were very complicated. Our marriage, which was previously picture-perfect, now looked like no picture you'd ever want to see. Yet our experience was that our relationship was expanding. Our love was growing, not diminishing. Michael and I began staying up until 2:00 in the morning, talking and sharing on a level of authenticity beyond any we'd ever known. I began to experience unconditional love for the first time, and I felt it transforming my psyche. I was becoming the woman I'd been destined to be.

My weekly night of dance had helped create changes in my life. Now it was helping me deal with those changes in a healthy way. I realized that if it hadn't been for Michael's other relationship, I wouldn't have had that time alone. I wouldn't have taken the time to go deep within and connect with my spiritual essence. My inner divine feminine might never have awakened. But now she was here and I was beginning to see that her consciousness was vast. Through dance she brought me such inspiration and self-respect that I could expand to accept life's challenges with love. Michael and I chose to remain in our marriage and see where our love might take us.

One night I felt a piercing clarity of purpose. I heard it as a voice saying, *Work with women, and bring forward dance.*

I found a catsuit—a sexy, black unitard with a zipped front, low back and long sleeves. It felt fabulous. Unconservative. Feminine. Creative. I wrapped my hips in silk and admired myself. My goddess was blooming. And soon I began to realize that this was my life's purpose: to share the experience of my awakening feminine with other women, always starting with the body's movement as the gateway to the divine.

As time passed I continued to experience a deep transformation. I was growing up, awakening spiritually and transforming my body. Having discovered the divinity within me, I was bigger, and my love was huge. Michael and I continued to grow happier together. And over time, we began to teach courses together, helping others awaken to their own divinity.

Today, over ten years later, my inner goddess is an integral part of my daily life. She has sung through me, moved through me, danced through me, loved through me. She has defined my life's expression and guides my work. And through her blessing, I live in loving relationship with everyone with whom I come in contact in this abundant world.

When I look back on those years of my life, I am grateful that I was able to navigate a difficult transition. I arrived at a place where I could see the perfection in all and the magnificent grace that has directed my path. Without Michael's love for another, I might not have looked within and discovered dance. Without dance, I might not have met my own inner goddess. Without this experience of my own divine feminine nature, I would probably never have birthed the work I am doing now—creating an online community, videos and audiotapes, and other products—all related to living life in a deeply intimate way. Today, as I approach my fifty-fifth year, I am living the life I was destined to live.

"For the first time, I had danced the dance that lived inside me, without thinking about what that looked like. It was free and real, and I knew it was beautiful."

—Christina Sukkal

25 · Surrender

I had just returned from a ten-day working vacation in Florida. I would have only two days at home before driving to Chicago for Book Expo of America, the annual book event I attend. The plan was to unpack; do laundry; repack; go through mail, e-mail and phone messages; and pay bills. I also had it in the back of my mind to squeeze in a little writing on this book.

The first thing I noticed when I drove in the driveway was that my grass was several inches tall. I had gotten the message while gone that the lawn had a fungus and needed to be treated before being cut, and I had made some calls to try to have things taken care of before I got home. Apparently, nothing had been done yet, and both grass and fungus were getting out of control.

Inside the house, the first thing I noticed was that the refrigerator was leaking. I left a message early the next morning for my neighborhood repairman, but when he called later in the day to come over, I was dashing out the door for an appointment, so we had to reschedule.

At work in my office, I could not for the life of me get my printer to work. From my laptop, I e-mailed myself documents so that I could print them from my desk computer, but that didn't work either. My computer man, one of the most accessible consultants I work with, did not answer his cell phone or e-mail.

I gave up the printer struggle to go to that appointment, only to find that they were running so far behind that they couldn't see me, and I'd need to reschedule for another day. So I went to the grocery store, where I quickly discovered that I had left my list at home.

There's more, but you get the point. Who hasn't had days like this? Of course, these "problems" are not really problems—they are completely insignificant when viewed in light of the plight of women struggling for survival in many countries. But, to paraphrase something Mother Teresa says on Ann Petrie's beautiful documentary, *Mother Teresa*, God puts you in the life you have, and whether you find yourself in a palace or a hut, you accept that. It seems ironic that however comfortable our circumstances, we still can find plenty of ways to be challenged by them!

What can you do when nothing seems to be going right? As the Borg on *Star Trek* say: "Resistance is futile." The frustration I feel in a situation like this comes only when it's not okay to let things be just as they are—or when I think I have the power to change them. The only way to experience peace in times like these is to surrender to "what is" at the moment. It's not easy, especially if you are strong-willed, like someone I saw in the mirror this morning.

But it seems to me that the events I described here might well have been signposts for me to *stop trying so hard*. I undoubtedly would have been better off adopting a more leisurely pace after getting back from vacation, perhaps doing a little writing and letting go of my obsession that bills and the lawn and all my e-mails couldn't wait until I got back from Chicago. When I really examined things, the only thing that absolutely *had* to be taken care of immediately was the refrigerator—and there was still time for that before I had to leave. It was a classic example of creating problems for myself by thinking that life needed to look and be a certain way—my way.

In our culture, surrender often implies giving up or giving in; we tend to view it as weakness. But I believe there are times when surrendering is the most powerful action (or nonaction) a person can take. This doesn't mean using surrender as an excuse for apathy or to avoid being responsible. Surrender in this case means to let go completely of whatever it is we're attached to or trying to make happen. If we can do this, even for a split second, we allow an opening in which the cosmic flow of life takes over, transforming frustration, anger or fear into a deep trust in something greater than ourselves.

And, as you will see in the following story, by Ciella Kollander, it could even mean a whole new life.

CIELLA KOLLANDER'S STORY
Song of the Warrior Spirit

From the time I can remember remembering, my whole family, mostly Scotch-Irish and Cherokee Indian, was passionately involved with music. My parents, both singers and musicians, took voice from some of the most respected teachers of the time. My mother played eleven instruments, and all three of us kids played several instruments and sang harmony as a matter of course. Our home was filled with the most famous singers and performers of the day, like John Charles Thomas and Marian Anderson, the first African-American woman to perform with the New York Metropolitan Opera.

From the age of four I studied with my mother, then other teachers, giving recitals in piano, voice, dance, accordion and violin. Music soothed everything in a life like ours; we had heard it from the time we were in the womb. In those days we didn't have television, so at family gatherings and picnics, we played and sang all day long—sometimes up to five or six hours at a time. Everyone brought their instruments, and so many people in our extended family could play the piano and organ that they would actually fight over who'd get to play them at our gatherings!

In addition to being a musician, my father was also a Protestant minister, as were my grandparents. I called him "the traveling preacher man," because we would travel to different parts of the country to build churches. My father would physically build them, fill them with a congregation and lead the choir, while my mother played the piano and organ and our whole family sang! Once a church was established and completely successful, we'd go somewhere else and do it all over again.

Growing up, I lived in ethnic neighborhoods and was exposed to a colorful life, including the fabulous music in black churches. Dad often looked for mixed neighborhoods for us to live in, because he thought it would make us better people to be surrounded by as many different races as possible. Once, we lived in a suburb southeast of Los Angeles. Every Sunday evening, when my father had finished preaching at his own church, he'd pile us all in the car and drive us into the city to a huge black church with a fabulous choir, called Echoes of Eden, for their Sunday evening radio broadcast service. They must have had a 500-voice choir—or so it seemed to me—and many of the musicians from the L.A. music scene came and played their instruments. I can remember the large matrons, dressed all in white like nurses, stationed at the end of every few pews to settle people down when they got too wild—the preaching and the music got people so excited and full of the spirit.

We were often the only white faces in a sea of black—and we were always welcomed with open arms. I loved the way the service started. It began at 10:00 P.M. with the preacher saying each line of the Lord's Prayer in his deep, rich, singsong voice. The choir would respond, singing each line back to him with all the glory of gospel music. By the end, the place was rockin'. My parents would stand me on a pew, and I'd sing and move my body to the rhythms. To me, this was religion that made sense! These people were so comfortable in their bodies, sensual, good-hearted, rhythmic and poetic. They loved to sing, and it felt like the real thing to me.

In those days, it was common for families to stand on street corners and sing. We didn't do it for money, just to inspire others. The preacher in those days was like the psychologist today, counseling and soothing the fevered souls of the people. As a minister's family, we would go to prisons and hospitals to sing for prisoners and the sick. I remember my dad and me often going alone together—I was cute, like a little Shirley Temple—and he'd stand me up on something because I was so little. I remember wearing my favorite dress, which was rich blue velvet with little satin ribbons, and my long curls, set by a curling iron heated on our big wood stove. I remember the sadness in the prisoners' faces.

I sang to them all—hymns and American songs, like camp songs and Stephen Foster songs. By the age of seven, I was singing radio commercials, which I had known I was going to do since falling in love with radio when I was only three or four years old.

And I *always* sang to the troops whenever my mother and I took the train across country from San Diego, where one side of the family lived, to Virginia, where the other side lived. It was WWII, and the trains were full of troops in uniform, either going to war or returning. They would ask me to sing and dance, and sit me on their laps, giving me presents like candy bars and pop—even

souvenirs like their military hats. They were such a source of enjoy-
ment for me, and I for them. I'm sure I reminded them of their
own deeply missed children.

When I was about thirteen my father left the ministry and went
to work for the U.S. government. By the time I was sixteen he had
become head administrator for the School for Allied Officers'
Training in the Philippine Islands, where I graduated from high
school. Radio was still the joy of my life, and by that time I had my
own 45s—a huge collection of rhythm and blues records. I was
bold enough to go down to the base radio station and ask the DJs
if they wanted to borrow my records! I ended up having my own
R&B show there, on which I got to talk and play my records.

I continued to sing and dance through my high school and college years. I was in every play and musical possible and, while performing with the U.S. Navy Dance Band, I fell in love with the lead
trumpet player—of course! We married and decided to move to
Las Vegas, one of the three places in this country besides L.A. and
New York where musicians and performing artists could make a
consistent living.

Life in Las Vegas was sometimes wonderful—and always wild. I
performed as a singer and dancer at the Riviera, Stardust, Harrah's
and many other hotels there and in Reno. On any given night, I
shared the stage with singers like Elvis and comedians like Don
Rickles, who loved roasting me from the stage! I often had coffee
between shows with Dan Rowan and Dick Martin from television's *Laugh-In*, two of my funniest friends. And Elvis's bass player
and I would go into our dressing rooms in Reno and read yoga
books together!

At the same time I was performing, I was raising a family, studying music theory and composition at the university, and managing
the only jazz club in Las Vegas, which I co-owned. Our club was a
place where jazz musicians—including greats like Steve Allen and
Bill Cosby—could come and play whatever they wanted, all night

long—unlike the big hotels, where they had to play what they were told to.

My husband was also performing. He was a "showroom" musician, playing with whatever orchestras came to town. He was good friends with Frank Sinatra, Jr., who often sang with or conducted the Dorsey Band.

When my husband and I split up, I moved to L.A., where I immediately became a studio singer and contractor with several big studios, hiring singers for the record and movie industries. My life was filled with hard work, but lots of celebrity and glamour. Andy Williams & The Osmonds, Bobby Darin, Paul Horn, Chad & Jeremy, John Davidson, country star Lee Greenwood and jazz greats Roger Kellaway and Tom Scott—I collaborated, performed and toured with them all. My daughter and Marie Osmond were little girls together, hanging out on private planes and schooling through correspondence, as we traveled all over the U.S. and Canada.

By this time, it was the sixties. My success seemed unstoppable, almost magical. I became a staff songwriter for A&M Records, with a studio of my own at the old Charlie Chaplin Studios. Many of my friends joined the cast of *Hair*, and another was the musical director for The Fifth Dimension. The group was looking for the last tune for their *Aquarius* album, and although famous people were submitting tunes for it, so far, the group wasn't satisfied with any of them. Then my friend happened to see my name on a tape at A&M Records, where they were recording. He pulled it out and listened to a piece written by my partner and me and recorded by the group I was in at the time. He played it for the Fifth, and they loved it! My song and arrangement got added to the album, which went platinum.

But things "in the biz" started getting crazy. I had made my fortune, and I was hanging out in publishing offices and mansions with pop icons like Dylan, the Byrds, the Beach Boys, the Monkeys,

Sonny & Cher and the Doors. The drug scene was inescapable. You'd go into a studio to record, and everyone was high, from the singers and musicians to the producers and engineers. We were often up all night for days at a time. The whole scene, even though exciting in the extreme, was wearing me down.

So when meditation came on the scene, popularized by the Beatles and other celebrities, it seemed like the answer to my prayers. Like so many of the musicians and "flower-children" of the sixties, I was drawn to the peace it offered—and the promise of stepping out of the rat race. I learned how to meditate and welcomed the silence and relaxation it gave me.

I soon trained as a meditation teacher and moved to Carmel, where I taught full-time and hung out with Clint Eastwood and some of his friends. My life was beautiful, and I continued to be surrounded by influential people, only now I was teaching them to meditate. I felt I was in the lap of the divine.

One day I was on my way to a follow-up meditation meeting and lunch in the Bay Area with the CEO of AMPEX Corp. It was December 27, 1974, and my car was filled with belated Christmas gifts for this wonderful man, his staff and family. It was about 11:30 in the morning, and as the first drizzle of the year began, the highway became slippery.

Suddenly, I lost control of the car. It spun across the median into oncoming traffic—where my small car and I were hit head-on. My car was thrown into a railing at the side of the road, which stopped me from going over the embankment into a canyon below. But it was serious. The other driver was kept overnight in the hospital for observation, but my car and I were totaled.

The first thing I realized after the collision was that my consciousness was leaving through the top of my head. I was in a huge field of light, and was filled with a palpable bliss beyond description. I watched the mechanics of the universe as it calculated the unfathomable equation of my destiny. I became aware—without thinking—that I had not finished my job as a mother or a teacher, and that I wasn't maimed so badly that I would be unable to recover. Yes, I would be able to heal. I watched as the decision was made that I would come back.

From far away I heard a moan and felt so much compassion. As I was drawn back into my physical body from this huge world of light and flowing love, I realized that the moan was coming from me. The pettiness of my life fell away after being cradled in that huge world of light, which I saw to be the unseen aspect of life that underlies everything that we see, everything that we think is real.

I should have been dead by the time the ambulance arrived. Two main arteries had been severed, and I had probably lain there for an hour by the time somebody called 911 and help arrived (we had no cell phones in those days!). When the ambulance got there, I heard someone say, "We're going to have to get a torch." I remember being aware of how nice they were being to me. From everything I had seen on television, I expected them to be rough and dispassionate. But they were loving and so gentle, and I, too, was having a very loving, compassionate awareness of them. When they finally blowtorched me out of the wreckage and carried me from the car to the ambulance, I could feel the rain as I slipped between life and death. The thought came to me, "You've changed," as if something was quietly speaking to me.

The damage to my body was extensive and devastating. The left side of my skull was crushed, as were my right elbow and arm, and my liver. My right lung had collapsed, and all the bones in my rib cage were sticking through my skin *and* my clothes. When I got to the hospital, I was aware that orderlies were actually fainting from the sight. I had approximately ninety breaks and fractures throughout my body. My jaw and pelvis were badly sprained, and the doctors considered amputating my right arm. But worse than everything: My vocal chords, trachea and esophagus had been virtually destroyed.

As the doctors performed the surgeries to try to rebuild my broken body, I saw gorgeous hands of light, dancing over the center of my body. The long, graceful fingers were reweaving the parts of me that had been torn into what looked like an intricate snowflake of light. Through it all, even though there were times with no vital signs, I remained fully awake inside and aware of everything that was going on in and around me.

Soon after the surgeries, when it became clear that my voice was not healing, the doctors gently told me that if I lived, I would never talk, much less sing, again. For me, one thing was clear: If I couldn't sing, I did not want to live.

In order to deal with the event—both the pain and what it meant for my life and future—there was only one thing I could do: surrender. What else could I do? My choices were to be in agony, angry and fighting reality, or to surrender to it. This was actually something I had been forced by circumstances to do all my life, so I was well prepared for it. When I looked back at the best and most successful things that had happened to me—my music, giving birth, traveling the world alone, facing huge audiences that both thrilled and terrified me—I could see that they always happened because I was willing to walk through the fear. I had been willing to surrender to the moment, to the unknown and to my own dreams.

Now my life had changed irrevocably, and I was being asked to surrender more deeply than ever before. I had lost my voice, which was my love and my career, and I had lost physical abilities, as well as my looks, which, like my voice, I had taken for granted. I didn't know if I would recover, and yet, surrender had started showing itself even in that car, when I was waiting for someone to help me. It continued now, and it kept bringing me an unspeakable bliss, like a river of liquid love. It was the most intimate, deeply familiar place imaginable, as if I had come home.

I meditated almost constantly, even as doctors and nurses came and went from my room. While still in the hospital, I began composing a love song to God in my head. I had seen that what animates us as human beings is so far beyond the little thinking mind that I was in a constant state of awe and gratitude.

The miracles continued. Occasionally a sound would escape through my vocal chords. And I was out of the hospital in only five weeks. Everyone was utterly astonished by my recovery. The doctors and nurses had said many times I'd gone way beyond anything they had learned in medical school to repair my body. They were skilled healers and wonderful to me, but I believe that ultimately, my healing resulted from constantly surrendering to the present moment, constantly letting go of outcomes and thoughts of the future.

I spent the next year resting, meditating, exercising, studying and working with a personal trainer. During that time, approximately two hundred surgeons, doctors, nurses and therapists started meditating because of what they had seen happen to me. Each one had had something to do with my case. I taught many of them myself, and was thrilled to be able to give something back to them. Several hospitals had conferences about my case, at which I was asked to speak about my experiences.

Thirty years later, I am still healing, both physically and emotionally. But life is good. I am writing, coaching professional and beginning performers, and composing and recording once again. I teach whole-body performing arts and consider this and my meditation practice the most significant elements of my ongoing therapy and healing process. And to my delight, I have recovered more than four out of five-and-a-half octaves of my former vocal range.

As a result of my accident, I now know that death is not something to be afraid of. It's full of light, full of love. It's bigger than anyone ever imagined! I'm no longer afraid to die—or to live. I also have more patience, more compassion and more willingness to simply accept things as they are—this is the real moment-by-moment surrender. My values have changed, and although I travel the world teaching, I make my home in a small town where I can tend my garden, ride my bicycle and teach young people in the local performing arts conservatory.

I sometimes have regrets about what could have been, and yet today I am creating the best music of my life. When I was a child, I thought I had to be on life's big stages, but life is simpler now. I have finally gotten to the music in me that feels like real medicine for the soul—the true purpose of art and music.

"I believe that ultimately, my healing resulted from constantly surrendering to the present moment, constantly letting go of outcomes and thoughts of the future."

—Ciella Kollander

26 · Authority

know a good speech when I hear one. Having been a "speaker" since age seven (as I described in chapter 17), I respond to speeches as any member of the audience might *and* with the professional's critical ear.

So when I tuned in to hear various speeches during our country's 2004 political conventions, I noticed two distinctly different kinds of presentation. One was delivered with intensity and the feeling that the words were being shouted *at* the audience. The other was delivered with passion and a sense that the speaker was connected with the words being spoken. The difference was heart—whether the speakers, men or women, genuinely owned what they were saying or whether they were just spewing words into the convention hall.

Each time that a speaker's words felt as if they were coming from the heart, I felt the presence of an authority that made me feel confident about the person's ability to lead, and I was much more likely to believe what I was hearing.

True authority is a natural quality of leadership in anyone who has achieved mastery within himself. A parent, for example, is a true authority when she can guide her child from a place of wisdom rather than control—and can herself model the same principles she aspires to teach her children. A nation's leader whose personal values are consistent with what he or she proclaims publicly has credibility—and authority. And a corporate officer who expects certain behavior from her employees must be able and willing to do the same, if she is to be respected and followed by her coworkers.

As I watched the conventions, hearing more women speak than I can ever remember at previous conventions, I felt the ever-increasing possibility of electing a woman president of the United States—and it felt good! It's not that we haven't had many great male leaders. But when a woman is elected, it will signal that the collective consciousness is ready for a shift in the direction of authority from the currently predominant domain of the mind to the deeper place of the heart.

Leading from the heart is a feminine attribute. This is not to say women always lead from the heart, nor that men never do. Certainly, some of the great women leaders of our time were as controversial as their male counterparts. But because the feminine is typically more lively in us, women are much more likely to look to the heart for leadership. And as Antoine de Saint-Exupery said, "It is only with the heart that one can see rightly; what is essential is invisible to the eye."

I believe very strongly that healing ourselves and the world depends on the ability to shift from competitive, aggressive models of behavior to those that are cooperative and inclusive. This means that feminine values will have to become more expressed in our culture, especially in the worlds of business and politics.

Linda Elliott experienced this in the events of the next story, and also demonstrated that, when leadership is backed by true authority, it leads others to their own power and self-awareness. In its highest form, leadership is an inner obedience to one's own truth and the ability to lead oneself in the direction of truth. In doing this, Linda Elliott models the kind of leadership I think all of us long to see more of.

LINDA ELLIOTT'S STORY
Running with the Bulls

W hen I arrived at work at 8:00 that morning, it clearly wasn't business as usual at Visa International. People were moving about quickly, looking grim, and the air was thick with tension. Almost immediately someone told me the news: We had had a three-minute card-servicing outage during the night.

Visa International operates the systems that process about two-thirds of all credit card transactions around the globe. If you use a credit card to buy a snorkel in Tahiti or rent a car in New Zealand, chances are, Visa International will verify and approve the transaction. When the systems for online, real-time verification of cards and credit limits were originally set up, it was groundbreaking. For the first time consumers could charge purchases and services in any currency, anywhere around the world, and the banks that issued the cards could verify whether the card was valid and the cardholder had sufficient credit.

Such dramatic changes are not brought to market by timid people or teams. Visa International was full of bold, dynamic, forceful professionals who knew their market as well as they knew their technology. To succeed in this environment, you had to run with the bulls.

I had been at Visa only a few months and was one of the newer managers controlling the development and support of these systems. Every morning at 8:00 we had a "flash" meeting to discuss every single systems event from the previous twenty-four hours— from small issues that might affect only a single merchant location to systemwide issues. When the entire system experienced a failure, no matter how small, the whole team was swept into a powerful set of events designed to determine exactly what had happened, how to correct it, how to prevent it from *ever* happening again and how to communicate about it to everyone connected to the system.

These actions were undertaken with the utmost urgency and seriousness. It was as if the system was a body and the problem represented a hemorrhage. A system outage of a minute was considered a near catastrophe. An outage of over two minutes could easily result in people losing their jobs and systems undergoing major overhauls. These systems represented the promise of the Visa brand, and the team took that completely to heart.

In my first days at Visa I had been surprised to see people getting so upset about one- or two-minute events. But I had learned quickly how devastating the effects could be. During an outage, merchants all over the world get no response when they swipe a card through their terminals—and they immediately ask the buyer if he or she has another card. The result is a loss of revenue in the millions for both Visa and the banks that issue the cards. Worse, cardholders tend to put a card that has been declined at the back of their wallets, never to be used again.

As I sat through the flash meeting, I felt something like terror rising in my chest. This enormous three-minute outage seemed to have been caused, at least in part, by the components for which I was responsible. That awful fact put me in charge of a multidisciplinary task force that would determine the root cause of the issue and take whatever action was necessary to eliminate it from the realm of future possibility.

An hour later at the first task force meeting, I found myself at the head of a table packed with grim-faced, determined and very powerful people, most of whom had been doing this for years. I looked down the long table at the twenty-four men and one woman. This was the mid-eighties and it didn't seem odd to me that there weren't more women at the table—it seemed odd that the two of us were there! Visa wasn't to blame; I had experienced firsthand their lack of bias against women and their willingness to give them responsibility. At this point in history, conference rooms were mostly full of men because women were still making the climb to this level of responsibility in corporate America.

I felt my male coworkers generally treated women fairly but doubted our ability to be tough enough to survive. There was no question but that toughness was required. The people around the table wanted answers, but also, in many cases, they were determined to place the root cause anywhere but in their own areas. This disaster was both an opportunity and a threat to every manager at the table. The corporate culture was that any blood in the water brought out the sharks. When something went wrong, people would dodge blame and try to find someone else to pin it on. If you were ever struck a blow you couldn't defend yourself against, everyone jumped on you in an often career-ending "shark attack." In the hour before this meeting, I had already heard several theories that were devastating to one group or another, including my own, and I knew the sharks were circling.

Everyone at the table was looking intently at me. What a target I was—new to the company, younger than most and a woman! I knew they thought I should be easy to control and run right over. Many a strong man had taken a tumble trying to make it in this environment; I didn't appear to present much of a problem. I'm sure they expected me to be in tears any minute, and it was true that inside I was terrified. I knew my job was on the line, and it didn't get more dangerous than this in corporate life. But outwardly I remained calm and showed no fear. I knew that I must be very strong, but I also knew—and this reflected both my upbringing and my values—that I must be careful and fair. I could accept the concept of running with the bulls, but attacking with the sharks didn't work for me.

I took a breath and began to speak. I told these strong and determined people that we had to have the full story, and that no piece of the story would be overlooked. Then I said the unthinkable. I said that if the problem was in my area, I would accept that and deal with it. And I said I expected the same of others. We would go by the facts, pure and simple, find the problems, fix them and not look for scapegoats. This was a problem we could solve together, and any background information or discoveries that came out of our investigation were not open game.

As I spoke I could almost see the scars that many of these warriors bore from past shark attacks. I knew their primary impulse was to save their skins at any cost, because I felt it strongly myself. But I knew it wasn't the right way to go. In short, I told these folks that I would not stand for any game playing, second-guessing or personal attacks once we knew exactly what had happened.

I finished my opening remarks and the room was quiet. Everyone was still looking at me, but their faces had changed. They were almost quizzical, and they were amazed. I had completely surprised them with this open, straightforward approach.

Since there was a hesitation, I simply moved forward with the steps we needed to go through, what input and data was needed from each group, and what our meeting schedule was going to be (basically every few hours until we got to the bottom of things). I suggested that we adjourn and all go get the initial information needed for the next meeting.

As we left the room, everyone seemed relieved and happy. From that day forward, I was accepted as a straight player, powerful and worth listening to. And to everyone's amazement, my simple, straightforward strategy worked. We found that there were several things that contributed to the problem. My group was the source of some faults, but so were several others. We all put forward our plans to fix the issues in our own areas, and then we worked together to refine those plans. We created a model for a new way of dealing with these crises, and it was productive without being destructive. No one lost their position or was discredited. There was no blood in the water, and no flashing of sharp teeth.

Within a few years, outages on the Visa systems became virtually nonexistent. For one period of five years straight there were no outages at all. This is a world-class company, and I feel honored to have been a part of it. I stayed at Visa for fourteen years, moving on to eventually become an executive vice president. I found it a great place to work and grow and learn about how women can have a positive influence in a corporate culture.

Perhaps one of the most significant things we can bring to the workplace is the understanding that fear isn't necessary in the exercise of power. People can run with the bulls, but they don't need to attack with the sharks. The committed efforts of good people are more than enough to achieve great things.

"Perhaps one of the most significant things we can bring to the workplace is the understanding that fear isn't necessary in the exercise of power."

—Linda Elliott

27 · Peace

I n several previous chapters, I have related stories about my decision to go into the Peace Corps in West Africa and my subsequent travels around the world after Peace Corps service. What a fortunate decision that was! The entire two-year period I spent in West Africa was one of the peak experiences of my life, a springboard for great learning and growth.

The town I lived in was Porto Novo, the capital of a small country in West Africa known today as Benin, at that time called Dahomey. Teaching English to young people whose neighbor was the English-speaking African giant, Nigeria, felt important and fulfilling to me. I submerged myself in the culture and was exposed to deeply religious Christians, naturalists and Muslims, all living in harmony. I was often awakened by drums in the night, and at times was invited to join the dancing in village celebrations. I loved my students passionately and delighted in their enthusiasm to speak with me in my language, their eagerness to teach me theirs and their obvious amusement at my American ways.

I also came to value highly the few native English-speakers I could talk with and the books written in English that I obtained from the Peace Corps library in Cotonou, the country's capital (not to mention American shampoo!). And one of the most significant things that happened to me in Africa was that one of the books that fell into my hands was Herman Hesse's *Siddhartha*, the story of a young man searching for the meaning of life.

I was deeply struck by Siddhartha's words, ". . . inside of you, there is a peace and refuge, to which you can go at every hour of the day and be at home. . . ." This book awakened in me a great longing for such peace, and so, instead of re-enlisting for a third year in Africa, I decided to travel to India, the site of *Siddartha*, in search of someone who might help me find it.

My journey continues to this day, and it has been glorious! Sometimes I feel I have found everything I ever wanted, and some-times I still long for more. Have I found inner peace? I'm not sure I could say that I was at peace recently when I spent eight hours in an emergency room in Toronto waiting to see if my eye symptoms indicated a detached retina! (They didn't, thank God.) Or when my husband and I decided to live halfway across the country from each other to pursue our creative dreams.

But underlying the ups and downs of life, behind the swings between joy and despair, I recognize the part of myself that does not change, the eternal aspect of life that is within me, and that I am within. Whatever part of the cycle of life I find myself in, up or down, I know that "this too shall pass"—because that is the nature of life. And the more I accept *everything* that happens in my life as simply part of the experience of being human, the freer I become.

This is exactly what happened to Lindy Jones, in our final story. I ran into Lindy one morning at yoga. It was the first time we had seen each other since her partner, Matthew, had passed away from cancer in the Philippines four months earlier. We held each other for a long time. I learned she was planning a road trip south to visit her family. Her first stop would be New Orleans, to carry cameras around the annual Jazz Festival for her father, a documentary photographer. I told her it was hard to believe I had grown up in Louisiana and never been to Jazz Fest. She unhesitatingly replied, "Come on down! You can stay with me."

Lindy is an extraordinary woman and a great singer-songwriter. I was excited about spending some time with her and meeting her family. But as we enjoyed Jazz Fest together, sharing mango ices and big bowls of shrimp étouffée, I gradually realized she was just going through the motions. On the surface she seemed happy, loving and interested in the people and events going on around her. But inside, the grief she was experiencing at the loss of her partner was overwhelming, and she had lost the desire to live. By the end of our time together, I knew she was in a place of deep despair.

A couple of months later, I invited Lindy to stay at my house in the Midwest while I was away on a business trip. When I returned, I found a different person from the woman I had spent time with in New Orleans. She was happy, vibrant and alive. Life seemed to flow through her in a way that felt magical to me. We came and went comfortably around each other, and at moments the day would throw us together unexpectedly. One night we found ourselves at midnight lying on a blanket on the golf course down the street from my house, looking at stars and fireflies. And we finally had time for the story of Matthew.

I think it confirms that it is possible to know peace regardless of the pain or joy in our lives.

LINDY JONES'S STORY
A Star-Filled Night

I had been with Matthew for a year and a half when he was diagnosed with advanced, aggressive gastric cancer and told he had just one to two months to live. Having been advised that any Western medical approach was likely to be futile at this point, we decided to fly to the Philippines to see some of the renowned psychic surgeons there. A friend of ours had been cured of three types of cancer by these surgeons five years before. Since then, he had advised ten friends to go there, seven of whom are now in remission.

Matthew was one of the three who didn't make it. When he died, I was left facing not only the grief of losing my beloved, but also the challenge of dealing with his death in a foreign country. I argued with officials to let me stay with his body when it was taken to the morgue. I traveled in the tropical heat with his body two hours to the nearest crematorium. I sat right next to the furnace in the crematorium, holding a vigil for Matthew for the six hours it took for his remains to be cremated. I found myself asking the question, *What's real?*

After the cremation, I went back to Baguio City to the apartment we had been living in when Matthew died. I threw myself into preparing a sacred space for Matthew's ashes. I took everything out of the room, turned the beds on end, washed the floors and cleaned the bathroom. Then I poured lavender oil over the parquet floor and rubbed it in on my hands and knees. I put the beds back down and put fresh linens on them, lit candles and incense, and sprinkled rose petals over the beds and floor. It felt like a purifying ritual for both of us. Friends called throughout the week and a close friend of Matthew's helped me, but most of all, I cherished the time I spent alone in ceremony of Matthew's passing.

In the days that followed, I found a beautiful ebony urn for the ashes and hired a local craftsman to carve the words "Into Love and Light" on the inside of the lid, along with the dates of Matthew's birth and death. It seemed important that the urn be made and carved there, in the Philippines—important to the transitions both Matthew and I were making. I was deeply touched by the simple sincerity and sympathy of the Filippino people I dealt with. When they learned what had happened, they would take my hand, look me in the eye and quietly say, "Condolences."

Finally, it was time to return to the States. Along with the death certificate and cremation papers, I would need documents for both Philippine and United States customs in order to take the ashes out of the country and into the U.S. I contacted the American embassy in Manila and made plans to be there at 7:00 A.M. the day of my flight back to California. It was a grueling trip to Manila, managing six pieces of luggage—mine and Matthew's—plus a wheelchair. But the physical exhaustion was nothing compared to the pain of the inescapable reality that I was leaving this country by myself.

I arrived at the embassy at 7:00 A.M., as I had been told to do—and found it closed for Martin Luther King Day. I panicked. I approached the guard at the door and explained my situation. When he told me the embassy was empty and no one was there who could help me, I felt a rising hysteria. I begged him to call the official who had told me to be there on that specific day and time. With a flood of relief, I saw a look of compassion in the guard's eyes and realized he was going to do everything he could to help me. Ultimately, the woman I had spoken with and her supervisor came in on their day off, opened their offices at the embassy, and began the paperwork I needed to get home.

Only staff were allowed inside the building, so the guard gave me a plastic chair to sit on in the courtyard inside the gate. For the next five hours I sat there, holding the urn with Matthew's ashes in my lap, and waited for the paperwork to be completed. It was a long wait, but I was surprised to realize that it didn't matter. I didn't feel bored or restless. As the hours passed, I asked myself if there was anything I'd rather be doing. Watching a movie? Sitting in a café, drinking tea? It came to me that I wouldn't want to be anywhere else at that moment. This moment was perfect as it was.

Suddenly it hit me: Every single moment, wherever I was, whatever I was doing, whomever I was with—*that* was my job. Never again did I want to be doing one thing while thinking about something else. I wanted to be able to give myself completely to what was happening in my life at every moment. At *that* moment, even though from one perspective everything was terribly wrong, I felt the deeper truth that everything was exactly as it should be.

That evening I flew to California, Matthew's home for most of his life. I felt numb and depressed, but I had promised Matthew to take care of his affairs and spread his ashes on Mount Tamalpais. That kept me going. I stayed with a close friend and volunteered a few hours a day at a local botanical garden, doing my best to talk to people and to function normally. But my life felt empty and pointless.

A few weeks later, I climbed a steep and winding path with an intimate group of Matthew's family and friends to a place we had chosen near the summit of Mt. Tam. In the clearing, we gathered at the base of a craggy old evergreen. On the ground was a circle of stones that looked like they had been there from the beginning of time. The light on the Pacific Ocean was shimmering, radiant and astounding. We all talked about how Matthew had changed our lives, and as we shared our stories, the day went through many changes—misty, clear, darkening, sunny. It was the most beautiful spot I had ever been in, and we all felt Matthew's presence there. It was as if he had come home.

A month later I walked through the door of Matthew's house in Iowa. I looked around the room. There were the chairs we had sat in at the kitchen table; there were the beans he had used to make coffee. That life was done. I sat on the chair nearest the door, and pain washed through me. I would have to live without Matthew, and the thought was unbearable. At forty, I had finally found a relationship that worked. I couldn't accept that he was gone.

The days went by but I didn't care about them. I wanted to die. One morning I was curled up on the living-room floor, hugging my knees, aching with sadness. Suddenly, I dropped into what seemed to be a well of grief. I began to fall deeply into it and discovered that it wasn't what I had thought. I had an experience— not so much heartbreaking or gut-wrenching, but visceral—of the poignancy of life, of the range, of the expanse, of the mystery of it, the depth, the breadth, the hugeness, the darkness of it that isn't really dark.

I realized that people think of grief as being dark and of darkness as being bad. But actually, it's just like night. It's beautiful. The electricity of it is like a star-filled night. It's not a bad experience. It's not a good experience. It's just a different experience. I began to see how I was going to survive.

In the weeks that followed, I rode huge waves of feeling that threw me from one extreme to another. One moment I'd be functioning normally, talking to someone or driving my car. The next moment, I'd be gasping from the wracking pain in my heart. Following experiences of grief, something would trigger exaltation, a state of extreme connection to, and love and appreciation for the amazing beauty of this world. I'd be sobbing, then, moments later, filled with ecstasy and gratitude at being able to see a sunrise, hear the sounds of morning, feel the warmth of a cup of tea in my hand.

Days passed, and then weeks and months. Today, as my heart continues to heal, I am more and more at peace. Sometimes I still feel angry. I did *not* want to lose the man I finally felt happy with. But I watch as emotions come and go, like a storm that blows in. It rains, the sun comes out, there's a rainbow. Another storm whips in, rips out a tree, then it's calm again.

My experience of losing Matthew was one of feeling completely smashed to bits, then discovering that what I really am cannot be smashed to bits. Knowing this, I can say that life has become deeper, more beautiful, more mysterious than I ever thought it could be.

"People's lives and deaths, the appearances and exits in our lives—all these comings and goings are not real in a sense. The part that feels real to me is the love, and that perseveres."

—Lindy Jones

Afterword

I am not the same person I was when I began writing this book. Working with the incredible women whose stories appear here—going deeply into the principles that lead to our greatest happiness and satisfaction—has made me more honest, more vulnerable and more real. I find myself making better choices about how I live my life. I often feel raw with gratitude for the unfathomable mystery of life. And my search for peace has reached a new depth as I find ever-increasing acceptance for what life brings.

When I was traveling around the world, a quote from T. S. Eliot caught my attention. In India I drew pictures of the simple scenes I was observing and wrote these words across the top: "We shall not cease from exploration, and the end of all our exploring will be to arrive where we started and know the place for the first time."

The only way we can know the "place" is to know ourselves. The principles of success described in this book are simply the expressions of a deeper understanding of ourselves. We do not need to practice them—we have only to know that they exist and that we want them to be part of who we are.

My heartfelt prayer is that we all have the ability to live in the here and now, to recognize how much we have to be grateful for, and to be at peace with what is. This is the soul of success—the source of our greatest authenticity and power.

Acknowledgments

My grateful thanks go to the following people, without whose love and support this book would not have been possible:

To the incredible staff at Health Communications, Inc., especially my publisher, Peter Vegso, and my editor, Allison Janse, for her invaluable insights and guidance.

To my editor Cindy Buck, whose feedback was brilliant and who was just plain fun to work with. Also to Carol Kline and Diane Frank for their editing of selected stories.

To Lilli Botchis, Ph.D., for her constant love and support, for listening to endless readings of every word of this book and sharing her invaluable insights, and for teaching me that laptops and beaches really do mix well. I couldn't have done it without her.

To Elinor Hall, for always being available at the drop of a hat to give feedback and highly valued opinions—and for decades of being my biggest fan. I am so grateful.

To Jennifer Claire Mayer, my dearest friend and guardian angel of this book from start to finish.

To the people who introduced me to some of the women whose stories are included in this book: Carol Allen, Lilli Botchis, Ph.D., Kent Crawford, Karla Christensen, Arielle Ford, Fredric Lehrman, Candace Freeland and Virginia St. Claire, Daniel Orion Hawthorne, Barbara Holden, Terry Johnson, Jennifer Moyer, Sheila Ross, Marci Shimoff and Christina Sukkal.

To the following people who advised me or allowed me to interview them, providing valuable contributions to the discussions of various principles in this book: Lilli Botchis, Ph.D., (various), Jeremy Geffen, M.D., and Kim Klein, R.N. (Medicine), Daniel Orion Hawthorne (Integrity), Fr. Tom Miller (Faith), Sgt. Karl Mohr (Listening), Janet Sussman (Grace) and Deborah Tannen, Ph.D., (Harmony).

To the women—and man—who read the manuscript in advance of publication and gave me invaluable feedback: Karen Burke, Sheryl Fulton, Leilani Gibson, Kim Antara Green, Ellen Greene, Elinor Hall, Amy Hawthorne, Daniel Orion Hawthorne, Nancy Leahy, Kelly McLoughlin, Yaniyah Pearson, Gabrielle Read-Hess, Maureen Read, Sheila Ross, Heather Sanders, Kristy Smith, Selma Sussman, Livy Ullman and Kari Wrede.

To Wendy Read, whose genius with spreadsheets provided a way to quantify and effectively make use of the readers' invaluable feedback.

To Barbara Warren Holden, whose joint research with me for our book *Diamonds, Pearls & Stones: Jewels of Wisdom for Young Women from Extraordinary Women of the World* provided many of the quotes used in this book.

To Paul Holden, for the creative and fun brainstorming sessions on the book's title.

To my greatest mentors, Marjorie Dyer, my high school speech teacher, and Jack Canfield, my coauthor on several books in the *Chicken Soup for the Soul* series, for opening doors and inspiring me to walk through them.

To the women who lovingly shared their personal stories and worked with me so that their voices were perfectly reflected.

And to the women I worked with whose stories do not appear in this book, who gave of themselves so generously and who represent the best of all that it means to be female. Thank you from the bottom of my heart.

Biographies

Nancy Bellmer is a wife and mother who enjoys meditating, teaching, making pottery, giving massage, exploring nature, and sharing loving relationships with friends and family. She offers her story with the hope readers will gain healing and expansion.

Chellie Campbell is the author of *The Wealthy Spirit: Daily Affirmations for Financial Stress Reduction* (Sourcebooks, 2002). She created the Financial Stress Reduction® Workshops on which her book is based and gives programs throughout the country. A professional speaker since 1990, Chellie can be contacted at *chellie@chellie.com* or at *www.thewealthyspirit.com*.

Catherine Carter has been a teacher, lecturer and workshop leader since 1976. She teaches the Transcendental Meditation technique and is a Vedic astrologer and Ayurvedic health educator. She received her degree in Vedic Science from Maharishi University of Management. She is coauthor of *The Healthy Home*, a guide to the principles of healthy home building, and co-created and performed on *Love Songs to Mother Earth*, a music CD inspired by Native American and ancient Vedic traditions.

Linda Chaé is founder of the nonprofit ToxicFree® Foundation. Ms. Chaé also consults for companies wishing to market pure, safe products including anti-aging, acne, hair, oral, baby, pet and household products. To order her toxic-free products, visit her product Web site at *jh.vivatoxicfree.com*. For consulting information or to book Linda for speaking presentations, contact her at *vickimartin@direcway.com* or phone her at 719-742-5288. For more information about toxic ingredients, visit *www.toxicfree.org*.

Eileen Dannemann is the founder and director of the National Coalition of Organized Women (NCOW). NCOW was founded in the early nineties as one of the first organizing forces opposing the genetic engineering of the world's food supply by the American company Monsanto. NCOW is primarily a strategic consultant and organizing support force for activist groups of all kinds, particularly those concerned with agriculture and food safety. Their motto is "From laboring women to labor unions, we move as one."

Vicky Edmonds is a poet and teacher who uses the art and practice of writing to bring the deepest, most authentic parts of ourselves to the page and to the world. Her published works include five books of poetry and two books of writing exercises. "Becoming Food," the poem in her story "Food for Each Other," is from her forthcoming book, *One Cell in the Body of God: Poetry as a Therapeutic & Spiritual Practice.* For more information, contact Vicky at 4742 42nd Avenue SW, #607, Seattle, WA 98116 or phone her at 206-937-0700. Visit her Web site at *www.ealloftheabove.com.*

Linda Elliott spent fifteen years with Visa International. As executive vice president she managed the technology that makes Visa cards work globally and created new systems for electronic commerce. Today, Linda is president of the PingID Network, focusing on frictionless, secure electronic interactions. Linda also consults and mentors, and serves on a number of corporate boards.

Pamela George, Ph.D., recently opened her painting studio in Durham, North Carolina, after serving as an educational psychology professor for three decades. While work assignments with the Peace Corps and the Fulbright program have led her to exotic places—Samoa, Portugal, China and Southeast Asia—she always comes home to her native South. George's paintings and contact information can be found at *www.pamelageorge.net.*

Leah Green, director of the Compassionate Listening Project, holds masters degrees in Public Policy and Middle Eastern Studies. She has taken hundreds of American citizens to the Middle East. She has produced three documentaries on the Israeli-Palestinian conflict and cofounded Jewish-German Compassionate Listening. Leah teaches Compassionate Listening to audiences worldwide. She can be contacted at the Compassionate Listening Project, P. O. Box 17, Indianola, WA 98342 or by phone at 360-297-2280 or via e-mail at *office@compassionatelistening.org.* Visit her Web site at *www.compassionatelistening.org.*

Ellen Greene received her Ph.D. from Berkeley in 1992. She is a professor of classics at the University of Oklahoma and specializes in the study of women and sexuality in ancient Greek and Latin love poetry. Her books include *Reading Sappho* and *The Erotics of Domination: Male Desire and the Mistress in Latin Love Poetry.*

Despina Gurlides was born in New York City in 1953. She received an MBA from New York University and spent the next twenty years working in New York. She moved to the Bay Area in California, where her life really shifted when she met her beloved teacher, Eli Jaxon-Bear. She now works for Eli's organization, the Leela Foundation, and lives in San Rafael.

Christine Horner, M.D., is a board-certified plastic surgeon with a special interest in natural medicine. She was honored by *Glamour* magazine and by Oprah after spearheading breast reconstruction legislation. Dr. Horner's book, *Waking the Warrior Goddess: Dr. Christine Horner's Program to Protect Against and Fight Breast Cancer*, is due to be released in 2005.

Ciella Kollander is an international gold-record recording artist, composer and teacher. She is currently writing her autobiography, *The Heart of a Singer*, producing her WholeBodySinging™ seminar video, and recording a CD with Roger Kellaway. She is also publishing short stories, articles and poetry. She can be reached at 641-472-SING! (7464) or via e-mail at *ciellathewriter@yahoo.com*.

Mackey McNeill's mission is to create an abundant universe by providing an opening to a new paradigm of money. Her book *The Intersection of Joy and Money* won the 2003 Most Life Changing Book Award from Independent Press. Currently a speaker, author and consultant, Mackey is widely regarded as "The Prosperity Advisor." She can be reached at *Mackey.McNeill@mmmpsc.com* or at her Web site at *www.joyandmoney.com*.

Sara O'Meara and **Yvonne Fedderson** are the founders of Childhelp USA, which serves thousands of children daily with many comprehensive services, including the National Child Abuse Hotline, 1-800-4A-CHILD. With the support of many kind humanitarians, they have opened several "villages" (residential treatment facilities) around the country for abused children, including one at an Arizona resort donated by Merv Griffin. To contact Childhelp USA, call their national headquarters at 480-922-8212 or visit their Web site at *www.childhelpusa.org*.

Catherine Oxenberg has appeared in twenty-eight movies, including the highest grossing independent film of 1999, *The Omega Code*, with Michael York. She has taken time off in the last three years to have two beautiful baby girls, Maya and Celeste. Her daughter India was born in 1991. Now back at work, she recently completed *Premonition* for the Sci-Fi channel with her husband, actor Casper Van Dien, in which they played husband and wife on-screen for the first time.

Yaniyah Pearson, M.A., has been working with young people since 1981 and conducts national leadership development workshops. She spent three summers touring with African-American, Latino, Asian-American and Native American young leaders throughout Russia and Uzbekistan. After twelve years with YouthBuild she now serves as a consultant to youth development organizations. Yaniyah is currently writing a novel, *Wind Island*, and a nonfiction work based on spiritual development for youth workers entitled *Working with the Sacred*, from which "The Beat" is excerpted. She lives in the mid-Hudson Valley of New York State with her life partner.

Deva Premal is known for her best-selling CDs, *The Essence, Love is Space* and *Embrace*, which feature the ancient form of Indian mantra in a contemporary setting. Together with her partner, Miten, she travels the world sharing her music in meditation concerts and voice celebrations. Visit her Web site at *www.DevaPremalMiten.com*, or contact her at *Connection@DevaPremalMiten.com*.

Alexis Quinlan lives and writes in New York City and teaches creative writing at William Paterson University in New Jersey. She has recently authored page-a-day calendars for 2004 and 2005 entitled *Dreams: A Daily Guide to Their Hidden Meaning*. Her poems have appeared in literary journals, including *The Paris Review*.

Wanda Roth, born in New York, currently lives in Fairfield, Iowa. After traveling in East Africa she moved to California to work with lions. While in California, Wanda also became a multimillionaire and multimillion-dollar realtor. One of her many passions is ballroom dancing. Wanda is also a teacher of Transcendental Meditation. She can be contacted at *rosalie@lisco.com*.

Susan Brandis Slavin has worked as an actress in film, television and theater to critical acclaim since her teens. She founded Susan Slavin Actors & Singers Academy at Carnegie Hall and is a produced playwright and director. Her new play has been optioned to be a feature film with Susan starring and writing the screenplay. She may be contacted at 212-330-8798 or *susanbrandisslavin@yahoo.com*.

Christina Sukkal is a pioneer in the field of human relations whose original teachings have positively impacted thousands of lives. She is the author of the e-books *Feeding the Feminine First* and *Essence to Essence: The Ebook of Intimacy*. She is also the creator of two Web shows, "Magical Living" and "Eros and Elegance." You may reach Christina through her Web site at *www.thetemple.tv*.

Lynne Twist—global activist, fund-raiser, speaker, author, teacher, mentor and counselor—has devoted her life to service in support of global sustainability and security, human rights, economic integrity and spiritual authenticity. Lynne has raised more than $150 million in individual contributions for charitable causes, and trained other fund-raisers to be more effective in their work for organizations that serve to end world hunger, empower women, nurture children and youth, and preserve the natural heritage of our planet. Her book *The Soul of Money* gives a new perspective on money. Visit her Web site at *www.soulofmoney.org*.

As a young girl, **Jacqui Vines** was passed around numerous foster homes and group homes, yet she set out on her own at the age of eighteen and worked her way up through the ranks of the male-dominated cable television industry. Tapped by Cox Communications to rescue a run-down cable system, she went in as vice president and general manager and oversaw its growth into a flourishing $150 million business with 550 employees. She loves her work and also her life with two little girls who call her "Momma Tia."

Ginny Walden was born in New Rochelle, New York, and received her B.A. at Hiram College in 1969. She then moved to Santa Fe, New Mexico, where she became a regionally known sculptor and performed classical flamenco guitar. After surviving cancer and receiving Chi-Lel training in China, Ginny relocated to Honolulu in 1999. Now finishing her book, *The Healing Power of Knowing*, about her healing journey, she continues teaching Chi-Lel and creating art and music.

Credits

We gratefully acknowledge the following publishers and individuals for permission to use the following material:

"They Can Be Like a Sun," from *Love Poems from God,* translated by Daniel Ladinsky, copyright ©2002 Daniel Ladinsky. Used by permission of Viking Penguin, a division of Penguin Group (USA) Inc.

"Well of Strength" is an excerpt from "Sufficiency: The Surprising Truth," from *The Soul of Money: Transforming Your Relationship with Money and Life* by Lynne Twist. Copyright ©2003 Lynne Twist. Used by permission of W.W. Norton & Company, Inc.

"Silence Broken" is an excerpt from "Chapter One: The Beginning," from *Silence Broken: Moving from a Loss of Innocence to a World of Healing and Love* by Sara O'Meara & Yvonne Fedderson. Copyright ©2003 Sara O'Meara and Yvonne Fedderson. Used by permission of Jodere Group, Inc.

The interview with Doug Henning used in "Chapter Eighteen: Humility" originally appeared in the October 1999 issue of MAGIC, *The Magazine for Magicians,* "Doug Henning: In His Words" by the interviewer, David Charvet. Copyright ©2004 David Charvet. Used by permission of MAGIC.

"The New York City Cabdriver" is based on an excerpt from a radio interview of Lynne Twist by Michael Toms for the nationally and internationally syndicated public radio series "New Dimensions." Copyright ©2004 New Dimensions Foundation. All Rights Reserved. The Web site for New Dimensions is www.newdimensions.org.

"Ithaca," the poem in Ellen Greene's story, "My Odyssey," was translated by George Barbanis from the original by C. P. Cavafy. Used by permission of George Barbanis.

Some names in selected stories have been changed for privacy.

About the Author

Jennifer Read Hawthorne is an inspirational speaker who delivers keynote addresses internationally.

She is coauthor of the No. 1 *New York Times* best-selling book *Chicken Soup for the Woman's Soul* and the No. 1 *New York Times* and No. 1 *USA Today* best-seller *Chicken Soup for the Mother's Soul.*

She is also coauthor of the best-selling books *A Second Helping of Chicken Soup for the Woman's Soul* and *Chicken Soup for the Single's Soul,* as well as *Diamonds, Pearls & Stones: Jewels of Wisdom for Young Women from Extraordinary Women of the World.*

For more information regarding Ms. Hawthorne's work, please visit her Web site at *www.jenniferhawthorne.com.*